Host

The Official American Youth Hostels Handbook

eling
USA

by Michael Frome

Published by The East Woods Press in association with the American Youth Hostels, Inc., Thomas L. Newman, Executive Director.

Library of Congress Cataloging in Publication Data

Frome, Michael.
  Hosteling USA.

  Edition for 1979 issued by American Youth Hostels, inc.
  Includes index.
    1. Youth hostels—United States—Directories. I. American Youth Hostels, inc. II. American Youth Hostels, inc. Hosteling USA. III. Title.
  TX907.A617   1981   647′ .9473   80-27546
  ISBN 0-914788-33-7

Typography by Raven Type.
Printed in the United States of America.

An East Woods Press Book
Fast & McMillan Publishers, Inc.
820 East Boulevard
Charlotte, N.C. 28203

About the Author

Michael Frome's long-standing and acclaimed career as a travel writer and dedicated environmentalist dates from his position as an airplane navigator in World War II.

Since that time, he has traveled and written extensively. His book, **Strangers In High Places—The Story of the Great Smoky Mountains National Park**, is regarded as a classic in the field of conservation. His writing combines the inspirational and practical and is designed to show the traveler what there is to see and how to see it. His devotion to the appreciation and preservation of the world's treasures is legendary and much of his time is spent lecturing and lobbying for this cause. He is the author of eleven books and numerous articles and columns for major magazines and newspapers. When not busy traveling he resides with his wife near Alexandria, Virginia.

Books by Michael Frome

Hosteling USA
Strangers in High Places
Rand McNally National Park Guide
The National Parks (with David Muench)
The Forest Service
The National Forests of America (with Orville L. Freeman)
Battle for the Wilderness
The Varmints—Our Unwanted Wildlife
Whose Woods These Are

Contents

I
Joining the Flow of Life

I set out to explore America when I was 17 and just out of high school. I wish there had been low-cost hostels along my route and the hosteling way of travel that young people can follow today. Mostly I hitchhiked, but I did a lot of walking, too, learning about America and its wonders and its people. I would spend the night where best I could, in farmhouses, with an uncle in Chicago, and once at a police station in Akron, Ohio, to which a friendly officer directed me after all else had failed.

Since then I've covered considerable distance and have slept in many different kinds of establishments, of various classes and quality, in America and around the world, developing along the way a certain expertise and a philosophy of travel as part of life.

The basic idea is not just to move from one place to another. That is really transportation. The faster one moves the less he sees, smells and feels of the environment around him. Flying can be essential to businesses, and it can be enriching to those who perceive the miracles and mysteries in skies, clouds and weather. But flying tends to encapsulate, and people don't speak much on airplanes.

Travel is a way of experiencing life, of finding new perspectives, of understanding one's own self better and of becoming a more positive person by relating to others. Speed has little to do with this creative process, since it is impossible to do any meaningful contemplation in a hurry. The idea is to slow down and reverse course from the usual way of doing things, joining the flow of life rather than simply observing it. This isn't only for young people, but for anybody who wants to be young.

It isn't necessary to go very far. I recall a fascinating article in a 1979 issue of the **New York Conservationist** concerning an expedition of the New York University Canoe Club. Its members would normally look for rivers, lakes and streams many hours drive away from New York, but on this occasion, they undertook to circumnavigate the most local of islands, Manhattan. In a crystal-clear sunrise, they left from the northern tip of the island and felt they could have been pushing off the Raquette River in the wild Adirondacks. Through the morning mist they spied the reddish cliffs of the Palisades across the Hudson River, small green fields and the

Canoeing on Western River.

wooded slopes of Inwood Park. Soon they were engulfed by civilization, but still there was beauty in it. Piers and docks were crowded with sunbathers, kite fliers and others out to enjoy fine weather. They passed the mammoth **Queen Elizabeth 2** getting up steam before leaving her berth, and they felt the wake of tugboats. Sun sparkled on the water, and a steady breeze brought the smell of fresh salt air. The voyageurs passed by the towers of the World Trade Center, the United Nations Building and under the bridge made famous by Simon and Garfunkel's "Fifty-Ninth Street Bridge Song." After contending with primitive forces of nature—wind, waves and tides—in a setting of supercivilization, they completed their trip in early evening peacefulness. It took thirteen hours, an exciting, uplifting interlude in anyone's lifetime.

It takes time and patience to recognize close-at-hand blessings of the American landscape. One must first analyze the components of a scene and then piece them together to understand the whole. Years ago, I traveled as a member of a horse party in the Bridger Wilderness, on the western slope of the Continental Divide in Wyoming. The trail led through a natural kingdom of tall timbers and clear lakes, alongside living glaciers and flowery alpine meadows, among massive rock formations like those in Yosemite Valley. Given a road, we probably could have driven the same route of ten or twelve days in three hours and seen virtually nothing. Driving through a wilderness is like watching a movie without the sound: you're trying to perceive an idealistic landscape, pretending that nature is represented by waterfalls but not stagnant swamps, by butterflies but not black flies, and by clear moonlit nights but not bone-chilling darkness and drenching downpours.

Perpetuating these notions only alienates travelers from the natural world. On the other hand, the slowness of non-motorized transportation allows one to appreciate the fullness of what lies at hand. Walking is even better than horseback riding. The idea is not to move from one point to another in the shortest possible time. Never mind the straight-line mile, if the crooked mile seems more appealing.

That to me is what hosteling is about: taking to the trails, traveling simply and lightly in search of fitness and health, fellowship and expanded horizons. It's not a question of dropping out of modern society, but of making it more complete and livable. Social improvement begins with personal improvement. Hosteling is part and parcel of a healthy lifestyle, the foundation on which an individual can network with others to make the world respond and feel better about itself.

II
The Best Cures
Come Before Illness

My travels accelerated with World War II. I discovered the American South when I was sent for training in Alabama, Georgia, Tennessee, Louisiana and Coral Gables, Florida. Once I completed the course and became an aerial navigator, I went on to several other stations across the country.

Each of these assignments was an eye and mind opener about another part of America. Ours is such a diverse country. People speak with many different accents, yet we are all the same. To think of crossing an entire continent without being asked to show a passport or required to change currency is something special in the world.

My actual mission was not to see America, but to navigate transport planes to overseas destinations and return. I covered a lot of oceans, islands and continents: across the Pacific to Australia and, at the end, Japan; to South America and across the South Atlantic to Africa, Italy, the Middle East and India; and across the North Atlantic to England and France.

Navigation taught me a basic lesson about what one might call cosmic unity, an idea that has stuck with me ever since and that bears on the essence of hosteling. The celestial navigator draws on astronomy and mathematics, or celestial mechanics, and meteorology in order to steer a course. When I was shooting celestial fixes with an octant, finding guidance from stars and planets and transposing the infinite of distances into lines of position on a plotting table, I felt that the technology of navigation had brought me close to the heavens, that I could sense the harmonious pattern of the universe and my own part in it.

Charles A. Lindbergh, whose life epitomizes the age of technological achievement, expressed much the same idea. "In wildness I sense the miracle of life, and beside it our scientific accomplishments fade to trivia," he wrote. "The construction of an analogue computer or a supersonic airplane is simple when compared to the mixture of space and evolutionary eons represented by a cell. In primitive rather than in civilized surroundings I grow aware of man's evolving status, as though I were suddenly released from a hypnotic state. Life itself becomes the standard of all judgment."

Dr. George Sheehan, the literate cardiologist and runner's runner, targets technology for what it is—both good and bad, a force that frees us from drudgery, shortens the work week, transforms society and gives us leisure to become onself. "At the same time," writes Dr. Sheehan, "technology has removed physical stress, atrophied our legs and bodies, and allowed us to gain weight as only affluent societies do. It has taken over the decision-making process in our day-to-day living."

The current surge in hosteling is part of the response to technology by people who want to recapture the decision-making process in their lives. Hosteling is more than a place to stay or a way of travel. It is a point of view. It relates to the individual's appreciation of himself or herself as a whole person willing to accept responsibility for his or her destiny as a member of the community of the earth.

People jog, run, cycle, canoe, walk, ski cross-country and contemplate nature because they want to be fit, to be in control of their lives and to be attuned to rhythms and cycles that bind human life to the stars and seas and all living things. Dr. Paul Dudley White, the famous heart specialist (and first honorary lifetime president of American Youth Hostels) was an apostle of self-respect and self-reliance. By treating President Dwight Eisenhower for heart disease, Dr. White became a celebrity and media personality, qualified to address the National Press Club in Washington. He arrived for his speech at the Club by walking up 13 stories of the National Press Building, straining the minds of his audience much more than his own body. "It's simple," he told the newsmen. "Never ride an elevator when you can take the steps."

In 1962, at Homestead, Florida, Dr. White dedicated the nation's first bikeway, while enthusiastic cyclists cheered. It was the dawn of the fitness revolution that has swept across the nation and the world.

Health is a process and a goal, a harmonious integration of body, mind and spirit. The idea is both ancient and as modern as tomorrow. According to the New Testament, Jesus Christ and three disciples once undertook a retreat on a high mountain on the northern boundary of Palestine, probably Mount Hermon. It was a kind of hosteling experience, in which they sought to rise above hazards to achieve self-improvement. They sought no shortcuts and would have spurned any offered to them.

Thousands of years ago Chinese physicians spoke of the values of diet, exercise and preventive natural medicine. An ancient maxim says, "The superior physician cures before the illness is manifest, while the inferior physician can only treat the illness he was unable to prevent." The Chinese learned to live according to the Tao, "the ultimate principle," or the harmonious law of nature. When disharmony occurs, it manifests itself in physical or psychological disease; thus therapy must reestablish balance and harmony for long-term effectiveness.

American Indians have held much the same principle. The power of Indian medicine is psychosomatic, derived from its direction at the entire person, mind, body, and faith. Natural remedies made from roots, herbs and barks of various trees are enhanced by varied paraphernalia and ritual, which lead the patient to believe in the efficacy of the cure and the authority of the shaman, or medicine man, who acts as an intermediary between the afflicted person and supernatural world.

While Orientals demand fresh foods and use natural medicines to treat the whole person in body and spirit, the affluent West relies upon refrigeration, air conditioning, motor cars, television, packaging and patent medicines. And computers, too. As Dr. Sheehan comments: "Computers now tell us what to eat, how to sleep, what shoes to wear, how hard and how long to exercise. We merely establish what we want done, and the experts can program us for it. No need to use, for instance, our inborn power to perceive exertion; they will do that for us with a treadmill. No need to trust the signals we are getting from our body; they will run a printout of eighteen tests which will tell us exactly how we feel."

Holistic health, or holism, or wellness, happily emphasizes responsibility of the individual for his or her health. It stresses the importance of mobilizing one's own health capacities, rather than treating illness only from the outside. Hosteling is truly holistic, since it combines daily exercise, sound nutrition and diet, upbeat friends, a good night's sleep, cheerful mental attitude and belief in oneself. Oddly enough, it's an idea that even the Hilton Hotels chain has picked up. In 1980, Hilton engaged Frank Shorter, the marathoner, as "fitness consultant." His advice to traveling executives who stay at Hilton hotels is simple: eat lightly and exercise. Shorter himself apparently settles for one well-balanced meal a day.

It wasn't long ago that all food was what is now called "health food," grown without artificial fertilizers and with few additives. Today, by contrast, the chemical feast fills the table with too much food but almost nothing to eat. Processed foods lack critical nutrients; they are loaded with petroleum-based preservatives, pesticides, artificial colors and flavors. Even at some of the best restaurants, the cuisine is apt to be rich and heavy, highly seasoned, starchy, the red meat fattened with DES, a cancer-related chemical. Studies of menu misrepresentation reveal many cases where the maple syrup is not really made from maple sap, the fresh shrimp is frozen, turkey is substituted in chicken a la king, the 16-ounce Delmonico is 12 ounces of beef round, Roquefort is domestic blue cheese and canned fruit is mixed with fresh.

Hostelers are wise when choosing to eat to live, rather than live to eat. There is nothing better than fresh vegetables and fruit, granola, nuts and dried fruit, GORP (Good Old Raisins and Peanuts) as a source of energy or yogurt instead of ice cream.

By its very nature, the philosophy of hosteling encourages sound nutrition and energy efficiency. Bikeways, footpaths and canoe trails are definitely "environmental trails." Hostelers who follow them use little energy except their own, and few if any petro-dollars. They don't pollute the air. Again and again, cycling is proving itself to be a practical means of sightseeing and touring for all ages. And bike lanes cost the taxpayer less than highway lanes.

Travel involves more than the collection of place names or the pursuit of leisure for its own sake. It should be the means to perceive the ways of the world, the cultural distinctions of people, the genius of humble life forms, the wonders of weather in all its moods. The ideal experience is to feel a part of nature rather than to view it through a picture window in padded comfort. You may be able to say that you've been to a place, but unless you apply some leg work, you can't say you've experienced it. Personal contact helps develop the harmonious naturalist view.

Being a participant, as in hosteling, yields the satisfaction of doing something rather than watching others do it. In Norway, professional athletes are unknown, yet that country's vast natural areas are heavily used for recreational travel and participant sports. The average Norwegian between the ages of 15 and 74 heads for the outdoors more than 50 times a year—to ski, skate, hike, fish, boat or swim, often staying in hostels enroute. Little wonder the hardy Nordics enjoy the longest life expectancy on earth.

America is making progress. In the last five years Americans bought more bicycles than automobiles. The Na-

16

tional Trails System is now emerging. Within a few years, thousands of miles of pathway will extend across mountains, deserts, forests and prairies, along riverbanks and lakeshores. Likewise, cities, counties and states are expanding their bikeways—a course that comes none too soon to meet rising expectations.

Hosteling is a way of travel that helps to stretch across counties and states and across boundaries dividing one country from another. It stimulates good neighborliness and comradeship, rather than hostility and false competition. For many years Americans have hosteled in other countries. Now visitors in rising numbers are coming to our shores. Hosteling provides them with the means to tour the United States inexpensively, to meet Americans of similar interests and to gain insights into our way of life.

Perhaps the best thing about hosteling is the basic premise to leave a place better than you found it. It reminds me of the old days in camping. When one camper reached a remote site, firewood would be waiting. The camper would, in turn, leave firewood on departure. There was no need to lock anything, for mutual trust and mutual help were the common creed. We can use a rebirth of the sense of respect and responsibility born of sharing and interdependence.

Chamounix Mansion

Mansion, Philadelphia International Youth Hostel

III
Hosteling, A Simple Idea that Spread World-wide

Each hostel is distinct and different. Together, they comprise a substantial national and worldwide chain of accommodations, but they are not at all like chain hotels or motels. None would make it as a five-star facility on the Mobil Guide scale of ratings, but then no Mobil five-star hotel would make it as a hostel.

Hostels are located in choice scenic, cultural and recreational settings. They are basically simple and cooperative, as well as inexpensive.

Hosteling is a part of a social movement. The International Youth Hostel Federation, representing national hostel associations throughout the world, defines its purpose as follows:

"To promote the education of all young people of all nations, but especially young people of limited means, by encouraging in them a greater knowledge, love and care of the countryside and an appreciation of the cultural values of towns and cities in all parts of the world, and as ancillary thereto to provide hostels or other accommodations in which there shall be no distinctions of race, nationality, colour, religion, class or political opinions and thereby to develop a better understanding of their fellow men, both at home and abroad."

That is the best kind of travel that any organization, private or public, could possibly encourage. It stimulates awareness, respect and responsibility that others may miss altogether.

The history of hosteling reveals its compatibility with a wholesome environment. The youth hostel idea was conceived in 1909 by Richard Schirrmann, an elementary school teacher in an industrial center of Germany. He led his city pupils on walking trips into the countryside to enjoy the treasures of nature. To provide overnight shelters on long excursions, Schirrmann developed a plan for use of schoolrooms, private homes and barns and a Twelfth Century castle operated as a museum. The concept caught on quickly, and by 1911 there were 17 youth hostels scattered throughout Germany (by 1939, more than 2000).

The first hostels were established by gifts of hiking and recreation clubs, wealthy patrons and local communities. The 1920s and 30s brought a rapid spread of hostels into other countries. Hostels in Poland were organized by the government agency dealing with physical education and school hygiene. (Even today the Hostel Association's president is the deputy minister of education, and many hostels are located in schools.)

French hostels were founded by the head of the Catholic Peace Movement, Marc Sagnier. Those in England and Wales were established under the auspices of the National Council of Social Services. In 1932 the first International Hosteling Conference was held in Amsterdam to develop common standards.

Since then hosteling has spread to 50 nations. The International Youth Hostel Federation is said to offer more beds to travelers than any hotel chain in the world. These include nearly 3,000 on the continent of Europe and 600 on the islands of Japan. Foreign visitors are always welcome, regardless of age, sex or occupation, as long as they are hostel association members and carry cards, or passes, that verify membership.

Hostels are highly developed in England and Wales. There are 250, including five in London. Scotland and Ireland have 150 hostels between them. They range in size from a dozen beds to more than 200 and originally served such diverse functions as shepherds' huts, farm buildings, water mills, mansions and even a Norman castle. Some, though, were built specifically as hostels. One of the most interesting recent additions is the old Coalbrookdale Institute at Ironbridge, in east Shropshire—the birthplace of the Industrial Revolution and a fantastic place for learning history.

Learning, in fact, is a key function in English hostels. Since most are in rural areas, they are well suited for study of botany, geography, geology and other field courses. School groups visit hostels as a normal part of their curriculum, and subjects that may seem dull in the classroom spring to life in natural surroundings. Imagine the opportunities at a hostel like the one at the Wildfowl Trust at Slimbridge, in Gloucestershire, with the largest array of swans, ducks, geese and flamingoes in the world. Teachers may plan their own courses, but most take advantage of the expertise offered by the Wildfowl Trust.

Although not directly involved in environmental activity, the Youth Hostels Association in England and Wales has supported efforts to protect the beautiful, endangered moors in Exmoor National Park and has opposed deposit of nuclear waste in national parks. Hostel associations both there and

The House of Grace Youth Hostel, Newcomb, N.Y.

elsewhere play a continuing role in environmental education.

Designed for active countrygoers, most English hostels are closed during the day. They are graded as Simple, Standard and Superior, according to international standards, and provide dormitories, washing facilities, a common room and fully equipped kitchen where hostelers can cook their own food (though some hostels also have cooked meals available).

The same system is generally in effect in Japan. Of its 600 hostels, 75 were built with government subsidies and are managed by local public bodies. The remainder are under management by Japan Youth Hostels, Inc., or under contract with it. There is much variation in the government-subsidized hostels in the Tokyo and Kyoto areas and the private hostels farther west.

Japanese hostelers are warm and friendly. They save a seat for a stranger at the dining table and introduce him or her to the routine. There are set times for rising in the morning, meals, taking baths and lights out. In many hostels, a loudspeaker calls at 7 a.m., allowing time to dress, make beds, clean the room, and breakfast before heading out and closing at 10 a.m. Doors open again at 3 p.m. and are locked at 8 p.m. with lights out at 10. A number of small private hostels offer an intimate homelike atmosphere; while the Seiunso Youth Hostel in Unzen-Amakusa National Park is more of a low-cost luxury resort, with heated swimming pool and picture windows that bring natural beauty indoors.

Elsewhere in the Orient, Hong Kong is known for some of the world's best hotels. The classiest and most expensive in the Kowloon district is the Peninsula. Its neighbor on Salisbury Road, the YMCA hostel, is quite modern, comfortable and attractive, offering a range of dormitory, double and family rooms at modest prices, with access to pool, gym, tennis courts, sauna and library. Another hostel has been opened at a prime site on the heights of Mount Davis on Hong Kong Island, made available by the government at nominal rental. With four and one half million people, plus refugees entering steadily from China, Hong Kong may be the most crowded city on earth. For all its wall-to-wall humanity, the colony is enriched by an outlying network of "country parks" in emerald green hills and islands. The casual visitor caught in the bustle of the city would find it difficult to believe that the Hong Kong Youth Hostel Association operates a Mountain Adventure Training Course and is active in protecting and preserving the remaining mountain countryside.

Despite Western influence, the cuisine, customs and

culture are fundamentally Chinese. The Hong Kongese like to eat in groups, leisurely, considering each of the many courses an adventure. Fresh chicken, duck, fish, meat seem more varied than western food. No matter how simple the dish, the idea is to make it pleasing to both the eye and palate. It struck me that in Chinese custom all life is conceived as an art. Eating is designed to better body and soul, so food must be fresh, freshly prepared, cooked and served.

The same idea holds true in medicine. Chinese pharmacists patiently told me how illness is considered "the loss of oneself inside oneself," and how their jars filled with roots and plants and animal fragments are used to enlist natural forces in treating the whole being for inner harmony and outward calm. It takes a little time and effort to understand that ideas are different than those of the West, but it's well worth it. A Hong Kongese with whom I became acquainted cited a revealing parable: "When I ride a donkey and observe another riding a horse, I look behind me. There I can always find someone else pushing a loaded cart." The moral, he explained, is: Do not wish for what you cannot have at that moment, for there are others wishing to have what you already possess.

Hosteling cuts across barriers of prejudice, false notions and political ideologies. During mid-1979, youth travel associations of the Socialist countries of Eastern Europe hosted a delegation of 27 representatives of associations of Western Europe. They studied youth centers in four nations that provide accommodations for young visitors from all over the world, starting in Moscow and finishing in Sofia, Bulgaria. Then, in the fall, a similar group of Eastern representatives visited Austria, Federal Republic of Germany, Switzerland and France to acquaint themselves with the youth hostels there and to consider ways of increasing East-West youth travel.

Another area where youth hostels are playing a role in promoting understanding rather than conflict is South Africa. A pilot youth hostel in the small nation of Lesotho has made it possible for groups and individuals of different races from adjacent South Africa to meet in a free and friendly atmosphere. With establishment of a multi-racial government and elimination of racial segregation in Zimbabwe/Rhodesia, the existing network of youth hostels is likely to be integrated into the worldwide hostel system. Hosteling in such activities is a people's movement that opens the way for politicians to do better things.

23

Friendly Crossways Youth Hostel Littleton, MA

(Drawing BY Charles H. Harris)

IV
Hostels In America

Hostels in the United States come in diverse shapes and sizes. They are located in private homes, churches, YMCAs, schoolhouses, college dormitories, country inns, farmhouses and historic mansions, and some have been built specifically as hostels. A number are unusual adaptations, like the venerable Coast Guard life-saving station on Nantucket Island, Massachusetts.

These lodgings extend in a network across America, reaching to Alaska and Hawaii. The heaviest concentrations are in the scenic areas of New England, the Adirondacks, Pennsylvania Dutch country, the Great Lakes area and the Colorado Rockies, with new facilities emerging in major cities, the West Coast and other regions. They now total more than 240.

Hosteling in America was begun by Isabel and Monroe Smith, who led a group of students to Europe in 1933 and discovered the phenomenon. They returned to Europe the following summer with another contingent and this time hosteled through Germany, Austria, Switzerland and Holland, ending at the International Youth Hostel Conference in London.

The first hostel was established in Northfield, Massachusetts, in late 1934, followed by others in neighboring New England states. Most early hostels were located on farms, with farmer and wife serving as houseparents to young visitors. The oldest hostel in continuous use, the Mount Everett Youth Hostel, in the Berkshire Hills of western Massachusetts, was chartered in 1936. It provides access to the Appalachian Trail, the famous summer music festival at Tanglewood, Stockbridge, Chesterwood and other attractions of the Berkshires.

"I was brought up on this sort of thing and realize the need for hosteling," declared president Franklin D. Roosevelt in 1936, when he was honorary president of American Youth Hostels. "From the time I was nine until I was seventeen, I spent most of my holidays bicycling on the Continent. This was the best education I ever had, far better than schools."

European hosteling has been more advanced than in the United States. Recreation and vacationing are recognized abroad as a human right and social need—national policy encourages people of all ages to get outdoors and keep fit. But we are getting there. It's encouraging to observe hostels emerging in national parks and state parks. California in 1976 voted to support a string of hostels along its coast, and Oregon, Washington and Alaska have enacted similar legislation. With new hiking trails and bikeways, hosteling is becoming the order of the day.

Like a hotel, a hostel provides travelers with respite—a place to sleep, wash and eat. However, where the hotel places people in private rooms and at private tables, the hostel brings them together, in a rendezvous of people of different nationality, social background and opinion.

The simplest youth hostel, in a rural district frequented by cyclists, walkers or climbers, provides simple basic requirements: dormitories, washrooms, sanitary facilities and kitchens where travelers can prepare their own meals. On the other hand, a large, modern hostel in a city or major tourist center may offer comfortable bedrooms with four to eight beds, hot showers, recreation rooms and a restaurant or cafeteria. Some hostels have accommodations for families and married hostelers, but most often families will have to conform to dormitory-style arrangements, with men and women in separate rooms.

Each hostel is supervised by adult houseparents, usually a married couple, who do this work because they like it—hosteling is their career. Houseparents are more than innkeepers; their role and goal are to bring strangers together into a friendly community, based on mutual trust and understanding.

Simplicity is the rule. It enables keeping costs at a minimum and stimulates self-help and self-reliance. Hostelers usually reserve space in advance. (Some hostels require reservations at all times, some only for groups; but it's always wise to reserve, especially in the busy season.) They usually buy and cook their own food and share common cleaning chores. Beds are equipped only with mattress and blankets, each visitor bringing a sheet sleeping sack (sanitary protection for mattress and blankets).

Hosteling appeals to all ages. While in a few countries a strict age limit is applied, in the United States all ages are welcome.

To insure sound administration, admission to hostels is limited to members, each of whom is issued a membership card. Membership is open to all at a very modest charge (graded according to age) and introductory membership cards are available for first-time visitors who want to test the experience before going all out. Individual membership cards are accepted at hostels in every country affiliated with the International Youth Hostel Federation.

American Youth Hostels, Inc., or AYH, founded in 1934, is the U.S. affiliate of the international federation. As a non-profit organization, AYH is supported by membership and program fees, contributions and foundation grants. Approximately 100,000 members enjoy access to hostels in this country and overseas. More than 30 regional councils, chartered by national AYH and operated mostly by local citizen volunteers, sponsor outdoor trips and service hostels in their areas.

In recent years, the use of and interest in hostels have expanded. AYH has responded with plans for new hostels, based on a set of operating standards designed to serve broad public needs and desires. Hostelers have traveled millions of miles under their own steam, by foot, bike, canoe, skis and horseback. This type of transportation is not always feasible in reaching popular distant city destinations. Thus transportation by car, bus, plane or train is acceptable where it's appropriate, but the idea is still to live and travel simply, in the esprit of fitness and friendship.

The back part of this book carries a complete list of AYH hostels in the United States. The Explanation of Symbols and Abbreviations, on the inside of the back cover, helps to understand a lot about them. These establishments cover a wide range, basically in the following three categories:

Hostels—low cost, supervised overnight accommodations; each has maximum fees set by AYH, resident houseparents (in or near the hostel building), separate dormitories and washing/toilet facilities for the sexes, a kitchen, a dining room and common room.

Home Hostels—facilities in private residences with usual elements of a hostel. The home hostel has only one to eight beds (compared with 10 to 100 in a hostel). The kitchen is usually the homeowner's private kitchen and meals may be provided. AYH sets maximum donations for each overnight stay, supper and breakfast provided.

Supplemental Accommodations—provided in particular areas with a high demand for hostel-type accommodations but where hostels do not exist. An SA is apt to be a YMCA, school, camp or hotel, generally lacking one or more typical hostel element. Usually there is no users' kitchen, meal service being offered instead. Rules differ with regard to reservations, arrival, check-out, lights out and closing times. In

Monroe Smith Memorial Hostel, Northfield, MA.

place of a houseparent, there may be a staff of desk clerks. The overnight charge is generally higher than the maximum hostel rate.

The hostel listing includes grading symbols that tell the hosteler what kind of facility to expect. Grading takes into account convenience and comfort items: per-person floor space in dormitories; ratio of toilets and washing facilities to beds; comfortable seating capacity in dining room and common room; work space in the kitchen, and information furnished about local attractions.

Hostel grading differs in its goals from grading systems used by Mobil Guides, American Automobile Association or Guide Michelin, in that it refers only to the level of the facility, not to the value of the experience—the simple outdoors encounter has superior value in itself that virtually defies grading.

Here are the four grades of hostels, with symbols for easy recognition:

⌂ **Shelter**—without full facilities, in a place or remote area where full facilities are not practical. A shelter is valuable because of location, but it may fall below minimum hostel standards in the following ways: more bunks in a smaller area; cots, or pads or mattresses on a floor, instead of bunks; dormitories shared by males and females; inadequate heating; only one toilet to 20 people; no electricity; "pack it in, pack it out" garbage disposal.

⌂ **Simple**—meets minimum AYH requirements, including: at least 24 square feet of floor space per person in dormitories; bunk beds of standard design; laundering schedule for all bed covers and linens; washing facilities with at least cold running water; fully equipped kitchen; and heating system capable of maintaining 55 degrees Fahrenheit in winter.

♠ **Standard**—more than meets minimum requirements by providing: at least 30 square feet of floor space per bed in dormitories; hot running water; showers or tubs; and comfortable dining and common rooms.

🏠 **Superior**—usually a large hostel where: at least some dorms have six or fewer beds; at least 40 square feet of floor space per bed in dormitories; sheet sacks and linen rentals available. In addition, there may be: daytime access to the hostel; separate game rooms; quiet rooms and common rooms; vending machines; and washers and dryers.

Certain equipment is essential for hosteling, notably the AYH Pass, sheet sleeping sack (sanitary protection for mattress and blankets, required at every hostel, and not to be confused with a sleeping bag), and personal eating utensils. Beyond that, anyone who has to carry a pack on his back, in a canoe or in bicycle panniers knows that lighter is better. I always find that, no matter how I travel, the less I carry the easier it is to pack in the morning and the less I'm likely to lose.

Hostel reservations should be made in advance, with one full night's deposit for each person and a self-addressed envelope for houseparents' reply included. Arrival time is customarily between 4:30 and 8 p.m. and checkout by 9:30 a.m., following breakfast and cleanup. Most hostels are closed between 10 a.m. and 4:30 p.m.; lights are out and bunkrooms are quiet from 11 p.m. to 7 a.m. The use of alcoholic beverages and illegal drugs is not permitted. Smoking is usually not allowed, and never in dormitories or dining areas.

Many hostels in the United States are fascinating for what they have been in times past—old mills, small factories, large dwellings and barns—as well as what they are today. More than a dozen are listed on the National Register of Historic Places. And no two are alike.

There is the Star of the Sea Youth at Nantucket Island, Massachusetts. It was built in 1873, as the first government lifesaving station on Nantucket and remains one of the few such buildings still standing. It was erected during a time when shipwrecks off Nantucket's dangerous shoals were frequent. The outside of the building, designed in the popular, romantic Stick Style, was painted red so it could be seen easily from the sea. Originally the first floor was used for boat storage, with a separate mess area for the crew, and the upper floor served as the crew's dormitory, with cots and blankets for the rescued.

Since its acquisition by AYH in 1963, Star of the Sea has been one of the most popular hostels. In recent years, guests have included entire school classes participating in the environmental studies program sponsored by the Nantucket Conservation Foundation. A major restoration funded in 1979 by this and other foundations and by the Massachusetts Historical Commission should insure the hostel's future. In one direction, ocean swimming is only a walk away; in another, a paved bicycle path leads to Nantucket's whaling museum, the cobblestone main street and the cluster of elegant ship captains' homes that hearken to the glory days of Nantucket whalers.

The Bowmansville Youth Hostel, at Bowmansville, Pennsylvania, 13 miles south of Reading, is another living museum. It was built in 1820, by Samuel Bauman as a country store, the first structure in what was to become a village. In 1837, a post office was established there with Mr. Bauman as the postmaster, to handle the weekly pony express service. This was the start of Bowmansville, named in his honor. The building was opened as a hostel in 1937 as one of a chain along the Horseshoe Trail, a scenic hiking and horseback riding trail in the heart of the Pennsylvania Alleghenies. The hostels are spaced roughly at 15-mile intervals. There is also a 40-mile loop trail starting from Bowmansville. The hostel itself is in the center of a Mennonite community; on Sunday mornings hostelers can hear the clickety-clack as Mennonites ride to church in their horse-drawn carriages.

In the great Southwest, the Weatherford Hotel, in downtown Flagstaff, Arizona, is another kind of hostel. In its heyday, the hotel hosted such notables as Theodore Roosevelt, William Randolph Hearst, Zane Grey and Thomas Moran, the artist of classic Western landscapes. Wyatt Earp is believed to have gambled there. The decline of the Weatherford was part of the demise of downtown Flagstaff, which came when the automobile replaced the train as primary transportation and visitors shifted to motels along the highways. The Weatherford's restoration as a hostel has helped in the recovery of old Flagstaff. The hostel preserves a balance between past and present. Situated one block from the Amtrak station and three blocks from the Trailways bus depot, it is easy to reach. And it provides access to the Grand Canyon, 80 miles north.

These are three examples that underscore a point about hostels. They not only make it possible to see America, they **are** America.

V
National Parks

For 30 years I have been traveling among the national parks. Hiking, canoeing, following rangers and naturalists on the trail, riding on horses and in automobiles, sleeping on the hard ground and in the best lodges—I've done all these things as part of my career of reporting on what the parks are like and advising people how best to enjoy them. Every day, whether researching or writing about national parks, discussing or simply contemplating these special places, I learn something new and wonderful about them.

National parks are places where young and old can exercise their minds and bodies and appreciate marvels of life beyond human control. The major parks are crowded, that is true, but mostly at core areas where people congregate because they are used to urban ways. Only a short distance away lie solitude and discovery. Walking, cycling, canoeing, ski touring cost little and cause minimal disturbance. Hosteling uses the parks as they were intended: to provide respite from sights, sounds, smells and pressures of supercivilization.

With their hundreds of museums, or "visitor centers," trailside exhibits and guided walks, national parks constitute the single most important influence in cultivating the art of travel as a reawakening of our sensitivity to nature. They cover about 30 million acres of native landscape and are administered as living museums where even such noncommercial activities as hunting and berry-picking are not allowed. Not only do these areas enrich our lives, they also give a breadth of unity to the nation and furnish guidelines for protecting and restoring the environment beyond their boundaries.

Here we find a gallery of living American treasures, an endowment of riches that makes our country the envy of the world. Few people realize it, but the national park idea was born in the United States and from here has spread around the world.

Today, more than 90 nations have their own system of national parks. The Galapagos Islands are now protected as a national park. Other national parks include the great game ranges of East Africa and South Africa; the heart of the Southern Alps in New Zealand; the highland moors of Dartmoor and Exmoor, the Lake District and Peak District in

England; the Vanoise high peaks in France and neighboring Alps in Italy; and one-fifth of the little island of Bonaire in the Netherlands Antilles, appropriately named Washington National Park. All these derive from the daring dream evoked at a Yellowstone campfire.

In the fall of 1870, only five years after the Civil War, a group of explorers accompanied by a small military escort spent a month amid the high mountains, plunging waterfalls, majestic canyons and geysers of the Yellowstone country—the wild frontier of western Wyoming. These explorers made many of the first maps of the region and named many of the features, including Old Faithful. They realized the benefit that sharing these treasures would bring to humanity.

Two years later, Yellowstone National Park was established by Congressional action. From that beginning an entire system has emerged, extending from Alaska and Hawaii across the mainland to Puerto Rico and the Virgin Islands in the Caribbean. Only Connecticut and Delaware are not represented. The system includes more than 40 national parks as well as national monuments, historic and battlefield parks, seashores, lakeshores, parkways, rivers and national recreation areas. Among these are some of the most famous places on earth: the Grand Canyon, Yosemite, Glacier, Great Smoky Mountains and the Everglades; Mesa Verde, Chaco Canyon and other archaelogical sites left by early Americans; shrines like Jamestown, Independence Hall and Gettysburg; and mammoth Lake Mead National Recreation Area—nearly two million acres of tawny desert, deep canyons and lofty plateaus bordering man-made reservoirs in Arizona and Nevada.

Although Yellowstone is still a magic word, I've learned that national parks can no longer be considered all things to all people. Crowds, congestion, noise, intrusions of man-made structures, pollution of air and water all interfere with enjoyment of the natural scene. To be fully enjoyed, the parks must first be fully preserved.

In many parks, the automobile lessens the quality of the visitor's experience, although the increasing use of shuttle buses is a help. There are some provisions for bicyclists, but there should be more, considering the compatibility of cycling with preservation. A number of parks are forced to operate under a permit system, rationing use of popular backcountry areas during peak seasons.

It's little wonder that rising numbers of visitors ask, "Where can we go to escape the crowds? Where are the na-

Regrouping after rapids on Kalamath River.

Warren Asa Photo

tional parks with space and elbow room?"

The questions are valid, but the answer is not simply a matter of where but of how—**how** to look at national parks as sanctuaries, **how** to absorb the wonders of nature they preserve, **how** to reorient one's patterns of travel and of thinking.

It's a matter of outlook and attitude, a willingness to adopt an unhurried approach. Observing a rock or stone in a national park, or wherever it may be, proves revealing and rewarding. Such observation leads to a point of view and demonstrates the value of Henry David Thoreau's idea that the earth is not a mere fragment of dead history.

This is evident on a small scale or on a grand scale. National parks become classrooms in volcanism, soil formation, erosion, glaciation, flooding, the effects of climate and climate change. Each time I visit the Grand Canyon, immensity is the first overwhelming impression, immensity of breadth and depth. Then I find it accented by flaming color. Looking more closely I can see how the open earth sinks down from the rim, through age by geological age, precipice to precipice, until it reaches the Colorado River—the straw-colored thread running through dark rocks formed in the first cooling of earth. The rock layers exposed to view are pages in the book of earth: gray Kaibab limestone walls, formed of shells, corals and sponges of a long-gone sea; buff-colored Coconino sandstone, solidified remains of sand dunes where ancient lizards left imbedded footprints; red and green shales, with traces of primitive cone-bearing plants and fossil ferns—layer upon layer which enable me to span millions of years within a matter of days, or in less than a mile down.

Those who try to see the maximum number of parks in the least time miss the message. They make it through the parks, touching only the centers with little chance to explore the uncrowded, unhurried corners.

A slower pace expands the dimensions of time, especially in a natural environment. It isn't a question of how extensively or expensively one travels, but how intensively and perceptively. Visiting fewer parks, staying longer at each one, leads to better appreciation and more enjoyment. It doesn't matter how one arrives, but the use of self-generated energy in the park—walking, cycling, canoeing—is great for nature viewing, and the exercise is beneficial.

To me that's what national parks are all about. They are communities of native life, safeguarded so that visitors may understand the mechanism of natural systems and learn to respect it. Often it's the concept of little things, rather than the spectacular, that count most. As massive monuments to the forces of nature, the peaks of the Rockies, Sierra Nevada Range or Mount McKinley in Alaska delight the eye, but there's as much majesty in the humble lichens, mosses, tough grasses and sedges.

The same is true in the redwood country. Motorists may whiz along U.S. 101, the Redwood Highway in northern California, and think they have seen the redwoods, but only by getting off the main road and wandering afoot can they grasp the meaning and beauty of these tallest living creatures on earth. In a secluded grove, the visitor can become his own ecologist. It's astonishing how you can train your eyes to note things others ignore—for example, that the redwoods never grow alone but always in company with other trees and with a lush undergrowth of plants, lichens, ferns and moss.

Consider the weather, which modern travelers expect to be perfect. Yet fog and rain are nourishments upon the earth, creating magic moods in the process. As Thoreau expressed in his choice of seasons at Cape Cod (now a national seashore): "A storm in the fall or winter is the best time to visit it."

Time of day is important. Twilight makes a choice time to walk, as deer feed on open hillsides and coyotes serenade the skies. Early morning and evening are best for birdwatching.

What makes a national park area truly special is the quality of human experience it provides. A few years ago, a friend of mine, Boyd Evison, who was then superintendent of the Great Smoky Mountains National Park, in the southern Appalachians, decided to focus on this particular point. He placed the emphasis on camping for self-reliant tenters who walk to their sites. Instead of building roads, Superintendent Evison converted them into "quiet walkways," bridges to the edge of wilderness.

Hostels are ideal for national parks and there should be more. There are some hostels, operating under special-use permits in converted government structures, and there may soon be more as the result of a policy adopted by the National Park Service in 1980. The sooner, the better.

The Little America Youth Hostel, at Truro, Massachusetts, in Cape Cod National Seashore, is among those that have proven popular and valuable. It lies 10 miles south of Provincetown, where the **Mayflower** made its first landing in 1620. From the picture windows in the dining hall, hostelers can see marshes, spectacular sand dunes and wide ocean beach. The National Park Service offers guided walks along the shore and around the marshes, guided tours of the Seashore Museum, and campfire talks. The northern section of the park has an excellent eight-mile bicycle path. Hostelers can pause along the Great Beach, which was given its name by Thoreau ("A man may stand there and put all America behind him," he wrote), then continue through the dunes to Race Point. Orleans Hostel lies 18 miles to the south of Little America, and Hyannis Hostel another 22 miles beyond. From Hyannis or Woods Hole, daily ferries lead to Nantucket and Martha's Vineyard hostels on nearby islands. Or you may follow the bike trail from Cape Cod to Boston and northeast to Gloucester on Cape Ann, visiting Salem National Historic Site enroute.

The Old Mine Youth Hostel, at Layton, New Jersey, has a choice setting along the banks of the Delaware River in the heart of Delaware Water Gap National Recreation Area. The famous gap—a break in the Kittatinny Range of the Blue Ridge Mountains, threaded by the river—is a forested canyon astride the Pennsylvania-New Jersey border at the edge of the Poconos. The hostel provides a base for fishing, swimming and canoeing and for reaching two national trails: directly adjacent is the East Coast Bicycle Trail, which runs from Boston to Richmond, and seven miles away lies the celebrated Maine-to-Georgia Appalachian Trail. This is an excellent area for birdwatching, especially during spring and fall migrations, since the hostel lies beneath a major flyway (and doubles as a bird banding station). Winter has its own appeal with ski touring and snowshoeing. The Peters Valley Craft Village, three miles away, is a living crafts center where visitors are encouraged to explore studios of blacksmiths, weavers, potters and jewelers.

Hostel in the Forest, at Brunswick, Georgia, is an aptly named modern private hostel providing access to Cumberland Island National Seashore, southernmost of the Golden Isles. This national seashore is distinctive with luxuriant moss-draped forests and 18 miles of golden beach. The island is open for day use and limited overnight camping and is reached via National Park Service ferry. History buffs will especially enjoy a visit to Fort Frederica National Monument on St. Simons Island (easily reached via causeway). Though now in ruins, it was once the largest, most costly fort in America. In 1742, the Spanish fleet and army attacked, but General James Oglethorpe scored a decisive victory in the

Sierra Mts., CA

Battle of Bloody Marsh.

Coronado Lodge Youth Hostel, at Porter, Indiana, lies within Indiana Dunes National Lakeshore, on the southern shore of Lake Michigan—a natural sanctuary 35 miles from Chicago. The clean sandy beaches, backed by huge sand dunes, bogs, marshes and woodlands, have long attracted interest and attention. This varying habitat includes the northern edge of the range of many birds and plants as well as several bogs representative of cooler climates. Besides the naturalist program conducted by the National Park Service, facilities at adjacent Indiana Dunes State Park include picnicking and swimming.

H Bar G Ranch Hostel, at Estes Park, Colorado, converted from a former livestock ranch, lies three miles from the east entrance to Rocky Mountain National Park. This park embraces 412 square miles of the Front Range, one of the highest regions of the country—untamed, rough and spectacular, the first wave of the Rockies to rise from the central Great Plains. The valleys are about 8,000 feet above sea level, and within the park are 59 peaks reaching 12,000 feet or higher in elevation. The hostel is ideally located for day use of the national park. The Visitor Center at Estes Park is a beautiful low building of reddish-pink stone, which contains a relief model of the entire area, natural history displays and a theatre where an introductory film is shown. This is the place to learn about guided nature walks and trails threading the park, some designed for a half-hour's leisurely walk, others for strenuous exploring.

Rocky Mountains Youth Hostel, at Kalispell, Montana, lies 35 miles from the western gateway to Glacier National Park, crown jewel of the Northern Rockies. The scenery here is overwhelming to everyone who comes this way. Glacier is one of the last strongholds of the grizzly bear, the symbol of Western wilderness. Bighorn sheep, mountain goat, mule deer, moose and elk are other large American mammals to be seen along the trails, covering 700 miles in all directions. Kalispell is interesting in its own right. The restored Conrad Mansion represents an authentic example of frontier luxury and architecture at the turn of the century. Flathead Lake, south of Kalispell, is the largest natural freshwater lake west of the Mississippi, bordered by the mighty Mission Mountains and foothills of the Salish Range.

Point Reyes Hostel, in Point Reyes National Seashore, California, provides access to a peninsula noted for its long beaches, sand dunes and lagoons, tall cliffs, forested ridges, grassland and brushy slopes barely 35 miles northwest of San Francisco. Hiking trails start from the Visitor Center at Bear Valley and from the Palomarin Trailhead, near the Point Reyes Bird Observatory. They spread over old ranch roads to Drake's Bay on the coast and to the summit of Mount Wittenberg. Birdwatching is outstanding, with more than 300 species, ranging from sea voyagers to dense forest dwellers.

The Lodge Youth Hostel, at Ashford, Washington, lies only a quarter mile from the Nisqually entrance to Mount Rainier National Park. Within this 40 square miles of icy, glacial rivers stands Mount Rainier, the loftiest volanic peak of the Cascade Range. Rainier is a gleaming landmark visible for hundreds of miles in all directions when the weather is clear. At close range, the mountain is a rendezvous for hikers, climbers, wildflower lovers, birdwatchers and glacier watchers. The broad dome of Mount Rainier includes the longest and largest by overall size glacier in the United States, south of Alaska. Mount Rainier offers 300 miles of trail, including Wonderland Trail, one of America's top hiking experiences. It completely encircles the mountain, a long 93 miles with steep climbs and descents, and takes between 10 and 14 days of backpacking. Mountain climbing is one of the thrills of the park, which served as training ground of the 1963 Mount Everest expedition. It is truly a "world class" park.

VI
National Forests

National forests provide low-density, low-key recreation of the kind that hostelers like best—hiking, biking, river running, trail riding, ski touring and snowshoeing. National forests cover a vast territory, in almost every part of the country, and are readily accessible from major cities, including Atlanta, St. Louis, Denver, Albuquerque, Phoenix, Los Angeles, Portland and Seattle. The Angeles National Forest, in fact, is only 20 miles from downtown Los Angeles and covers 25 percent of Los Angeles County.

The national forests hold their share of spectacular features. Of 21.4 million acres designated for protection in the National Wilderness Preservation System from 1964 to 1980, more than 17.6 million acres are in national forests (the remainder are in national parks and national wildlife refuges). The largest unit in the Wilderness System was approved by Congress in 1980: the River of No Return Wilderness in central Idaho, embracing more than 2.2 million acres of rugged peaks, flowery alpine meadows, highland lakes and forests, and portions of the wild Salmon River flowing through deep granite gorges.

I've been down this river in a rubber raft alternately crashing through ripples and boiling rapids and then cruising through calm and lovely pools, a sheer adventure amidst towering scenery typical of wild places

"There is absolutely nothing like it on the North American continent," says Clifton R. Merritt, director of the American Wilderness Alliance. "The River of No Return Wilderness is larger and wilder than Yellowstone, with a greater variety of plants, fish and wildlife." Ted Trueblood, one of the nation's leading outdoor writers, is even more enthusiastic, convinced as he is that the River of No Return Wilderness is the most fabulous parcel of unspoiled nature on earth. "Why, the water is so clear you can count the spots on a trout beneath six feet of it," he says.

The wilderness is not a park like Yellowstone, Glacier or Grand Teton. It is a composite of near pristine public lands covering portions of six national forests: Bitterroot, Boise, Challis, Nez Perce, Payette and Salmon. They are part of a system of 154 national forests and national grasslands extending from Alaska to Puerto Rico, from Maine and New Hampshire to the southernmost part of California.

Tosrvphoto

Beginning in the 1890s, millions of acres were set aside as forest reserves in order to save them from short-term private exploitation. Today, national forests are spread over 187 million acres. They are administered by the Department of Agriculture (national parks come under the Department of the Interior) on the principle of conservation through use. Logging, grazing, mining and various forms of recreation are permitted as long as they do not preclude future use. That is the theory, anyway. It sometimes proves difficult in fact. Logging on steep slopes, and unstable, erosion-prone soils make the future highly uncertain.

National forests are life musuems, too, with their vast array of trees, plants, geological forms and wildlife, and in wilderness areas they are largely protected. No mechanized equipment is permitted (except in emergencies or when necessary for administration). Trees are not cut, nor permanent roads built. Virtually all developments, except trails and shelters—simple facilities to allow use without damaging the wilderness resource—are prohibited. The emphasis is on keeping (and restoring) wilderness in its natural state.

The idea of setting wilderness aside through classification began in the Forest Service. In 1924 the first wilderness area was established as a part of the Gila National Forest in the southwest corner of New Mexico, primarily through the influence of Aldo Leopold, then a field official of the agency, later renowned author of **Sand County Almanac**, the classic work on the "land ethic" and "ecological conscience." During the same period, Arthur Carhart arrived at Superior National Forest in Minnesota as a Forest Service landscape architect with an assignment to lay out a recreational development of roads and lakeshore summer homes. But he foresaw instead an expansive parcel that could be "as priceless as Yellowstone, Yosemite or the Grand Canyon—if it remained a water-trail wilderness." He fought for this objective and the establishment of the Superior Primitive Area, later to become the Boundary Waters Canoe Area, famous because it remains roadless.

From these beginnings, the wilderness movement blossomed. In 1964 the United States became the first nation anywhere in the world to declare through law a recognition of wilderness as part of its culture and heritage. The adoption that year of the Wilderness Act, providing for establishment of the National Wilderness Preservation System, reinforced the public feeling for nature and the desire to enjoy recreation with a feeling of self-sufficiency and physical challenge in a biologically healthy environment.

Wilderness use has become so popular that permits are now required and the number of visitors is limited in order to save many areas from being loved to death. Deeply concerned outdoor clubs have devised guidelines and codes of ethics, urging members to try not to tread unnecessarily on delicate plants in fragile alpine communities; to walk or climb where possible on bare rocks of streambeds, slides and mountaintops to reduce damage to the ground surface; to camp in designated areas only; and to leave camping and hiking areas cleaner than they found them.

In 1968 Congress enacted two additional laws with wilderness potential: the Wild and Scenic Rivers Act and the National Trails System Act. In a 1965 message that furnished the spark for the Trails System, President Lyndon B. Johnson called walkers, hikers, horseback riders and bicyclists "the forgotten outdoorsmen." He declared, "For them we must have trails as well as highways. Nor should motor vehicles be permitted to tyrannize the more leisurely human traffic."

The Appalachian Trail and Pacific Crest Trail were designated in the 1968 Act as the initial links in the Trails System. Both of these run extensively through national forests, as do other trails established since then. The Forest Service has made trail development a priority activity, with plans underway for 60,000 miles of national recreation trails; 20,000 miles of trail near population centers; a bikeway, now under construction, from Denver to Colorado Springs, and more of such facilities where participants can know and experience nature in an energy-efficient manner.

The Appalachian Trail (AT) extends 2,044 miles from Maine in northern New England down the crest of Appalachia to Georgia in the Deep South. If you were to walk the entire trail, averaging a brisk 17 miles per day, it would take you 119 days. You would cross eight national forests spanning 840 miles (White Mountain, Green Mountain, George Washington, Jefferson, Pisgah, Cherokee, Nantahala and Chattahoochee), as well as two national parks (Shenandoah and Great Smoky Mountains), state parks and private lands. You would be within 150 miles of six of the country's largest cities—Atlanta, Washington, Baltimore, Philadelphia, New York and Boston—walking in the company of wildflowers and birds, tumbling brooks and timbered ridges. You would reach the highest elevation (almost 6,000 feet) in the Great Smoky Mountains and the lowest (sea level plus a foot or two) at the Hudson River.

The AT is more than a footway. It is a concept of recreation brought to reality through the efforts of volunteer trail clubs which for years administered the trail with the cooperation of public agencies. When private development encroached on some portions of the trail to an alarming degree, the trail clubs asked the federal government to take a more active role, particularly in purchasing critical rights-of-way. In 1968, when the AT was designated as a national scenic trail, about 220 miles were on private land within national forest boundaries. By 1981, virtually all rights-of-way had been secured and all but 80 miles of the entire Forest Service mileage constructed or reconstructed to standards.

In the West, the Pacific Crest Trail extends 2,350 miles between Mexico and Canada along the mountain ranges of California, Oregon and Washington. It is located for the most part in national forests (including the Gifford Pinchot National Forest in southern Washington, the scene of volcanic activity of Mount St. Helens). The Continental Divide Trail is even longer, 3,100 miles along the backbone of the continent, through a spectacular mountain setting, over passes followed by Indians, explorers and pioneers. Most of it runs through national forests and superb national parks—Glacier, Yellowstone, Grand Teton and Rocky Mountain.

A number of youth hostels are convenient and handy to national forest adventures. Following are a few of them.

Juneau Youth Hostel and Ketchikan United Methodist Church, Alaska, are next door to Tongass National Forest, the largest national forest anywhere in the country. It covers a major portion of Southeast Alaska, including scores of islands and a mainland coast deeply cleft by bays, inlets and large rivers. You can reach this area from Seattle via one of the best overnight ferry systems in the world. Operated by the State of Alaska, the ferries run throughout the year, arriving at Ketchikan, the first port of call, in 40 hours. The ferries take vehicles of all sizes, from bicycles on up. Once in Alaska, there are many opportunities to get off a ferry at one community, paddle with a kayak to another community and pick up another ferry.

In 1978 President Carter designated two major sections of the Tongass to be administered as national monuments. Admiralty Island, the better known, roughly midway between Juneau and Sitka, is legendary among outdoor enthusiasts. You can travel by canoe for days over freshwater lakes and streams, crossing the paths of few people, looking up at snowy mountains, and at eagles, too, as Admiralty has the

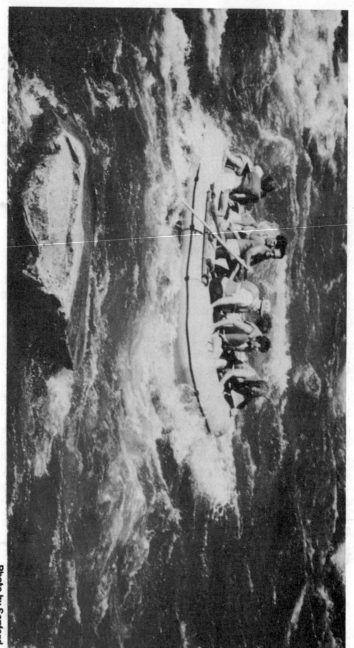

highest density of nesting bald eagles in the world.

Misty Fjords National Monument, in Alaska's southernmost corner, covers two million acres of rain forests, steep granite fjords, hidden glaciers, alpine meadows and snowfields. A canoe trail is in the making on the sparkling Gokachin Lakes and river system of which Ketchikan is the jump-off point for outfitters and guides using floatplanes and boats.

Crested Butte Youth Hostel, at Crested Butte, Colorado, a picturesque and historic mining town, lies in the heart of the Colorado Rockies, south of Aspen. Fabulous national forests—Gunnison, Grand Mesa, White River, San Isabel and Uncompahgre—lie on all sides, with scenic vistas and snowy peaks. These include Mt. Elbert, the highest point in Colorado (14,433 feet). East of Crested Butte, the old mining town of Tincup is just below the Continental Divide.

Seagull Outfitters Hostel, on Seagull Lake, 54 miles northwest of Grand Marais, Minnesota, is at the eastern gateway to the Boundary Waters Canoe Area, which comprises about one-third of Superior National Forest. The BWCA, and its Canadian neighbor, Quetico Provincial Park, comprise a series of endless lakes that merge into one another. For overnight stays in the Boundary Waters, the Forest Service maintains about 200 primitive campsites. Canoeing equipment is available for rent.

Nantahala Outdoor Center, near Bryson City, North Carolina, has the Appalachian Trail just outside its door and the rugged mountain wonderland of Great Smoky Mountains National Park and Pisgah and Nantahala National Forests within walking distance. Joyce Kilmer-Slickrock Wilderness, astride the North Carolina-Tennessee border, includes within its 15,000 acres a magnificent virgin hardwood forest, abundant in wildflowers and flowering shrubs, and the steep, sculptured valley of Slickrock Creek. Within easy reach of the hostel lies the most challenging wild river in the East, the Chattooga. It begins under the shadow of Whiteside Mountain in the Nantahala, then flows through other national forests forming the state boundary between South Carolina and Georgia.

Mt. Everett Youth Hostel Sheffield, MA
(Drawing by Charles H. Harris)

VII
America's Rural Back Roads

Freeways have changed America and Americans. They dominate transportation and tourism and have caused the disuse of the back roads of rural America.

Interstates should be diligently avoided while exploring America. Designed for the benefit of large trucks instead of private automobiles, freeways are congested and unsafe. The rural road, however, requires a slower pace as it dips, curves and winds through the land; you can appreciate fences and flowers and chimneys etched against the sky.

A century ago the bicycle was the principal means of transportation in rural America. This human-powered mechanical marvel was so popular that Colonel Albert A. Pope amassed a fortune by building the famous Columbia brand.

Biking is the best way to appreciate the landscape. A press release issued by the Kentucky Department of Tourism on biking the back roads in that attractive state states:

"Many of Kentucky's back roads are well suited to bikers' needs. In fact, although the roads are shared with motorists, the bikers seem more at home. These roads—most of which are paved—take the tourer through the hundreds of small communities that populate Kentucky, many of which have only the ever-present tiny grocery store and perhaps a house or two. While these spots are ignored by motorists who whiz by looking to refuel their machines, they are a boon to bikers who are constantly on the lookout for places to refuel their bodies."

The same idea can apply in motoring. Stopping at a crossroads village to pass the time of day is likely to lead to all kinds of fascinating information about the landscape and lifescape that others miss.

Trains and buses provide leisurely, low-cost public transportation. Amtrak has been improving but it is still far behind the trains of Europe that go virtually everywhere and often. There are now some fine trains and long trips in America. The **Southwest Limited** runs from Chicago across the prairies and southwest into Los Angeles. And there's no train better than the **Coast Starlight** between Seattle and San Diego, at any time of year. Even in February, riding north from Los Angeles to Santa Barbara, you're likely to see the first wildflowers of the year and, in the ocean just beyond, gray whales in winter migration. With winter temperatures often in the sixties, you can spend a pleasant interlude at Santa Barbara's colorful waterfront and visit the historic mission, courthouse and museums of art and history. Or you can rent a bike at the foot of Stearns Wharf and head out Cabrillo Bikeway to the Clark Bird Refuge.

Buses are tops for short distances and visiting smaller locales. They're still the cheapest way to see the country, and you can meet the whole gamut of backbone America. Buses serve more than 15,000 communities, with an enviable record of keeping on schedule. You need to get to the bus terminal only a few minutes before departure. Most tickets are valid for one year so you can stop along the way. Greyhound and Trailways both sell low-cost passes, valid for unlimited travel for varying periods of time.

However you get to the country, let your eye enjoy treasures of graphic arts and architecture waiting to be discovered, appreciated, and preserved. Some of the choicest attractions are functional expressions that have sprung out of the web of American life. Walt Whitman had a special talent for perceiving beauty and art in matter the rest of us would consider manifestations of industrial ugliness. Other individuals have unearthed treasures long forgotten and demanded recognition for them, or discovered meaningful qualities in something too current to be accepted as significant. A subjective experience on the part of the observer counts as much as the established values of the objects themselves. In other words, forget the experts.

How many contemporaries of the cigar-store Indian thought it would become a collector's item and museum piece? How many experts of a century ago looked at the odd fixtures on barns and taverns and foresaw that one day they would be glorified as "folk art"? It takes a certain independence of judgment to envision the metallic skeleton of an oil rig in the Oklahoma landscape or the taut, thin line of a barbed wine fence glinting in the sun across the Western range as art expressions of our age.

Farms, barns and fences form a culture all their own. Among wooden fences there are the pioneer split rails of rough-hewn logs, followed by post and rail, post and plank, the more advanced capped picket and pointed picket, and the elegant white plank fences that enclose thoroughbred horse farms and cost well over a dollar a running foot.

One day in Kentucky I watched a workman while he was repairing stone fencing. He told me he was the third or fourth

La Anna Youth Hostel, La Anna, PA.

generation in a family of stonemasons. In the old days, he said, such fence building served a dual purpose. First, people would gather loose rock from the fields to clear them for plowing. Then they would set the rocks in place to serve as fences, a task requiring infinite patience as no mortar was used. Such fences are perhaps not art at close range but certainly part of the artistic pattern of the landscape.

Various types of barns offer an excellent study of the history of rural America. In the early days barns were often built better than houses, since protection of crops and animals was critical to survival. Depending on where you travel, you can see examples of the Pennsylvania barn, salt-box barn, mountain barn, tobacco barn and horse barn.

The brick-end barns of southeastern Pennsylvania are classics of rural American architecture. Built by the Pennsylvania Dutch, these barns were traditionally decorated. The average age of those still standing is about a hundred years. In their day they were symbols of affluence. The painted barns with the so-called hex signs have been widely celebrated and copied, but the brickwork defies imitation. They derive their name from their construction: both ends, and occasionally the sides, are made of brick, the interiors of timber frame, usually hand-hewn oak. The ends are marked with handsome open-work designs that bring natural light to the interior and circulate the air (to reduce the chance of spontaneous combustion in the hay and straw lofts). The barns are equally impressive inside, where light filters through the walls and shapes its own design.

A barn's plain exterior might belie an intricate internal arrangement of timbers and beams supporting the roof and loft. One ingenious example of barn architecture is the cantilevered log barn found only in the mountains of eastern Tennessee. This barn gets its name from the fact that the loft extends out over the supporting log crib base on cantilevered beams, which are frequently tapered to reduce their weight. Because of the high rainfall of the area, the overhanging loft may have been devised to provide greater ventilation and to enhance drying or curing in wet spaces—an architectural response to environmental needs.

Midwest prairie barns display another personality. They reflect the toils and hopes of farm pioneers whose plows broke the plains. The older barns have higher peaked gables or gambrel roofs, a style that evolved around the turn of the century so that farmers could hang their meats high after butchering. The shape of the roofs also served to deflect the wind and to keep heavy snows from accumulating. Barns with hip roofs were considered showplaces. Later, the Victorian Gothic influence was apparent in the use of gingerbread.

Farm and ranch lands of Kansas and Nebraska, in the heart of the prairie country, have a beauty all their own with vast expanses of waving wheat and herds of grazing cattle. In spring the sun-drenched prairie comes alive with wildflowers: the freshness of the windflower, the blue of verbena and wild indigo, the yellow of goldenrod and sunflower and the bronze red of the tall grass with its waving seedhead.

There is no better area to absorb the spirit of the prairie than on the byroads and farm roads winding through the rolling Flint Hills between Topeka and Manhattan, Kansas. A choice route runs from Chautauqua north to Hanover, through towns rich in western history, like Cottonwood Falls, which has a French renaissance clock tower atop the courthouse. A large portion of this area has been proposed for a Tallgrass Prairie National Park.

Another choice destination is Red Cloud, Nebraska, just 20 miles north of the geographical center of continental United States. This is the region celebrated by Willa Cather, novelist of the prairies. After visiting the Willa Cather Memorial Prairie and Willa Cather Museum, one can appreciate her feelings for the land. She arrived from Virginia in 1883 as a child and years later wrote: "By the end of the first autumn that shaggy grass country had gripped me with a passion I have never been able to shake."

Most of the prairie has given way to cities, highways and huge farms, but fragments still remain scattered across mid-America. In 1978 Amtrak was preparing to clear its right-of-way in Michigan along the route between Detroit and Chicago, not realizing that this would destroy rare and beautiful prairie plants (including the delicate white lady's-slipper, Jacob's ladder, spotted phlox and birdsfoot violet) in the process. A young botanist at a nearby nature center observed that the areas were being mowed. She contacted the Amtrak district engineer, who appreciated her concern, and an agreement was signed with the non-profit Nature Conservancy.

Amtrak pledged not to plow, spray with herbicides, or damage vegetation on the six prairie tracts it owns, while the Nature Conservancy accepted responsibility to manage and protect the areas. Located in an active railroad right-of-way, the prairie parcels are not open to the public, but if rail passengers glimpse a splash of color amid tallgrass as their train speeds through southwest Michigan, they will have seen a reminder of the natural heritage.

Many early hostels were located on farms, and hosteling remains rooted in rural America. From almost any of the hostels in Vermont, for example, you can easily meet people involved in dairy farming (the state has 3,500 dairy farms), in raising sheep and horses, and in making maple syrup and cheese products. The state and Vermont Dairy Industry Council encourage such encounters by sponsoring the Red Clover Trail (marked with a red clover sign), leading to almost 100 participating farms.

The Cannon Hill Youth Hostel, north of Brickerville, Pennsylvania, is one of several hostels in the Pennsylvania Dutch country, a luxuriant and productive farmland. With Cannon Hill as a base, you can visit the Pennsylvania Farm Museum of Landis Valley, a restored village with craft shops, country store and schoolhouse, illustrating country life before 1900. You can see the Ephrata Cloister, left by a communal society known for its music, calligraphy and fine printing, and visit Lancaster, center of the Pennsylvania Dutch country. There are many commercial attractions but fine free points of interest, too, like the museum and planetarium on the campus of Franklin and Marshall College. It costs nothing to visit Lancaster's five farmers' markets, abounding with produce and local delicacies like schnitz and shoofly pie.

Malabar Farm Youth Hostel, outside Mansfield, Ohio, is on the property where Louis Bromfield, the novelist, developed a thousand-acre farm as a model of conservation. Now it's a state park, with the Big House, including the author's study and library, as he left it. Malabar is a center of education about the land—every Sunday, April through October, tractor tours are conducted over the farm.

The Anderson House Youth Hostel is part of a hotel at Wabasha, Minnesota, that has long been in the same family and that sustains the spirit of small town America. Wabasha is on a scenic bend of the Mississippi River, 70 miles south of St. Paul, with an abundance of byroads fanning into the rich farmland of southeast Minnesota. It lies at the northern boundary of the Upper Mississippi River Wildlife and Fish Refuge, where timbered islands and marshes are rich in animal and plant life. The western gateway to the bicycle trail that spans Wisconsin lies 40 miles south and across the Mississippi at La Crosse.

VIII
State Parks

To overlook the potential of state parks for hosteling pursuits and pleasures would be unpardonable. All states have them—and their national, historic and recreational values make attractions in themselves

There are non-government preserves, as well. For instance the National Audubon Society has 70 sanctuaries and nature centers spread across the country. They provide unparalleled opportunities for wildlife viewing and photography. Camping and picnicking are generally not allowed as priority must be given to protection of wildlife in undisturbed settings, but Audubon wardens will direct visitors to suitable areas nearby.

A few years ago, I was canoeing down the east branch of the St. Regis River, in the upper reaches of New York State with my friend and companion, Dick Beamish, one of the great outdoor persons I have known. "This is one of those hidden beauty spots," said Dick. "And the Adirondacks are full of them."

His comment made me conscious of the full dimensions of this huge natural sanctuary in the heart of the populous Northeast. The Adirondack Park covers about six million acres—an area equal in size to the entire state of Vermont. Bounded by the Mohawk Valley, the Canadian border, the St. Lawrence River and Champlain Valley, the park encompasses 2,300 lakes, 1,200 miles of rivers, 30,000 miles of brooks and streams and 46 mountain peaks more than 4,000 feet high.

About 60 percent of the land is privately owned, in large and small holdings, villages and hamlets (but no cities of size), where use is regulated by state law to sustain a harmony with the 2.3 million acres of public owned state lands, officially called the Adirondack Forest Preserve.

The Adirondack Park and Forest Reserve constitute a recreational resource unique in eastern America. Summer communities like Lake George (which alone can accommodate 30,000 guests), Lake Placid, Schroon Lake and Lake Luzerne provide boating, swimming, sailing and golf. Even after the summer months, autumn colors match the best of New England, and winter is a time for skating, skiing (especially ski touring) and snowshoeing. Fort Ticonderoga, Saratoga, Plattsburgh and Lake George all have restored historic sites that reflect the early shaping of a nation.

Campers can choose from 135 public and private camp-

AYH photo

Leadership Training.

grounds and hikers and backpackers from more than a thousand miles of trail. There are hostels, too, in and around the Adirondacks, Blue Mountain Lake, at Hogansburg, Lake George, Lake Placid, Malone, Newcomb, Old Forge, Paul Smith's, Plattsburgh and Warrensburg.

Across the continent, California state parks constitute a significant network in themselves, embracing natural areas from the Anza-Borrego desert to redwood rain forests, beach parks along the Southern California coast, and historic parks recounting many phases of human history—including the homes of Jack London and Will Rogers, and the San Simeon Castle of William Randolph Hearst.

Covering almost half a million acres east of San Diego, Anza-Borrego is one of California's last frontiers. It ranges in elevation from 100 feet below sea level near the Salton Sea to 6,000 feet above sea level atop San Ysidro Mountain and in many places is as wild as when the first Spanish explorers found it. The traveler with patience and a sharp eye can find 600 different species of plants, many producing lovely flowers in spring. The park is a refuge for birds and many species of wild animals, including the rare desert bighorn sheep. There are developed campsites, but this is the only California state park where you can camp anywhere you wish.

In Northern California, if you stay at Arcata Crew House Youth Hostel, at Arcata, you will have access to great redwood state parks, including Richardson Grove, Humboldt, Grizzly Creek, Del Norte and Jedediah Smith—the last three are within the boundaries of Redwood National Park but still administered by the state of California. They are among 30 magnificent redwood state parks, comprising 135,000 acres, purchased by the Save-the-Redwoods-League, with large and small donations from private citizens, and by the State of California with matching funds.

In the Middle West, Porcupine Mountains Wilderness State Park is a substantial park with wide appeal to outdoors lovers. It covers more than 58,000 acres on the Upper Peninsula (20 miles west of Ontonogan), rising in elevation from the shore of Lake Superior to Government Peak, 2,023 feet, the highest point in the northern tier of states between the Adirondacks and the Black Hills of South Dakota. Miles of trail lead through protected hardwood and pine forests to beauty spots like the Lake of the Clouds.

While Porcupine Mountains is rewarding in its remoteness, it isn't necessary to go all that far to escape civilization. The Heavner Home Hostel, at Milford, Michigan, is only 45 minutes from Detroit. Yet here at Proud Lake State Recreation Area there are many wonders of nature for those who travel and look closely.

Oswald West State Park, north of Manzanita, Oregon, is one of the outstanding Pacific Coast beach areas, with panoramic rolling surf and rocky cliffs. Along the beach are caves and creeks, excellent surf fishing, swimming, clamming and camping.

Custer State Park, in the heart of the Black Hills of South Dakota, covers 58,000 acres, with one of the world's largest buffalo herds, as well as deer, elk and bighorn sheep.

Itasca State Park, Minnesota, covers 32,000 acres, much of it water, including Lake Itasca, the source of the Mississippi River. The Itasca forest is dominated by spruce and white pine, but it contains nearly every kind of tree, plant and wild animal native to Minnesota.

Cumberland Falls State Park, Kentucky, is noted for its outstanding falls. The water drops 65 feet, and on bright moonlit nights a moon bow can be seen in its midst. (The only other moon bow is in South Africa.)

A number of parks in many states have great appeal in winter, as well as other seasons. Porcupine Mountains, for instance, gets about 100 inches of snow, making it delightful for skiing and snowshoeing. If you stay at the Vermont State Ski Dorm, at Stowe, Vermont, you'll not only have modest priced accommodations in a classy ski resort, but also access to miles and miles of ski touring trails across state forests and lands administered by the Nature Conservancy.

The National Audubon Society's 70 sanctuaries and nature centers range in size from 10 acres, at Theodore Roosevelt Sanctuary, Oyster Bay, New York, to 27,000 acres of coastal marsh at Rainey Wildlife Sanctuary on the Gulf Coast of Louisiana. Before visiting any of them, it's imperative to recognize their basic role: to safeguard breeding grounds of rare or threatened species, including the forest or marsh or whatever habitat on which they depend. This means that certain critical sanctuaries are closed to visitors and certain others open only through special arrangements with the wardens. Wherever nature centers are part of the sanctuaries, it's another story. These are definitely for people, of all ages, to learn about the wonders of the outdoors in unspoiled settings.

Corkscrew Swamp Sanctuary, between Naples and Fort Myers, Florida, embraces one of the last large fragments of original Florida. Walk the trail on the raised boardwalk through the swamp and you'll see the largest remaining stands of baldcypress, some trees measuring 25 feet around, ferns and epiphytes thriving in the moist setting, alligators, turtles, snakes and fish in ponds and streams beneath the lush greenery. Foremost among birds are thousands of wood storks, the only American stork. During spring nesting season thousands of storks, more than in the nearby Everglades, nest on the tree limbs.

Aullwood Audubon Center and Farm, just 10 miles from downtown Dayton, Ohio, depicts scenes of Midwestern history. There's the working farm, complete with century-old barn, windmill, springhouse, garden, orchard, pasture and domestic farm animals. And there's the bordering forest and vestige of tallgrass prairie. Walks along discovery trails reveal 300-year-old oaks, the old sugarbush, snakes, turtles, toads, songbirds, owls and hawks.

Sable Palm Grove Sanctuary, on the Rio Grande River, near the popular resort of Brownsville, Texas, is one of the newest and most intriguing in the Audubon network. It protects a grove of the rare sabal palm trees, along with unusual birds, plants, brilliant butterflies, spiders and beetles that range only this far north from Mexico and Latin America. Between the Audubon sanctuary and nearby Santa Ana National Wildlife Refuge, you are apt to see the rare speckled racer, rose-throated becard, chachalaca, buff-bellied hummingbird and jacana, as well as trees such as ebony, anaqua, guayacan and retama. Late spring bird migrations include spectacular flights of 20,000 broad-winged hawks.

If you were to stay at the Ohiopyle Youth Hostel, 20 miles east of Uniontown, Pennsylvania, you would be close to the Bear Run Nature Reserve, in the forested Laurel Highlands. Maintained by the Western Pennsylvania Conservancy, trails wind through the Reserve and along the spectacular Youghiogheny River Gorge. One trail leads to Fallingwater, the architectural masterpiece designed by Frank Lloyd Wright as the private retreat of a wealthy Pittsburgh family (now open to the public), with sweeping balconies cantilevered from huge boulders and a lovely waterfall directly below the main terrace. There is rafting on the Youghiogheny River, or the "Yock," in Ohiopyle State Park—a 7½ mile float through deep woods, accessible only by water.

IX
Urban Pleasures

Each city is a world of its own. There are major differences in speech, appearance and atmosphere in cities as close as Baltimore and Philadelphia. New York is still "Bagdad-on-the-subway," even after all the years since O. Henry dubbed it as such, and Chicago is the stormy, husky, brawling City of the Big Shoulders, just as Carl Sandburg said long ago.

It isn't easy for a city to be itself. Pressures tend to make cities over to the point where they can't be distinguished from each other, what with urban freeways, convention centers, chain hotels and culture palaces variously called Lincoln Center, Kennedy Center and Chandler Pavilion—all out of the same mold. It isn't easy, but it helps to know how to look. A number of years ago when Ralph Rinzler, a friend of mine, moved to Washington to run the Folk Festivals on the Mall for the Smithsonian Institution, he took up residence in the unlikely Northeast section. He listened to what people were singing and smelled what they were cooking and found a folk festival on every block.

With a sympathetic eye you can create your own walking tour anywhere. A decent map and a guidebook will help for directions, dates and data, but the main idea is to look closely at the cityscape to get the feel of it. Hostels are located in many cities and will give you excellent starting points and sources of information and guidance.

Consider Los Angeles, the West's largest city, as an example. The Visitors and Convention Bureau, at 505 South Flower Street, makes available free maps and booklets telling about commercial attractions, parks, cultural institutions and historic landmarks. One of the best of the landmarks, the Bradbury Building, is the kind of place to spend some time. It was built almost a century ago as a pioneer skyscraper, all of five stories tall, with wood and cast-iron fixtures, an elevator with an open cage and a skylight that lets the light filter through the building. There is a pleasant, inexpensive place to eat on the second story, or you can walk across the street to the Grand Central Market, where stalls sell simple foods and Mexican specialties. Nearby (across Pershing Square), the Biltmore Hotel, dates from 1923 and its lobby is an example of the opulence of the day.

To see a glorious example of people's art, head for the Watts section of Los Angeles, where Sam Rodia, a tile setter by trade, lived at 1765 East 107th Street, a dead-end street. He began constructing what are now called the Watts Towers in his backyard in 1921. He worked quietly and alone, evenings and weekends, on his complex of open-worked, multicolored, and ornate turrets. His artistic use of seemingly useless materials is impressive. In his composition are 75,000 seashells, hundreds of broken dishes, thousands of pieces of broken tile, several truckloads of broken bottles: all fit into place in the mosaics or in the patterns adorning his spires and spheres. Experts have called Watts Towers the art treasure of California, the paramount achievement of 20th Century folk art, and a classic of architectural forms.

For contrast, you can take a bus to Malibu to visit the J. Paul Getty Museum. Designed as a replica of an ancient Italian villa destroyed by the eruption of Vesuvius, the museum houses such diverse art treasures as Greek and Roman statuary and paintings by Italian and Dutch masters. Getty is said to have personally approved or purchased everything the museum contains. Though it opened in 1974, he died in 1976 without seeing it. Nevertheless, Getty, the richest man in the world, left the bulk of his estate to this art museum, perched on a bluff overlooking the Pacific.

A city like Los Angeles has many sides. The Union Passenger Terminal was opened in 1939 as one of the last great rail depots and remains an Art Deco landmark worth exploring. Across the street, in El Pueblo de los Angeles State Park, walking tours are conducted regularly from the historic Plaza where Los Angeles began through the cluster of the city's earliest buildings. Straddling the eastern end of the Santa Monica Mountains, Griffith Park covers more than 4,000 acres. It has its share of attractions (including the zoo, observatory, open-air theatre and the West's largest collection of rail equipment), but most of the park is undeveloped and natural. Miles of trails lead through canyons and woodlands and up rugged slopes to the 1,625-foot summit of Mount Hollywood. One of the nicest parts of the park borders the Ferndell Nature Center, where trails lead past waterfalls and terraced pools and a landscape of ferns, ginger, acanthus, aranthus and other plants adapted to the cool, moist dell.

Chicago, the city and environs, is a living architectural museum. From the 19th century birth of the skyscraper through the supertowers of today, Chicago has erected a collection of buildings unmatched anywhere on earth. Here are the works of H.H. Richardson, who inspired the "Chicago School," Frank Lloyd Wright (with 75 buildings in the city and

Tosrvphoto

Annual Mother's Day Tour of Scioto River Valley, OH.

suburbs), Louis Sullivan, Daniel Burnham and Mies van der Rohe—men who have changed the world's cities. The Chicago Architecture Foundation (1800 South Prairie Avenue, Chicago, Illinois 60616) operates an outstanding tour program of 25 separate itineraries by foot, bicycle and bus. Prices are modest because the tours are led by volunteer guides—teachers, lawyers, secretaries and architects—who love their city.

There is no better way to get a meaningful overview of Chicago. Even if you'd rather get around on your own, you ought to visit the headquarters of the Foundation, formerly the John J. Glessner House, built in 1886 according to the plans of H.H. Richardson and the city's sole surviving example of his work. It is the nucleus of the Prairie Avenue Historic District, an innovative outdoor "museum of urban change." Look over the available literature and pick up a free copy of the program of tours. You might want to follow the itinerary of "Lincoln Park by Bike," or the "River Walk," tracing the history of Chicago from the site of Fort Dearborn to the world's tallest building (the Sears Tower), or walk along the banks of the waterway that flows backwards, or take the "Frank Lloyd Wright in Oak Park" tour, viewing the scenes where America's most famous architect lived and worked during the 20 years in which Prairie School architecture evolved.

One of the Foundation's most popular tours (whenever it's given) visits Graceland Cemetery, perhaps the most monumental cemetery in the nation, where Chicago's nabobs, like George Pullman and four generations of the Marshall Field family are handsomely entombed beneath marble and bronze memorials, designed by noted sculptors such as Daniel Chester French and Lorado Taft and by architect Louis Sullivan. Stop at the main building and ask for a map and location guide to the most famous graves. Allan Pinkerton's monument bears an inscription that begins as you might expect: "A friend to honesty and a foe to crime."

There are pleasures to be found in cemeteries. Many are like arboretums, softly landscaped, affording opportunity for contemplation and self-study. There is hardly a more beautiful springtime setting in the South than at Bonaventure Cemetery, at the edge of Savannah, Georgia, where weathered tombstones are shaded by ancient live oaks and bordered by pink azaleas, camellias and wisteria. Walk through the Old Burying Ground at Cambridge, Massachusetts, dating from 1635, and you'll become absorbed by the gravestones of early settlers, Revolutionary War veterans and the first eight Harvard presidents.

Many visitors to Washington, D.C. are fascinated by the Georgetown section, but few make it to Rock Creek Cemetery at the edge of Georgetown. Those who do are rewarded by the chance to view the bronze statue of "Grief," a memorial to Mrs. Henry Adams from her husband, sculpted by Augustus Saint-Gaudens. Mark Twain was so deeply moved he said the figure embodies all human grief, while Alexander Woollcott called it "the most beautiful thing ever fashioned by the hand of man on this continent."

This leads me to a favorite, but generally overlooked, building in downtown New York is the old Custom House, the bastion of Bowling Green. It stands near the tip of Manhattan among the banking halls and maritime palaces, occupying the site where the Dutch came ashore in 1626 to build Fort Amsterdam, and where Government House was constructed in 1790, when New York was the young nation's capitol.

The Custom House is a seven-story granite vintage piece of 1907. Cass Gilbert, its designer, embellished the exterior with 44 Corinthian columns, stone dolphins, masts, rudders, waves and a convention of statues representing the continents, races of mankind, and the ancient and modern seafaring powers. The building cost so much to erect ($5,000,000) that the Government ran out of money before decorating the rotunda above the main hall. During the WPA days, however, Reginald Marsh was put to work on a series of eight murals around the convex ceiling. For $90 a month, he depicted, with his excellent draftsmanship, energy and humor, an outstanding study of New York landings and departures. The whole building is, in fact, a monument to the saga of the sea and one of the world's major seaports.

All week lower Manhattan is a bustling commercial center. When the weekend comes, however, it becomes a region ideal for walking, bicycling and leisurely exploring. It is one of America's most historic corners. Trace a line from Federal Hall National Memorial, at Wall and Nassau Streets, commemorating the site where George Washington was inaugurated as the first president, to St. Paul's Chapel (where he worshipped), the Custom House, Trinity Church, Castle Clinton, Fraunces Tavern and South Street Seaport and you have New York's answer to Boston's Freedom Trail.

A cyclist will love it here on a weekend. Try City Hall Park, with a side trip across Brooklyn Bridge—on the pedestrian level for a gull's eye view of the East River. Or take the ferry

Pt. Reyes Hostel

from Battery Park to Staten Island. Cycle up to Soho, Washington Square and Greenwich Village. Sidewalks are wide so you can dismount and push or window shop. Bike shops are listed in the Yellow Pages, in case you need to rent one.

New York, for all its overpowering dimensions when taken en masse, breaks down into neighborhoods of manageable proportions. Mulberry Street is the center of Little Italy, where the streets are filled with aromas of Italian cooking and with sounds of Italian opera flowing from tenement windows. Various festivals during summer and autumn attract crowds with game booths, rides and lots of tasty Italian food and drink.

Next door to Little Italy is Chinatown, centered around Mott and Pell Streets. It is unmistakable with its pagoda-shaped telephone booths, Chinese pharmacies and grocery stores, tea parlors, and good cheap restaurants.

The Lower East Side, where Eastern European Jews settled soon after the turn of the century, still looks in some parts as it did then, though the area is shared now by Puerto Ricans, Cubans, blacks, and various others.

Uptown on the East Side, Yorktown, ethnically represents German and Eastern European influences, with plenty of beer halls and restaurants specializing in Wiener schnitzel and sauerbraten.

Theodore Roosevelt's brownstone birthplace and boyhood home can be reached by Lexington Avenue subway or Madison Avenue bus. The four-story house at 28 East 20th Street, a few blocks above Greenwich Village, is now Theodore Roosevelt Birthplace National Historic Site, largely restored to the period of Teddy's formative years, filled with family furnishings and memorabilia.

Subways provide access to museums, theatres, scenic attractions and architectural landmarks throughout four of the five boroughs. They make 458 stops, run largely above ground once out of downtown and will take you as far as Coney Island and Brighton Beach on the Atlantic coast. Lots of graffiti is in evidence on the trains and along the routes, though you may also find of interest the wall tiling of underground stations done long ago.

Bus lines serve practically every avenue and major street. The two Culture Bus Loops operate weekends and most holidays, taking you to the front door of virtually all major cultural institutions and tourist attractions for a single price, no matter how many times you get on and off.

You might also ride the Staten Island Ferry, from the Battery at the tip of Manhattan, to Staten Island, the city's last frontier. The 25-minute cruise gives close-up views of the bustling harbor, the Statue of Liberty and Ellis Island and costs only 25 cents for the round trip.

Cities tell fascinating stories about themselves through their public transportation. In New Orleans, the St. Charles Avenue Streetcar is a marvel of its kind. Believed to be the oldest continuously operating streetcar in the world, it is a National Historic Landmark in motion, traveling the full length of broad, boulevard-like St. Charles Avenue. It starts at the edge of the French Quarter, runs through the business district and out to the Garden District, University District and Audubon Park. It passes blocks of mansions built by wealthy planters, cotton traders and rivermen who spared nothing to rival the classic Creole homes of the French Quarter. The trip takes about 45 minutes one-way, but it's worth stretching it for hours, with stops at musuems, the zoo, shops and restaurants. Happily, the city has established a single price for a Streetcar Pass, valid for all day. You can count on a car passing almost every 10 minutes.

The July, 1981 launching of the first bright red streetcar out of the historic Santa Fe rail depot at San Diego marks completion of the first streetcar line built anywhere in the United States in 20 years. It's called the "Tijuana Trolley," since the 33-minute ride ends at Tijuana, Mexico, across the border. You can also ride streetcars in Boston, Newark, Philadelphia, Pittsburgh, Cleveland and San Francisco.

San Francisco's cable cars, clanking up and down steep streets, are the most famous streetcars in the world. Loved by residents and visitors, they carry 11 million riders yearly over their 10 miles of track. The Cable Car Barn on Mason Street is open to visitors, displaying the wheels pulling the cables in actual operation, along with relics of the early transit system (including the first cable car of 1873).

Another unique streetcar is the historic Duquesne Incline in Pittsburgh, one of few remaining funiculars in the world. It has operated in perfect condition since 1877 and was rescued by local citizens from annihilation in 1963. You may see the six cast-iron sheaves, weighing one ton each, which were installed as part of the renovation. The view from the observation deck at the 400-foot-high summit reveals the Golden Triangle—more spectacular at night than in the daytime—where the Allegheny and Monongahela Rivers merge to form the mighty Ohio, once the gateway to the West.

Actually, the Chicago Transit Authority's elevated system is a moving museum piece, too, one of the oldest still functioning. Note the different types of cars, track structures and station designs and how they blend into Chicago's history, architecture and atmosphere.

Seattle supports one of the country's most interesting transportation networks. For one thing, buses cover the entire city and all the suburbs. For another, the "Magic Carpet" service offers free rides in the downtown area. The city reimburses Seattle-King County Metro for this service; all you have to do is get on and off and forget about fares. Best part of all is the chance to ride the Washington State ferries serving Puget Sound and the San Juan Islands.

The ferries are as fine as anywhere in the world. They are a part of life for commuters and a delight for visitors. They go to the Olympic Peninsula, resorts, island state parks and ocean beaches; but even if you don't get off, or have no place to go, the ferries are still fun to ride. Nine different routes serve 45,000 travelers every day, or 18 million per year. They carry buses, trucks, bicycles, cars and walkers. Each ferry has a restaurant (where beer is served), observation deck, and miles of glass for inside viewing if weather turns inclement.

The all-day trip during summer from Anacortes, 83 miles north of Seattle, winding through the San Juan Islands to British Columbia, is one of the finest boat trips in the country. The San Juans, over 172 islands, are vestiges of unspoiled America. Among the four islands at which the ferry stops, Orcas Island is the setting of Moran State Park, with salt water beach, waterfalls and a trail to the summit of Mount Constitution, 2,454 feet high, overlooking a panorama of water, islands and the snowy peaks of the Cascades and Olympics. The ferry also stops at San Juan Island—where a national historical park memorializes the border confrontation of 1859-1872 between the United States and Great Britain—on its way to the port of Sidney, 17 miles from Victoria, the beautiful capitol of British Columbia. The run is popular with cyclists, bus travelers and foot passengers (especially since convenient bus connections are available to downtown Victoria).

Riding the ferries ties in handsomely with a visit to places along Seattle's waterfront, like Pioneer Square where the city began, and Pike Place Market, an absolute one of a kind. The Square was Seattle's main business district during the Alaska Gold Rush, the jumping-off point for the treasure hunters of 1898, and now partly restored to its former appearance with interesting galleries, bookstores and restaurants occupying the original buildings. As for the Pike Place Market, the celebrated Seattle chronicler, Jim Faber, sums it up in a single sentence: "Nowhere in America do so many farmers, tradesmen, artisans, and customers share a locale that is as earthily colorful and genuine as the time-wrapped labyrinth known to all Seattleites as simply The Market." It is exactly the kind of place that hostelers will enjoy.

X
Colleges and College Towns

Colleges and college towns are overlooked treasures. They may be off the standard travel circuits, but they are barometers to the direction America is taking.

Colleges have art galleries, museums, buildings of architectural merit, cafeterias, concerts and students willing to share their opinions. Many colleges and universities furnish guide services and all welcome visitors.

Apart from the campus, college towns frequently are attractive in their own right. They can be pleasant, economical vacation spots, particularly since student haunts are geared to undergrad allowances.

Westwood Village, as a striking example, may be next door to Beverly Hills and surrounded by the rest of Los Angeles, but it still retains many aspects of a village and college town. The college itself, the University of California at Los Angeles, offers some of the finest free activities and points of interest in the Los Angeles area.

These include the Museum of Cultural History, in Haines Hall, featuring folk art from all over the world, with hands-on exhibits for the blind. The Murphy Sculpture Garden, near the arts complex, contains pieces by Twentieth Century masters like Rodin, Matisse and Henry Moore in a garden setting. Free noonday concerts are given on the patio of Schoenberg Hall. Each Thursday afternoon a tour is conducted to a different campus attraction, and on Wednesday evening you can look through the 16-inch telescope at the observatory in the Math Sciences Building.

The campus at UCLA is a self-contained community covering 400 acres. Make your first stop the Visitor Center at the Student Union for directions. You'll learn that you're welcome for breakfast, lunch and supper at various snack shops, cafeterias and dining rooms, such as the Tree House in the Student Union, Bomb Shelter Deli in the Court of Sciences (with patio seating), the Coffee House in Kerckhoff Hall and North Campus Food Facility. Ask for a copy of the booklet, "University Garden," which outlines a self-guiding tour of plants and trees landscaping the campus. Pleasant activities in autumn include watching women's and men's soccer and lacrosse. There is lots of running, too, which you are welcome to join at the Drake Stadium track or the 18-station parcourse.

In the East, Princeton, New Jersey, has been called "the most beautiful college town in America." It has a little of the aura of Cambridge and Oxford in England. Nassau Hall, the oldest building on the campus, was home to the Continental Congress in 1783, while the capitol was briefly at Princeton. Over the years leaders in science, letters and politics, including Woodrow Wilson, Thomas Mann and Albert Einstein, have lived at Princeton and been associated with the University. Stanhope Hall is the center of guided tours, which reveal the works of Twentieth Century sculptors—Picasso, Nevelson, Calder, Epstein, Moore and others—in courtyards, plazas, lawns and lobbies all over the campus.

Picasso's work, "Head of a Woman," stands at the entrance to the University Art Museum. This museum contains outstanding paintings and art objects from ancient to contemporary times and offers gallery talks and guided tours of its own. The Natural History Museum will appeal to geologists, since it was founded by Professor Arnold Henry Guyot, who came from Switzerland to pioneer in geographic and geological studies of America.

Princeton is about an hour away from New York and Philadelphia. Once you arrive, there is pleasant bicycling in the vicinity. Nearby George Washington Crossing State Park commemorates the heroic crossing of the Delaware River by Washington and his army on Christmas night in 1776, enroute to turning the tide of the Revolution at the Battle of Trenton. Nature trails lead from the Visitor Center through forests and rolling hills to an overlook at the actual river landing area.

It isn't only the large, prestigious colleges that have something special to offer. Stay at the Springfield College Camp, a hostel outside Springfield, Massachusetts, and you will have access to the museums and restored areas of downtown Springfield. The Mattoon-Elliot Streets section shows townhouses of the past with slate roofs, ornate cornices, large octagonal dormers and stained glass windows. Springfield Armory National Historic Site, which had its beginning in the American Revolution, displays the largest collection of military small arms in the world. And on the campus of Springfield College, sports enthusiasts will find the Basketball Hall of Fame, complete with replica of the original gynmasium where Dr. James Naismith invented the game in 1891. He had come to Springfield as a physical education instructor. The game he devised was different than basketball today: there were nine men on a team and no dribbling was

Camp Warren. View looking over Lake Michigan from Vesper Point.

allowed; players shot a soccer ball at peach baskets 10 feet above the floor.

In the foothills of the Alleghenies, the campus of Salem College, 12 miles west of Clarksburg, West Virginia, includes Fort New Salem, a living museum representing a typical frontier settlement of the late 1700s. It's a community project involving people of all ages—a classroom in history, arts and crafts, conducted in 20 buildings, mostly log cabins, moved from different points in the area and reconstructed on the campus. You can set up a base at nearby Blackwater Falls State Park and take whitewater river trips, hike and ride in the mountains.

Berea College, at Berea, Kentucky, is another unusual small school, designed to provide higher learning to young people of the Southern Mountains. The students all work—in college offices, at handicrafts, at college-owned farms, and at an attractive campus hotel, the Boone Tavern.

Collges consciously strive for green campus landscapes. Stay at the University YMCA, the hostel in the center of the Madison campus of the University of Wisconsin, and you'll have at hand the 1,200-acre arboretum on the shores of Lake Mendota. This outstanding campus has abundant attractions outdoors and indoors, including the Planetarium, in Sterling Hall; Washburn Observatory, on Observatory Drive; the Geology Museum, and Elvehjem Museum of Art, with collections spanning man's creative talents from ancient to modern times.

Tosrvphoto

Or try the unique Student Housing Co-ops at East Lansing, Michigan, and you'll have access to the 5,100-acre campus of Michigan State University, beautifully landscaped with 7,600 different species and varieties of trees, shrubs and vines. Since Michigan State was founded as the country's first agricultural college (and the pioneer land-grant college), you will find such interesting features as the experimental farms, Beal Botanic Gardens, in continuous use since 1873, and the horticultural gardens with roses and tulips.

The Boulder International Youth Hostel is only two blocks from the University of Colorado, ideally located 30 miles north of Denver and 36 miles south of Estes Park, gateway to Rocky Mountain National Park. Boulder, in fact, is the only city in the world which obtains part of its water supply from its own glacier, Arahapo, 28 miles west. The University Museum, in the Henderson Building, displays natural history objects that furnish a worthwhile introduction to the Rockies. With the city-owned mountain park system, you needn't go far to enjoy Colorado's natural pleasures.

XI
Treading Lightly to
Leave Treasures in Place

Over the years I've watched the transformation of communities and whole regions from the impact of tourism. Aspen and Vail were once quiet villages in the Colorado Rockies. Today they are crowded and complicated, with traffic lights, hotels, gift shops, clothing stores and bars jumbled on top of each other. Forty years ago Gatlinburg was a Tennessee country crossroads at the gateway to Great Smoky Mountains National Park. Today the "number one mountain resort of the nation" is an obstacle course of neon-lit motels, commercial tourist attractions and gift shops, while the approach roads are ablaze with billboards.

The impact of tourism has had its adverse effect on people, as well. Placed in an unnatural condition, an individual is likely to respond unnaturally—which means that the friendly, fun-loving native who would give his all to a stranger in need can become hard and bitter after encountering tourists who feel that money buys anything.

Hosteling is another kind of tourism. It treads lightly on the land. Hostelers go places and do things under their own power which is a natural and non-harmful effort. I think of the difference between ski touring and snowmobiling. The skier exercises every part of his body, creating rhythm of motion within himself and harmony with the white world around him. The snowmobiler feels a sense of power, excitement, control, but his focus of attention is on the activity of riding the machine, as a game, an end in itself, rather than on nature or the scenery. He's unmindful of shattering silence on a wintry day or night, of polluting clean air with exhaust fumes. He doesn't notice, because he has scorned the challenge of hard work, the feeling of self-sufficiency away from a super-civilized world. When a person enters a machine, he relegates himself to being a cog in the machinery; he detracts from nature and natural recreation, rather than contributing to them.

Hosteling is economical. Hostelers are out to save money when they can, and their interest is in life as everyday people lead it. It's a shift in emphasis from superstandards of living to quality of life.

What will you bring home as a hosteler? The best souvenirs

are ideas of what the world should be like, based on healthful experiences and stimulating places hostelers visit.

There are some souvenirs that I would advise against bringing home. Scrimshaw would be high on that list. True enough, it's an old art form traditionally practiced by whalers producing intricate and often beautiful carvings during long periods at sea. They would carve mostly on the teeth of the sperm whale, a species which is now protected under the 1973 Endangered Species Act. According to the law, sperm whale teeth cannot be sold unless acquired prior to 1973, and unless the seller (or possessor) has a permit issued by the National Marine Fisheries Service.

Needless to say, a lot of scrimshaw is touted as being whale teeth acquired before 1973, or having been made from fossilized tusks of walruses or from elephant tusks. No doubt some of this is true, but plastic of ivory color labeled as scrimshaw creeps in, too. The point is that as long as consumers purchase items that look like genuine scrimshaw, they encourage exploitation and merchandising of the real thing, accentuating the endangerment of the endangered species.

This idea was driven home to me on a visit to Nairobi, Kenya, in 1977. "If there were no market for the product there would be no killing of elephants," an official of the Kenya government said quite simply. "Tourists encourage poaching when they fall in love with nonsensical items such as lion-tooth 'good luck charms,' elephant-hair bracelets and zebra-skin wallets."

Following our dialogue, I walked the main streets of Nairobi, observing the junk adorning shop windows and walls: stuffed heads of animals, skins of animals shaped into wastebaskets, feet and legs of animals for sale as bookends, ash trays, lamp stands and umbrella stands, teeth and claws as trinkets and jewelry. Since then the sale of such items has been outlawed, but the poaching goes on. The truth is that advanced nations have created an insatiable demand for products made from the wild animals of Africa. Prices have soared and so have imports in Japan, Hong Kong, France, Belgium, Italy and the United States. Tourists contribute to the damage, usually innocently, when they buy souvenirs made from parts of endangered species, often misrepresented one way or another.

Buyers scarcely know that exploitation of tropical seashells has caused disastrous ecological impacts upon portions of the Indian Ocean, the Caribbean and the Pacific. Or that scientists are alarmed by the trade in ornaments made from the blue wings of the giant Morpho butterflies of South America, a trade that has spread to many spectacular Asian and African species.

Consumers are often encouraged by guidebooks and travel articles that advocate seeking such items. In years past I may have written my share of this sort of thing, but no more. I realize the need for better guidance, that travelers should tread lightly and leave treasures in place. It isn't so much a matter of respect for law as for living species and their native environments.

Consider the queen conch, prominently displayed in nearly every shell collection. The conch is startling in its beauty, revealing nature's handiwork at its finest and most mysterious. From the frequency with which the conch is sold in souvenir shops in Florida and the Caribbean, you might assume it's one of the most abundant of molluscs. But this isn't true at all. The shell-producing coral reefs and sandy bottoms of Florida, the Caribbean, Bermuda and northern South America are being continually disturbed by collectors, divers, dealers, tourists and natives.

Shell collecting is a rapidly growing hobby. Each year energetic thousands flock to the beaches of Florida's West Coast and converge on the fragile islands known as the Keys. Shelling is getting worse as more people seek the treasures of the sea washed shore. But seashells cannot reproduce in shell cabinets and cigar boxes. And of those sold in stores, the best specimens are taken live in the western Pacific and then killed. Two of the commonest ways of collecting commercial supplies of shells are dredging the ocean bottom and dynamiting coral formations to expose the molluscs—both methods disrupting entire habitats.

Tortoiseshell, valued for its rare and lasting beauty, is another case. For centuries it has been fashioned into ornaments or inlaid in wood, bone or metal bracelets and boxes. In recent years the demand has multiplied manyfold. The shiny, mottled brown shell comes from one species of tropical sea turtle, the hawksbill, which can hardly endure this popularity.

The reefs of the world could last forever, delighting travelers till the end of time, but such special places demand special treatment. Our own country is enriched by coral reefs along the coasts of South Florida, the Keys, the Virgin Islands and Hawaii. Because the reef community flourishes in clean, clear, sunlit water, it is simple for human visitors to enter and enjoy. Innumerable scuba divers, snorkelers and sightseers

aboard glass-bottom boats visit coral reefs each year.

John Pennekamp Coral Reef State Park, extending out from Key Largo, has become a major asset to tourism in South Florida. Buck Island Reef National Monument, with its marked underwater nature trail opening the wonders of the reef to everybody, is to my mind the best attraction of St. Croix in the Virgin Islands.

When I enter a reef, I find treasures in every square foot: in the coral rising like trees, mountains and spires, the sea feathers and violet-hued sea fans swaying in the current, anemones carpeting the reef like shrubbery, the brilliant colored fish gliding through the network of caves, crevices and boulders or resting on stony branches.

The tiny coral animals exist in reef-producing masses only as long as they live in a healthy environment. Any sediment in the water cuts down on light penetration, and any silt reduces reproduction. This is exactly what is happening. In Kaneohe Bay, Hawaii, pollution in the form of sediment from land development and sewage from bordering towns is believed to have killed more than half the coral reefs. And the same forces have seriously affected the Florida coastal reef.

Still, there is further damage—from commercial coral harvesting and specimen collecting. Both Florida and federal laws prohibit the taking and selling of coral, but the practice continues. Souvenir shops are loaded with huge quantities.

Of course, it's fun to display "a piece of reef" on the mantle at home or to wear classy coral jewelry. But think of it this way: the world has coral reefs because reef-building exceeds the rate of destruction by natural factors. As long as that process continues the reefs will last. However, they cannot endure destruction by human factors. So leave the coral and take home memories.

On returning to your own hearth, let the contrast with faraway places help in better judging the particular place where you live—its streams, valleys, hillsides, architecture, vistas and vignettes of nature and man. Network with others to generate the sense of respect and responsibility born of sharing and interdependence. Apply your perspective toward improving and enriching the everyday quality of life around you, and hosteling will yield its lasting reward.

XII
Planning a Hostel Trip
Independent Travel

One advantage independent travel has over planned group travel is flexibility. There is a certain joy in being able to leave a hostel and travel with the wind at your back. Yet independent travelers would do well to remember the maxim of the AYH National Leadership Courses: **Prior Planning Prevents Poor Performance.** You will want to be certain of the following:

1. Hold a ticket for your return passage.

2. Make reservations at large city hostels during summer months and holiday periods. This is done by enclosing partial payment (see American and International handbooks for addresses and amounts) and, for overseas, two International Reply Coupons, available at any post office. These coupons assure you of a response via air mail.

3. Arrange for mail stops. Large city youth hostels will hold mail for hostelers. Main post offices will hold mail marked "General Delivery" in the language of the country. American Express offices around the world will hold mail for a fee.

4. Locate maps of the areas in which you will be traveling. State and national tourism offices are useful sources for free maps.

AYH Sponsored Trips

American Youth Hostels has specialized in small travel since 1934. Special group trips are arranged every year for summer and winter travel through the U.S., Canada, Caribbean area, Europe, Israel, and Japan. You will discover many advantages in a small, closely-knit group. The travel is informal and personal; on-the-spot decisions can be made to take immediate advantage of local situations. You will go places and see things impossible in larger, less flexible groups.

Hosteling is a special kind of educational travel. Youth Hostel groups are small, 7-10 people, and are under the direction of trained adult leaders. Groups are organized, insofar as possible, according to age and interests. In small AYH groups, individuals become skilled in cooperative living, each bearing a share of the responsibility while maintaining individual freedom.

AYH group leaders are trained and experienced hostelers who have completed the AYH National Leadership Course. Typically, they are teachers, graduate students or social workers who have come up through the ranks as group members. They practice a personalized approach to meet individual needs. Leaders are selected for their ability to work with a group, to handle group funds, and for their practical hosteling experience. It is up to the group, with the aid of the leader, to discover and choose the activities in which the group wishes to take part.

AYH trips feature both out-of-the-way spots and well-known places. Hosteling trips operate on the "do-it-yourself" principle and offer a wide variety of activities including hiking, cycling, canoeing, skiing, sailing, horseback riding, and camping in many countries. Buses, trains, planes, ships, vans, and station wagons are used to reach hosteling areas or to bridge great distances. These programs are described in a pamphlet entitled "Highroad to Adventure," obtainable from National AYH Headquarters.

In addition, AYH local Councils sponsor year-round hosteling programs and several also arrange trips abroad. Write your local Council (see page 214) for further details.

Equipment Checklist

Keep your pack and everything in it as light as possible. For cycling, canoeing and horseback 30 pounds is maximum; for hiking or skiing, it's 10-25 pounds, depending on your size and strength. Keep these things in mind; climate, season, mode of travel, length of your trip, and area it will cover. Select only what is necessary to your well-being and comfort under these conditions. Most of the clothing and other standard equipment needed can be obtained at local stores. Many Councils carry additional items of equipment which hostelers desire. Write your nearest local Council for its price list, or to the Metropolitan New York Council Equipment Supply Service, 132 Spring St., New York, N.Y. 10012.

The check list which follows is to help you remember what you might overlook. **Don't try to take everything.**

Current AYH Pass properly signed and with your picture securely attached; plus completed medical information form.

Sheet Sleeping Sack. Not to be confused with a sleeping bag, the sack is a sanitary protection for mattress and blankets and is required at every hostel. See below for pattern.

AYH and Foreign Handbooks and Maps.

Passports, Visas, validated international certificates of vaccination for overseas travel.

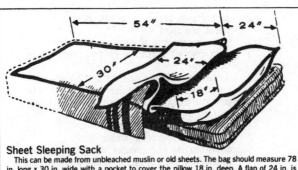

Sheet Sleeping Sack
This can be made from unbleached muslin or old sheets. The bag should measure 78 in. long x 30 in. wide with a pocket to cover the pillow 18 in. deep. A flap of 24 in. is needed to protect the upper blanket, and a gusset each side of the bag adds roominess and prevents tearing. Many AYH councils sell ready-made nylon or muslin sheet sleeping sacks.

Water-repellent money bag or pouch for AYH pass, passport, traveler's checks.

Saddle Bags. Roomy, water repellent double bags that are easily carried on the bicycle or over your shoulder while walking.

Sleeping Bag and Waterproof cover. The maximum weight should be three pounds; approximately 6" in diameter and 14-16" in length when rolled up.

Cycling cape, or water repellent parka.

Space blanket or heavy plastic sheeting, to cover sleeping bag and pack when cycling in the rain.

Clothing

Clothes should be of good quality and able to withstand stress and strain. Washable, perma-press, **quick-drying**, lightweight items—dacron, nylon, or other synthetics are strongly recommended. Do not bring clothes which require ironing or dry cleaning or which cannot be washed. Choose dark, solid colors for slacks and shorts. Match your sweaters, jackets, blouses, etc. so they will go with either informal or dress clothes.

Consider the geography and climate of the areas in which you will travel.

Your biggest temptation will be to bring too much clothing. Keep in mind that you are responsible for carrying your own luggage, and pack accordingly.

Clothing List

Women:

Tops 2-3   drip dry, in colors or prints. Knit or cotton shells are good.

Shorts 1   pair dacron/wool or dacron/cotton shorts.

Pants 1   dark colored cotton or perma-press slacks or jeans.

City Wear 1   outfit, either dress or skirt and blouse combination of drip-dry, quick-drying materials.

Footwear 1   pair comfortable shoes for cycling, walking and hiking.

  1   pair for city wear

  2   pair light wool/cotton socks

Cosmetics . . . .   keep liquids and creams in plastic bottles and jars with tight-fitting lids. Try to limit the amount you take, since you can always buy these while on the trip.

Men:

Shirts 2-3   of the sport or polo-shirt variety, synthetic or perma-press cotton dress shirt and tie.

Trousers 1	pair, dark color in perma-press cotton or blue jeans.
Shorts 1	pair, dark color.
City Wear	perma press, wash and wear, dacron/cotton slacks and sport jacket.
Bandana 2	
Footwear 1	pair sturdy, comfortable shoes for cyling, walking, and hiking.
1	pair for city wear
2	pairs of dark socks, lightweight wool or wool/cotton
Razor	battery operated, or safety razor with blades and shaving cream.

Both:

Pajamas 1	pair quick-drying
Underwear 3	sets quick-drying
Swimwear 1	bathing suit, cap (some pools require caps for men and women)
Towel 1	lightweight, dark-colored, medium size bath towel & wash cloth.
Toilet Articles	toothbrush, toothpaste, plastic bag, soap with container, coldwater soap for clothes, deodorant, comb, shampoo, suntan cream.
Raingear 1	Cycle cape or poncho for bicycle trips. A parka, water-repellent and lightweight, for other types of trips.
Sweater 1	cardigan, all-purpose
Belt 1	strong belt for your money bag
Head Covering ...	for protection against sun and rain while cycling.

Cooking and Camping

Metal Mess Kit or Cup, Plate, Fork, Spoon and serrated-edged knife.

Combination Jack knife and can opener.

Dish towel.

Matches, waterproof case.

Soap. Some hostels and campsites have cold running water where you will not have a chance to soak clothes in detergent. Cold-water soap is highly recommended.

Flashlight. Get one that is attachable to the bicycle.

Toilet tissue (carry flat)

Scouring Pad, copper mesh.

Water bottle or canteen.

Bottles and jars for liquids and creams, plastic

First Aid Musts
Small scissors.
Antibiotic Cream.
Band Aids.
Adhesive tape.
Rolls of 1-inch gauze.
Phisohex soap.
2-inch gauze bandages.
Aspirin.
Burn Ointment (for burns and/or sunburn).
Absorbent cotton.

Possibilities
Bicarbonate of Soda.
Triangle bandage.
Paregoric or Bismuth Compound.
Laxative.
Boric Acid Ointment.

Vaseline.
Calamine Lotion.
Ace Elastic Bandage.
Salt Tablets.

**Packing and
Organization**
AYH Wander Bag (handle-bar bag).
Nylon String Shopping Bag.
Plastic Bags — heavy duty. A quantity of various sizes for clothes, laundry, etc.
Elastic or Webbed luggage straps, elastic preferred. Take at least four.

Personal
Songbook.
Writing, sketching supplies, ball point pens.
Camera supplies.
Sun Glasses. Those wearing glasses should bring an extra pair or the prescription, for long trips.
Insect Repellent.
  Clothesline, clothespins.
Small sewing kit ... Include buttons, safety pins, heavy dark thread

Bicycle Equipment
All metal rat-trap luggage carrier with tubular side supports, either with lock washers bolting carrier to seat post, or regular clamp type with non-slip device. Ring clamp carriers are inadequate and cannot be used with the non-slip device.
Bicycle pump. Invest in a good one.
Bicycle bell or horn.
Tail light. Be sure your bike has a reflector or tail-light.
Combination or long cable lock.
Spare innertube to fit your tire.
Bike repair patch kit and tire irons.
Small adjustable 6-inch wrench.
Small pair pliers, screw driver.
Small roll friction tape or plastic electrical tape.
Spare brake blocks.
Extra valve cores and caps.
Assorted screws and nuts.
Cotton cloth for cleaning.

Hostel Customs

1. HOSTELING means traveling under your own power—biking, hiking, canoeing, skiing, and horseback riding—living and traveling simply in a spirit of fun and friendship, and using youth hostels as overnight accommodations. School and "outdoor" hostels as overnight accommodations. School and "outdoor" education trips are encouraged. Many hostels have facilities for large conference, youth and student tour groups as well.

2. EVERY HOSTELER carries for use at all hostels his own AYH Pass, sheet sleeping sack, and personal eating utensils—plate, cup, knife, fork, spoon and dish-towel.

3. MAKE RESERVATIONS IN ADVANCE and enclose a standard self-addressed envelope for houseparents' reply. **All Reservations must be accompanied by One Full Night's Deposit for each person. (Also for Groups)**

Houseparents may require 100% of total overnight fee to be deposited in advance and may exercise the following refund policy; give full refund for cancellations received 30 days or more before first arrival date; no refund for cancellations received after two weeks before first arrival. Specific exceptions to this rule applicable to some hostels are indicated in the write-ups for these hostels. Reservations not held after 8:00 p.m.; if unavoidably detained, notify houseparents.

4. ARRIVE BETWEEN 4:00 and 7:00 p.m., give membership card to houseparents, show sleeping sack, sign registration book, and pay overnight fee listed in write up and on charter. Hostels customarily are closed between 10:00 a.m. and 4:00 p.m. Kitchens closed after 9 a.m. and 9 p.m.

5. MAXIMUM LENGTH OF STAY at any one youth hostel is 3 days, unless permission is obtained from the houseparents.

6. LIGHTS OUT and bunkrooms quiet from 11 p.m.-7 a.m., but houseparents may extend it. Houseparents may collect a double overnight for violation of this custom.

7. COOKING, CLEANING, and general hostel duties are shared by all hostelers.

8. Check out by 9:30 a.m. If hostel facilities are used between 9:30 a.m.-4:00 p.m., a day fee of 50¢ is charged.

9. ALCOHOLIC BEVERAGES and the use of illegal drugs are not permitted on hostel property.

10. SMOKING usually not allowed in hostels but where the houseparents permit smoking, it is prohibited in sleeping, food preparation and dining areas.

11. MOTOR TRANSPORTATION may be used in connection

with hosteling activities as follows: (1) as transportation to the first hostel of a chain; (b) as transportation to a single hostel only if hiking, bicycling, skiing, canoeing, horseback riding, etc. in the area is intended; (c) as transportation to hosteling activity in cases where time or distance make traveling under your own power unsafe or impractical.

By special arrangement, youth groups touring by auto or bus, may use hostels if (a) they stay two nights at each hostel used; (b) if they spend the intervening day in hosteling activities; and if (c) they make advance arrangements through AYH local Councils and/or National headquarters, and make reservations with houseparents.

12. COLDS OR OTHER ILLNESSES developed on a trip should be reported to houseparents.

13. HOUSEPARENTS MAY WITHHOLD CARD for failure to follow customs. They will inspect the hostel to make sure it is neat and clean before returning membership card. AYH reserves this right when the best interests of the organization are endangered.

14. BEFORE GOING ABROAD become fully acquainted with youth hostel customs of the countries you intend to visit and plan to abide by them. Only **individual** cards are available abroad—not family or group cards. Be sure your card is validated with the proper year stamp.

15. CITY HOSTELS may have somewhat different rules and practices with regard to reservations, arrival, check-out, lights out and closing times, depending on local conditions and requirements. City and Holiday hostels usually charge a higher overnight fee.

16. NEITHER HOSTELS NOR HOUSEPARENTS assume any responsibility for loss or theft of property.

17. Have your snapshot on your pass, or be subject to a 25¢ fine per night.

XIII
The Hostel Directory

The descriptions of hostels are listed in the following pages alphabetically by state and location within each state. For easy reference, the Explanation of Symbols and Abbreviations used in the listings is printed on the following page and again on the last page of the book.

Please note that information on hostels is subject to change. American Youth Hostels, Inc., tries to keep the material as up-to-date as possible. If you find errors or omissions in the individual hostel descriptions or if you think a new map or changes in an existing map are advisable, please send your ideas, corrections, sketches, etcetera, to

Director of Hostel Development
American Youth Hostels, Inc.
National Administrative Offices
1332 I Street NW—8th Floor
Washington, D.C. 20005

Updated information on specific hostels may also be obtained by writing to the above address.

Happy hosteling!

Explanation of Symbols

🛖 Shelter grade hostel
⌂ Simple grade hostel
♠ Standard grade hostel
♨ Superior grade hostel
⌂ Home hostel
SA Supplemental Accommodation
♤ Name of houseparents or managers
☏ Hostel telephone number
━ No. of beds with blankets; ♂ males, ♀ females
─ No. of other beds: ♂ males, ♀ females
♦ Hostel not open all year, open . . .
♦ Advance reservations required during . . .
◑ Address during hostel closed period
● Overnight charge
SN Special rule or condition at this hostel
▲ Hostel owned and/or operated by (If different from hostel or houseparent name)
♨ Type of showers
⋒ Nearest grocery/Name and/or distance
♥ Type of kitchen, or fully equipped
🚌 Location and/or distance of nearest bus station
🚃 Location and/or distance of nearest train station
🚲 Nearest bicycle shop
🚗 $ Nearby parking and fees, if any
✈ Location of nearest airport served commercially, distance
⏶ Camping on hostel grounds
✳ Special attraction and distance from hostel
✳✳ Any special features of the hostel facility
✦ Special accommodations available for families
🎫 Hostel is AYH pass selling agency
⟍ Meals provided I Breakfast and $ II Lunch and $ III Supper and $ I-III inclusive price
⌕ Price for rental linens or sleeping sacks
↦ Any interesting historical fact about hostel
♨ Nearest hostels—by name of town and distance

NOTE: Symbols for which information is not available or which do not pertain to a particular hostel will not appear in the listing.

Most of these symbols are used internationally and have the same meaning when used in the International Youth Hostel Handbook, Vol. 1 & 2.

ALASKA

Alaska Council, Box 1543, Juneau, AK 99802

ANCHORAGE 🏚 Anchorage Youth Hostel, 9500 Jewel Lake Rd, Anchorage, AK 99502.

🏚 Varies

☎ (907) 276-9522; info: 243-3456

🛏 38 ♂ 25 ♀ 13

🏕 Yes. If groups, in summer.

● $5 S, $5 W. Group rates in winter.

SN No pets.

▲ Robert & Liz Auer, Pat Faherty

🚰 Hot and cold

🛒 Carrs or Safeway, 2 blks

🍴 Yes

🚌 Bus stop in front

🚂 1st Ave. & D St, 3 mi

✈ International Airport Rd

⛺ No

* Tennis courts and park next "door"; bowling alley 4 blks, swimming pool & roller rink 1 mi, lots of restaurants, fast food places, 2 shopping centers, car rental 4 blks and bakery. Bicycle rental 2 blks.

** Laundry room facilities

★ No

🏠 Yes

🏚 $1

↦ Anchorage, the Crossroad of the Air World is the gateway to special wilderness experiences via plane, train, bus and water.

DIRECTIONS: Corner of Minnesota Drive and 32nd Ave., 1 blk S of Benson Blvd.

⛪ Nome 500 mi NW, Juneau 500 mi SE

JUNEAU Juneau Youth Hostel (SA, no cooking facilities) Northern Light United Church, 11th & B Sts, Box 1543, Juneau, AK 99802

🏚 Janet & Don Kussart

🛏 ♂ 20 ♀ 10

🏚 June 1-Sept 1

● Box 1543, Juneau, 99802

● $2

▲ Northern Light United Church

🛒 Foodland 1 blk

✈ 9 mi

⛪ Ketchikan 230 mi S by ferry, Sitka 156 mi S by ferry

KETCHIKAN Ketchikan Youth Hostel (SA, no kitchen) First United Methodist Church, Grant & Main St, Box 8515, Ketchikan, AK 99901

🏚 Social Concerns Committee,

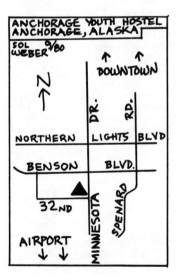

United Methodist Church
- 907-225-2833
- 35 ♀ & ♂
- Memorial Day to Labor Day
- $2
- SN Open 7 PM to 8:30 AM only. No reservations accepted or required.
- ▲ First United Methodist Church, Box 8515, Ketchikan AK 99901
- ⌂ Hot & cold
- ⊓ Schenk Mart 2 blks
- ⇔ local only
- ♨ 1 blk
- 🚗 Adjacent Street
- 🛬 3 mi
- * Boating, fishing 1, Camping 7, Pulp Mill 7, Trails 1, Museums ½.

DIRECTIONS: Methodist Church at Grant & Main Sts in center of town.
- Juneau 230 mi N by ferry or plane, Sitka 200 mi by ferry or plane

NOME Community United Methodist Church Youth Hostel, Box 907, Nome, AK 99762
- John J. & Barbara Shaffer
- 907-443-2865
- ♀ 8 ♂ 8
- ♀ 2 ♂ 2
- $5
- ⊓ Stop shop & save 3 blks
- ♨ yes
- 🛬 Nome 1 mi
- * Bird watchers paradise, reindeer herds, Eskimo gathering place, dog sled races, panning for gold.
- yes
- included in overnight fee
- Located in gold rush town founded in 1899.

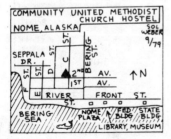

DIRECTIONS: 2nd & C
- Ketchikan 1200 mi SE, Juneau 1000 mi SE, Sitka 1000 mi SE, Anchorage 500 mi SE

SITKA Sitka Youth Hostel, (SA, no kitchen), Sitka United Presbyterian Church, 505 Sawmill Creek Blvd., Box 479, Sitka, AK 99835
- Sitka Youth Hostel Comm.
- (907) 747-6332
- ♀ 10 ♂ 10
- June 1-Sept 1
- $2 S, $3 W
- ▲ Sitka Youth Hostel Committee
- ⌂ Hot and cold
- ⊓ Market Center Super 1 blk
- ♨ Viking Home Center ½ mi
- 🚗 Hostel
- 🛬 Sitka Airport 3 mi
- * St. Michaels Cathedral 3 blks; Sheldon Jackson Museum 3 blks; Totem National Park 4 blks; Harbor Mountain 7 mi.
- yes

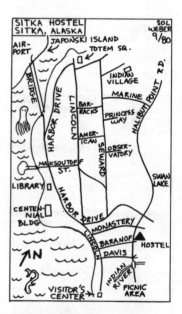

DIRECTIONS: Sitka United Presbyterian Church, corner of Sawmill Creek Blvd &

Baranof St.
🏠 Ketchikan 200 mi S by ferry

or plane, Juneau 156 mi NE
by ferry or plane

ARIZONA
Arizona State Council, 14049 N. 38th Place, Phoenix, AZ
85032. (602) 922-6482.

FLAGSTAFF 🏨 Weatherford Hotel, 23 N. Leroux, Flagstaff, AZ 86001
🏠 Lloyd Taylor
☎ 602-774-2731
🛏 40
🍴 60
🔓 Open all year
● $6.24 members, $8.32 non-members
▲ Lloyd Taylor
♨ Hot & cold
🍴 Food Town 4 blks
♿ yes
🚲 4 blks
🚌 3 blks (Trailways)
🚂 1 blk (AMTRAK)
🚗 Across street
✈ Flagstaff Airport 5 mi S
* Grand Canyon 80 mi
🔑 I 2.50, II 2.50, III 2.50
🔒 $1
➡ Listed on National Register of Historic Places

☎ (602) 524-6770
🛏 ⚦ 15 ⚨ 15
🍴 36
♿ Yes, for groups.
● $4 S, $4 W
🚲 6 blks
🚌 Greyhound 3 blks
* Petrified Forest National Park 19 mi, Painted Desert 25 mi, Navajo, Hopi and Apache reservations.
🔒 50¢

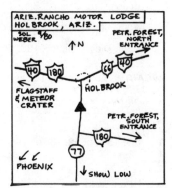

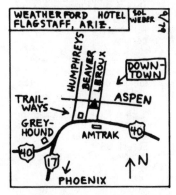

DIRECTIONS: One blk N of AMTRAK station; 2 blks E, then 1 blk N from Trailways Bus Depot.
🏠 Phoenix, 140 mi S, Holbrook 140 mi SE

HOLBROOK Arizona Rancho Motor Lodge, 57 Tovar St, P.O. Box 695, Holbrook, AZ 86525
🏠 Mrs. Lloyd M. Taylor

PHOENIX 🏠 South Mountain Hostel 1346 E South Mountain Ave, Phoenix, AZ 85040

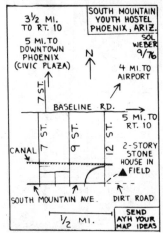

ARIZONA

⌂ David & Phyllis Harkins
🕭 (602) 268-9949
⊨ 24 ⚐ 10 ⚐ 10
⬤ $4.50
SN Buses stop running at 6 PM, none on Sundays. Open 5 PM. Close 8:30 AM. Non-smoking.
▲ City of Phoenix
ᵮ yes
🚍 6 mi
🚲 10 mi
🚶 10 mi
✈ 7 mi
✳ So. Mtn. Park. largest city park in world, 2 blks, Heard Museum, 6 mi (anthropology), Grand Canyon (200 mi) Indian reservations, (20 mi)
✳✳ Quiet area in park
🏠 yes
� Historic stone house built by Sears in early 1900s.
DIRECTIONS: ½ mi S of Baseline Rd. Enter from 7th St. From downtown, take bus to 7th St & S. Mtn Ave.
🏠 Flagstaff 140 mi NW

CALIFORNIA

Central California Council, PO Box 28148, San Jose, CA 95159
(408) 298-0670
Golden Gate Council, Bldg. 240, Ft. Mason, San Francisco, CA
94123. (415) 771-4646
Los Angeles Council, 1502 Palos Verdes Dr., N., Harbor City, CA
90710. (213) 831-8109
San Diego Council, 1031 India St., San Diego, CA 92101.
(714) 239-2644

ARCATA 🏠 Arcata-Crew House, 1390 I St, Arcata, CA 95521
⌂ Cliff Harvey
🕭 (707) 822-9995
⊨ 6
⊢ 14
🏠 June 15-Sept 19, 1981
⬆ Suggested
⬤ $3.75 S
SN Checkout by 9 AM
🚰 Hot and cold

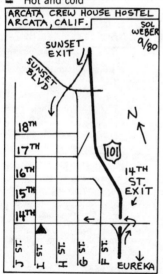

🍴 Arcata Coop 5 blks, Larry's Market 2 blks
ᵮ yes
🚍 Greyhound, 10th & G, Arcata 6 blks; Amtrak in Redding 120 mi; Arcata Transit, 10th & G, 6 blks
🚲 Life Cycle, 17th & H, 4 blks
🚗 At hostel $ no charge for parking
✈ Hughes Airwest, 6 mi at Arcata Airport, McKinleyville
✳ Redwood National Park, 35 mi; Pacific Coast Bicentennial Bicycle Trail, 4 blks; Humboldt State University, 6 blks; Pacific Ocean, 5 mi; Trinity Alps Primitive Area and Six Rivers National Forest, 35 mi.
✳✳ Bicycles available for rent
★ yes
🏠 yes
➤ House is old Victorian, featuring some fine woodwork in redwood burl.

DIRECTIONS: Hostel is at the corner of 14th & I in Arcata.
🏠 Bandon, OR 200 mi; Shasta, CA 175 mi; Point Reyes 200 mi; San Francisco 280 mi

BONITA, 🏠 Creepy Hollow Hostel. Reservations: 3440 Valley Rd, Bonita, CA 92002

(S of San Diego)

🏠 Mr. & Mrs. Edwin Campbell

📞 (714) 475-1573

🔑 Reservations required year around.

🌐 $3 S, $3 W

SN Folk music participation encouraged. No smoking allowed

🚰 Hot & cold

🏪 ½ mi

🚲

🚌 ¼ mi, city bus stop

🚆 San Diego AMTRAK, 10 mi

🚴 1½ mi

🚐 at hostel

✈️ San Diego, 12 mi

⛺ yes

* Mexico, 8 mi. One of the most Southwesterly areas in the United States.

** swimming pool, hot tub

👪 families welcome, but no special accommodations.

🍷 Yes, but weekends only.

💰 I $1, II $1, III $2, I-III $6

🏠 Map of hostel will be mailed with confirmation of reservation.

🏠 Armed Services YMCA, San Diego, 10 mi; San Diego Point Loma Hostel, San Diego, 14 mi

JULIAN (A) 🏠 Camp Stevens Hostel P.O. Box 367, Julian, CA 92036

🏠 Peter & Vicki Bergstrom

📞 (714) 765-0028

🛏 20 ♂ 12 ♀ 8

🌐 open from Sept. 15 to May 15

🔑 recommended; required for weekends

🌐 $3.50

🏪 Jack's Market, 2 mi in Julian

🍷 yes

🚌 Julian, Main St, 2 mi M-F from El Cajon

🚆 Oceanside 60 mi

🚴 Kirk's Bike Shop, Ramona 25 mi

🚐 hostel

✈️ San Diego 65 mi

* State Parks 15 mi, Julian, gold town, 2 mi

** 80 acres of forest

👪 with advance reservations

🏠 not available

DIRECTIONS: 2 mi east of Julian on Hwy 78, turn at Camp Stevens sign, go to house

🏠 Camp Marston 5 mi W, San Diego Point Loma 70 mi SW

JULIAN (B) 🏠 Camp Marston Hostel Pine Hills Road, Julian, CA 92036

🏠 Robert Anderson

📞 (714) 765-0642

🛏 20 ♂ 12 ♀ 8

🌐 $3 S, $3.50 W

🚰 Hot & cold

🏪 Jack's Market, Julian

🍷 yes

🚌 3 mi, Julian, Main St. M-F from El Cajon

🚆 Oceanside 60 mi

🚴 Kirk's Bike Shop, Ramona,

🚐 hostel

✈️ San Diego 60 mi

* State parks 15 mi; Julian, gold town, 3 mi; at camp — canoeing, horseback riding, swimming, fishing.

👪 with advance reservations

🚆 yes

CALIFORNIA

DIRECTIONS: 1 mi W of Julian on Hwy 78, turn at Pine Hills Rd for 2 mi to camp entrance.

🛎 Camp Stevens 5 mi E, San Diego 60 mi SW, San Diego Point Loma 65 mi SW

LAKE PERRIS (Riverside County) proposed. A new 30+ bed hostel will open in early 1981. Contact San Diego Council, AYH for date.

LOS ALTOS 🛎 Hidden Villa Ranch 26870 Moody Rd, Los Altos Hills, CA 94022

🛏 Patricia & Curtis Schneider

☏ (415) 941-6407

▬ 32

🛏 Sept 1-June 14

🔺 Weekends

● $3 S, $3 W

SN Childrens camp in summer, room for 4-5 hostelers.

▲ Hidden Villa, Incorporated. P.O. AH, Los Altos, CA 94022

⌂ Whitecliff Market, 342 1st St, Los Altos 5 mi

🚩 yes

🚌 2 mi located at Foothill College

🚲 10 mi via Santa Clara Transit

🚴 Los Altos Bike Works, 369 State St, 5 mi

✈ Nearest airport 20 mi

* Great America Amusement Park 12 mi; Stanford University 10 mi

** Hostel is located on a

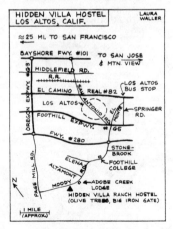

HIDDEN VILLA HOSTEL
LOS ALTOS, CALIF.
LAURA WALLER

2000-acre ranch, much wilderness; hiking trails available

⌂ yes

🛏 50¢

↦ Hostel was the first chartered on the Pacific Coast (1937). It was begun by hosteling pioneers Frank & Josephine Duveneck.

DIRECTIONS: 26870 Moody, Los Altos Hills. 2 mi from Foothill College. No public transportation from college.

🛎 Ft. Mason SE 45 mi, Saratoga Hostel 15 mi

LOS ANGELES, (A) 🏠 Los Angeles International Hostel, 1502 Palos Verdes Dr N, Harbor City, 90710

☏ (213) 831-8109

▬ ♂ 40 ♀ 30

● $4

▲ Los Angeles City Dept. of Recreation & Parks

⌂ 1 mi W of Hostel 3 J's Ranch Market

🚩 yes

🚌 Long Beach Greyhound 10 mi Los Angeles Greyhound 20 mi

🚃 Union Station 20 mi

🚴 ½ mi NW of hostel

🚗 On grounds

✈ Los Angeles International Airport

* Surfing, swimming, sailing 5-10 mi from hostel. Disneyland, 20 mi. Marineland of the Pacific, Cabrillo Marine Museum, Lomita Railroad Museum, Queen Mary, Manhattan Beach, Redondo Beach, Hermosa Beach, 5-15 mi. Palos Verdes Peninsula coast line, Point Vincente, Portuguese Point, Inspiration Point, Royal Palms State Beach, Point Fermin, Cabrillo Beach 5-10 mi

⌂ yes

🛏 $1

DIRECTIONS: Hostel is 20 mi S of LA International Airport, 20 mi from downtown Los Angeles. 10 mi N of Long Beach. 20 mi from Disneyland.

🛎 Hollywood YMCA Hostel, 30 mi NW, Westchester YMCA Hostel 20 mi NW

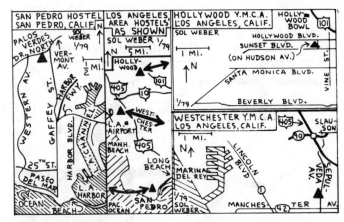

LOS ANGELES, (B) Westchester YMCA 8015 S Sepulveda Blvd, Los Angeles, CA 90045

🏠 Richard Rothenberg
☎ 213-776-0922
🛏 35 ♂ 20 ♀ 15
🏠 June 1-Sept 15
🔒 Advance booking for groups
💲 $4.50 (members), $5.50 (non-members)
SN over 18 years old only
♨ Hot & cold
🍴 Hillmart 2 blks
🚌 one hour from bus st RTD no. 871 to Manchester & Sepulveda; walk 4 blks N
🚃 one hour by bus
🚲 Manny's cycle 1 mi S
🅿 on premises
✈ Los Angeles Airport 1 mi S
✱ Hostel is located 15 mi from downtown Los Angeles; 2 mi N of LA Airport; RTD 88 or Culver City Bus no. 3; 2 mi from Playa Del Rey and Marina Del Rey Beaches; 1 mi from highway 405
🎿 I $1.75, II $1.75
🚿 25¢
DIRECTIONS: San Pedro 20 mi S Hollywood 15 mi N

LOS ANGELES (C) Hollywood YMCA International Center (SA no kitchen), 1553 N. Hudson Ave, Hollywood, CA 90028

🏠 Margaret Johnson, Claude Bazoge
☎ (213) 467-4161
🛏 ♂ 26 ♀ 20
💲 $3.50 S, $3.50 W, non-AYH

$5
SN Over 18 years old only. Reservations are not accepted.
🍴 Safeway ¼ mi
🚌 Greyhound ¼ mi
🚃 Downtown LA, 7 mi
🅿 on premises $ 75¢
✈4 Los Angeles International 16 mi
✱ Scenic attractions include movie studios, major theaters, Griffith Park, Hollywood Bowl. Easy access to Disneyland and all major Los Angeles attractions.
✱✱ Access to track, gym, swimming pool in facility, evening hostel lounge & siteseeing, trips occasionally.
➡ This hostel made available by American Savings Mark Taper Foundation
DIRECTIONS: Downtown Hollywood; 4 blks W of Vine, 1 blk S of Hollywood Blvd. 7 mi N of Downtown LA; 40 minutes from Los Angeles International Airport.
🏠 San Pedro Youth Hostel 30 mi SW, Westchester Youth Hostel 16 mi SW

MILL VALLEY—Proposed Muir Woods Hostel in Mt. Tamalpais State Park is due to open July/August, 1981. 1 mi from the town of Muir Beach, the hostel which is expected to provide 28 beds is equidistant from the beach and the Muir Woods National

CALIFORNIA

YOU ARE WELCOME IN THE CITY OF THE ANGELS
VISIT THE THREE YOUTH HOSTELS IN THE AREA

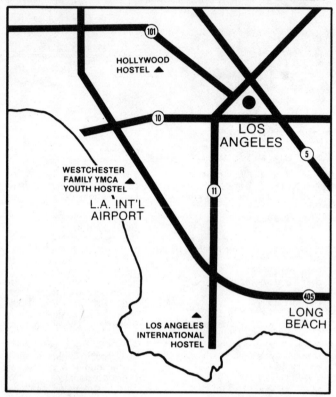

HOLLYWOOD YMCA HOTEL
1553 N. Hudson Avenue
Hollywood, CA 90028
(213) 467-4161
Open year round

WESTCHESTER YMCA HOSTEL
8015 S. Sepulveda Blvd
Los Angeles, CA 90045
(213) 776-0922
June 1 through Sept. 15th

LOS ANGELES
INTERNATIONAL HOSTEL
1502 Palos Verdes Dr. North
Harbor City, CA 90710
(213) 831-8109
Open year round

For details send stamped,
self addressed, legal size envelope to:
LOS ANGELES COUNCIL, AYH
1502 Palos Verdes Drive North
Harbor City, CA 90710
(213) 831-8846

102

Monument. For more information contact AYH Golden Gate Council, Building 240, Fort Mason, San Francisco, CA 94123, Tel. (415) 771-4646.

MONTARA ⌂ Montara Lighthouse Hostel, P.O. Box 737, 16th St. at Cabrillo Hwy (1), Montara, CA 94037

MONTARA LIGHTHOUSE
25 miles South of San Francisco
Operated by Golden Gate AYH

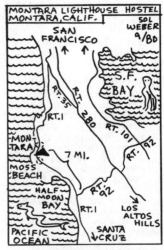

⌂ Lee Collins & Rich Lilley
☎ (415) 728-7177
▬ ♦ 10 ♦ 10
⬆ Reservations recommended during summer
● $3.50 members, $5.50 non-members
SN Advanced booking required for groups
▲ Operated by AYH Golden Gate Council; leased from CA Parks & Recreation Dept.
≙ Hot and cold
⌒ Deli 9 blks N
⚑ yes
🚌 Local county, 8 blks 6th & Hwy (1) N
🚲 BART, Daly City 18 mi; SP, Hillsdale, 19 mi
🚗 Coastside Automotive & Bikes 3 mi S
🚗 10 spaces on premises
✈ San Francisco International Airport 30 mi E
⛺ no
✷ Montara St. Beach North ½ mi S; J.F. Fitzgerald Marine Reserve, Moss Beach, ½ mi; Pillar Point Harbor 3 mi; Half Moon Bay Pumpkin Festival (October) 7 mi; Bicentennial Route along Hwy (1);

Horseback riding stables 5 mi S; skin diving.
✷✷ Ocean & lighthouse
★ yes, by reservation
🏠 yes
⌶ 50¢
➡ Victorian structure built in 1883
DIRECTIONS: Located on the Pacific Coast Hwy (1) between Santa Cruz and San Francisco 7 mi N of Half Moon Bay. ½ mi between the towns of Moss Beach & Montara at 16th & Cabrillo Hwy (1).
⌂ San Francisco International 35 mi N; Hidden Villa, Los Altos 23 mi N

MONTEREY, Monterey Peninsula Youth Hostel, 404 El Estero, Monterey, CA 93940
☎ (408) 373-4166
▬ ♦ 8 ♦ 8
▬ ♦ 22 ♦ 22
⌶ June 20-Aug 20
● $3.50 members, $4.50 non-members
▲ YMCA
≙ Hot & cold
🚌 Greyhound Bus Line
🚲 Salinas 10 mi W
🚗 Monterey 10 mi E
🚗 Immediate Area
✈ Monterey 6 mi from Hostel
✷ Canoeing on El Estero Lake, horseback riding at Carmel Valley Beach (horses can be

rented, many hiking trails, biking trails, Monterey Jazz Festival in Sept, Carmel Bach Festival in July, theater.

🚿 yes
🔥 50¢

DIRECTIONS: Southbound on 101, take 156 to Hwy 1; Northbound on 101, take 68 to Hwy 1; N & S take Marina (Del Monte) exit to Reindollar (right), turn left at Zanetta Ave, right on Hillcrest Ave. (Los Arboles Junior High School Gymnasium) 294 Hillcrest Ave, Marina, CA

🛏 Santa Cruz 50 mi N, San Francisco 70 mi

Call YMCA as hostel may be relocated in 1981.

MT. SHASTA 🛏 Shasta Hostel, 200 Sheldon St, Mt. Shasta, CA 96016
🏠 John Richard Welke
☎ (916) 926-4896
🛏 16 ♂ 8 ♀ 8
🔥 no
● $4 S, $5 W
🚰 Hot and cold
🔁 Cowels ½ mi
🐎 yes
🚌 Mt. Shasta 1 mi
🚃 Dunsmair 8 mi
🚲 Fifth Season 1 mi

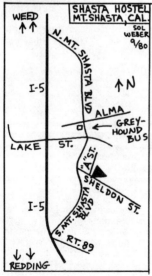

🚗 on site
🚌 Redding 48 mi
* Mt. Shasta 18 mi
** Wood stoves

DIRECTIONS: I-5 exit for Mt. Shasta City. Turn at Sheldon St. from Main St at Lamplighters Restaurant
🛏 Arcata Crew House, Arcata 200 mi

NORDEN, Ski Inn, (SA No kitchen) P.O. Box 7, Norden, CA 97524
🏠 Mayo & Melva Torgerson
☎ (916) 426-3079
🛏 In Dorms ♂ 40 ♀ 40
🛏 8 Pri rooms—2-3 per room
🔥 by reservation only
● $3.50 S, $5.50 W, in Dorm, Sleeping bag accommodation. Private room rate $14 double S, $16 double W
🚰 Hot & cold
🔁 Norden 1 mi
🚌 Greyhound 3 mi
🚃 Truckee 11 mi
✈ Reno 41 mi; small craft Truckee 12 mi
* Recreation room, quiet room, fireplace, sun deck, horseshoes, tether ball, outdoor fireplace, swimming 4 mi ($1). Sailing ($4 per hour), horseback riding (June through September ($4 per hour), hiking, bike trails, skiing, ice skating.

DIRECTIONS: From Sacramento E on I-80, 90 mi to Donner Summit; Take Soda Springs, Norden Exit, Go 3 mi to Ski Inn on right.
🛏 Sacramento 100 mi S.

PESCADERO ♠ Pigeon Point Lighthouse, Pigeon Point Rd, Pescadero, CA 94060.

PIGEON POINT
LIGHTHOUSE HOSTEL
53 miles South of San Francisco
Operated by Golden Gate AYH

☎ (415) 879-0633
▬ 30
● $3.50 members, $5.50 members
▲ AYH, Golden Gate Council
♨ Hot & cold
⌂ Williamsson 10 mi N
☂ yes
🚌 15 mi
🚗 San Mateo 35 mi
🚲 Santa Cruz 38 mi
🐾 on premises
⛵ San Francisco 49 mi
⛺ no
* Beach/lighthouse. This

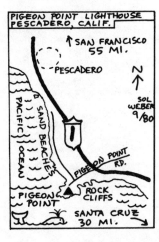

PIGEON POINT LIGHTHOUSE
PESCADERO, CALIF.

↑ SAN FRANCISCO 55 MI.

PESCADERO

N ↑

SOL WEBER 9/80

PACIFIC OCEAN

SAND BEACHES

PIGEON POINT RD.

PIGEON POINT

ROCK CLIFFS

SANTA CRUZ 30 MI. →

hostel made available by special arrangements with the State of California, Dept. of Parks & Recreation. Bicycle storage.
★ yes
🏠 yes
🛏 50¢
↦ Second tallest free standing lighthouse in U.S.
DIRECTIONS: On coast 38 mi N of Santa Cruz & 22 mi S of Half Moon Bay. Look for only 120 ft. lighthouse.
🏠 Santa Cruz 39 mi S, Montara Lighthouse 28 mi N

PT. REYES 🏚 Pt. Reyes Hostel P.O. Box 247, Pt. Reyes Sta. CA 94956.

POINT REYES HOSTEL
45 miles North of San Francisco
Operated by Golden Gate AYH

🏠 Jules & Meryl Evens
☎ (415) 669-9985, 8-9:30 AM & 4:30-9 PM
▬ ▮ 20 ▮ 20
🛏 4:30 PM-9:30 AM
🔒 Good idea weekends
● $3.50 members; $5.50 non-members
SN Group Day Use w/ advance arrangement
▲ AYH, Golden Gate Council
♨ Hot & cold
⌂ Palace Mkt. 8 mi E, Inverness Deli 7 mi E
☂ yes
🚌 Limited bus service by Golden Gate Transit to Park Hdqtrs. 7 mi
🚗 Oakland 50 mi
🚲 Seashore Bike Shop 8 mi

CALIFORNIA

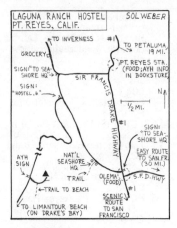

LAGUNA RANCH HOSTEL
PT. REYES, CALIF.
SOL WEBER

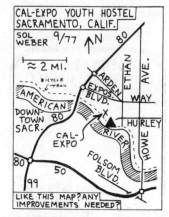

CAL-EXPO YOUTH HOSTEL
SACRAMENTO, CALIF.
SOL WEBER 9/77

LIKE THIS MAP? ANY
IMPROVEMENTS NEEDED?

- Outside
- SF Int'l. Airport 60 mi
- 1 Family Rm.
- yes
- 25¢
- Located in Pt. Reyes National Seashore
- Golden Gate Hostel 40 mi S, SF Int'l. 50 mi S

SACRAMENTO ♠ Sacramento Hostel, P.O. Box 13907 Sacramento, CA 95813

SACRAMENTO HOSTEL
90 miles East of San Francisco
Operated by Golden Gate AYH

- Corine Luce
- 916-927-3819
- ♦ 6 ♦ 6
- $3.50 members, $5.50 non-members
- AYH, Golden Gate Council
- Hot & cold
- Corti Bros. ½ mi, closed after 7 PM & on Sunday

- yes
- Greyhound 5¾ mi
- Amtrak 6 mi
- within 2 mi of Hostel
- Parking available on grounds
- approx. 18 mi
- yes
- Bike and jogging trail ¼ mi public swimming pool 1½ mi Old Sacramento 6 mi, Golden Bear Raceway 1/8 mi
- Buses stop running at 9 PM weekdays, 6 PM weekends
- yes
- 50¢

DIRECTIONS: 6 mi from downtown bus depot, take bus no. 10, 23, 24, 25 or 29 on 8th & K St to Arden Fair Mall, get off, walk to corner of Arden & Ethan Way (Standard gas station on corner) proceed on Ethan Way, turn right on Ethan Way into service gate no. 12 Cal Expo Fair Grounds. Hostel to your right just inside gate no. 12.
- San Francisco 90 mi

SAN DIEGO (A) ♠ San Diego Point Loma Hostel, 3790 Udall St, San Diego, CA 92107
- 714/223-4778
- 54 ♦ 34 ♦ 20
- $4 S, $4 W
- San Diego Council of AYH
- Hot & cold
- Alpha Beta 1 blk
- yes

🚌 Greyhound 6½ mi
🚃 Amtrak 6½ mi
🚲 1 mi
🚗 on street
✈ 3½ mi
* Ocean 1 mi, downtown San Diego 6½ mi, San Diego Zoo 7½ mi E, Balboa Park 7½ mi E, Sea World 1½ mi N
✶ with advance reservations
🏕 yes
🛏 $1

DIRECTIONS: By car: see map. By bus: from airport, take no. 2 bus to downtown San Diego & transfer to no. 35 bus going W to Voltaire St. and Worden St., walk 1 blk SW to Udall St.
🏠 Camp Marston, Julian, 60 mi NE; Camp Stevens, Julian, 65 mi NE; San Diego Point Loma Hostel 6½ mi SE

SAN DIEGO (B) Armed Services YMCA Hostel (SA, no kitchen) 500 West Broadway, San Diego, CA 92101
🛏 Mr. Michael Waggener, Mrs. Anna Mae Wright
📞 (714) 232-1133
🛏 24 ⚥ 16 ⚥ 8
💲 $3.50 S, $3.50 W with own linen or sleeping bag
SN Space for 100 in private rooms.
🚿 Hot & cold
🚌 3 blks E
🚃 1 blk W
🚲 2 mi
🚗 On-street parking during evening hours
✈ 2 mi NW
* Balboa Park (San Diego Zoo) 2 mi, ocean swimming 5 mi, Sea World 4 mi NW
** Storage, checking of backpacks at 50¢ per day
🏕 yes
🍴 yes. Available on premises in coffee shop
🛏 50¢

DIRECTIONS: On Broadway, 1 block E of Amtrak Depot & 3 blks W of center of San Diego (& bus terminals)
🏠 Camp Marston Hostel, Julian, 65 mi NE; Camp Stevens Hostel, Julian, 65 mi NE; San Diego Pt. Loma Hostel 6½ mi NW

SAN DIEGO (C) YWCA, 1012 C St, San Diego, CA 92101
🛏 Pat Downey
📞 (714) 239-0355
🛏 12
🛏 preferred
💲 $4 S, $6 W
SN Hostel is part of YWCA residence. For women only, 18 & older.
🎵 3 blks
🚰 yes
🚌 Greyhound 8 blks
🚃 11 blks
🚗 2 blks
* Balboa Park 2 mi
🛏 $2
DIRECTIONS: Located on NE corner of 10th & C Sts in downtown San Diego. 3 blks S of 10th St exits, 15 end of Rt 163.
🏠 Point Loma, San Diego 5 mi W

SAN FRANCISCO (A) 🛏 San Francisco International Hostel, Building 240, Fort Mason, San Francisco, CA 94123

SAN FRANCISCO
INTERNATIONAL
Operated by Golden Gate AYH

🛏 Joe & Phoebe Pummill
📞 (415) 771-7277 ("P-A-S-S")
🛏 130
💲 $5.50 members, $7.50 non-members
▲ AYH Golden Gate Council, same address
🚿 Hot & cold
🎵 Safeway Marina 4 blks
🚰 yes

CALIFORNIA

🚋 Market & 7th 4 mi
🚃 Townsend & 4th St 5 mi
🚲 1.2 mi
🚗 limited at hostel & 2 blks away
✈ SF Int'l Airport 14 mi
✱ Museums, theaters, parks, symphony, opera, restaurants, mountains, beaches, etc.
✱✱ Inside national park, containing theaters, restaurants, view of bay, bike trail, etc.
✱ yes
🛏 yes
🚪 50¢
🏛 Registered federal historic building, former Army dispensary, 100 yrs. old

DIRECTIONS: 2 mi N of SF Civic Center, entrance at the corner of Bay & Franklin. Bicycles on Pacific Coast Bicentennial Route—take Lincoln Blvd. E from the SF end of the Golden Gate Bridge. Go approx. 2 mi on Lincoln & turn left on Lyon St. Go 1 blk to Chestnut & turn right. Follow Chestnut 1 mi and turn left on Franklin. Follow Franklin straight into Ft. Mason. From Transbay Terminal or from SF (railroad) Station—Bus 42 to Ft. Mason.

SAN FRANCISCO
INTERNATIONAL
HOSTEL

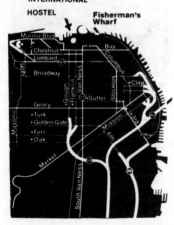

From Greyhound Station—any bus (except No. 5) on Market or Mission W to Van Ness; transfer on Van Ness to Bus 42 or 47, northbound to Ft. Mason.
🏠 Golden Gate Hostel, Sausalito 8 mi N; Montara 20 mi S

SAN FRANCISCO (B) 🏠 Golden Gate Youth Hostel, 941 Fort Barry, Sausalito, CA 94965

GOLDEN GATE HOSTEL
8 miles North of San Francisco
Operated by Golden Gate AYH

BY EDIE BROWN

🏠 Mark & Nena Ahalt
📞 (415) 331-2777
🛏 60 ♂ 35 (2 family) ♀ 25
💲 $3.50 members, $5.50 nonmembers
SN Day use fee $1//person, minimum 15 people, advance reservation necessary
▲ AYH, Golden Gate Council
♨ Hot & cold
🍴 Golden Gate Market 5 mi NE
🍷 yes
🚋 Golden Gate Transit 3 mi
🚃 San Francisco 8 mi
🚲 Bicycle Odyssey, 2001 Bridgeway, Sausalito 6 mi
🚗 Plenty available at hostel
✈ 20 mi
✱ Rec Room with ping pong & games, tennis, swimming (7 mi), sailing (5 mi), horseback, hiking & cycling trails, water bird sanctuary, marine mammal rehabilitation center.
✱✱ laundry facilities, bike storage
✱ Reservations suggested June-Sept
🛏 yes
🚪 50¢

108

Welcome to
SAN FRANCISCO
BAY AREA HOSTELS

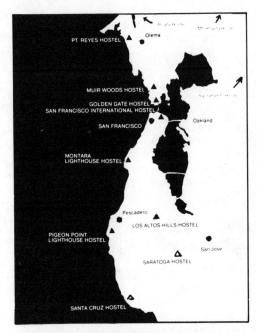

AMERICAN YOUTH HOSTELS
Golden Gate Council

Building 240, Fort Mason
San Francisco, CA 94123
(415) 771-4646

Affiliated with IYHF

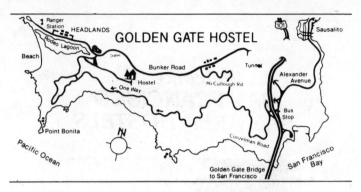

GOLDEN GATE HOSTEL

➡ National Register of Historic Places, 1902, Previously Officers' Headquarters
🏠 San Francisco 8 mi S, Pt. Reyes 45 mi N

SANTA CRUZ Santa Cruz Hostel Project (SA, no kitchen), P.O. Box 1241, Santa Cruz, CA 95061
🏠 Staff
🌐 Hostel Society Office (408) 423-8304 or 425-9915 (evenings only)
🛏 50 ♂ 25 ♀ 25
🛏 10
🗓 June 21-Aug 20 (approx.)
💲 $4.50 S
▲ Santa Cruz Hostel Society
🚰 Hot & cold
🚌 Santa Cruz local & Greyhound 1 mi
🚲 Bicycle Center ½ mile
🚗 varies
✈ San Jose 30 mi
* Hostel located in schools. Hostel on busline; near beaches, redwoods, theater, shopping, restaurants, concerts, parks & colleges.
** free light breakfast
⛺ yes
🔦 50¢
🏠 San Francisco 75 mi N

SARATOGA 🏠 Sanborn Park Hostel, 15808 Sanborn Rd, Saratoga, CA 95070
🏠 Jay Hudson
🌐 (408) 867-3993
🛏 36
🚪 recommended on weekends
💲 $3 S, $3.50 W
SN First 20 beds opened 1980, remaining beds will open '81

SANBORN PARK HOSTEL
SARATOGA, CALIF.

▲ Santa Clara Valley Club of American Youth Hostels, P.O. Box 28148, San Jose CA 95159
🚰 Hot & cold
🍴 several 3 mi
⛽ yes
🚌 County Transit (no. 27 & no. 54) & Greyhound, Saratoga 3 mi; Greyhound, San Jose, 13 mi
🚃 Amtrak, San Jose, 12 mi
🚲 Saratoga Cycle Center, 3 mi
🚗 at hostel
✈ San Jose 12 mi
⛺ no, but at park camp grounds 1 mi
* Beautiful hostel set in magnificent redwood, oak & madrone forest. Hiking trails lead all the way to Pacific Ocean through Coast Range mountains.
✱ yes
⛺ yes

- 🛏 50¢/night
- ➞ Main hostel building is historic Welch-hurst, large redwood log building from 1908, on National Registry of Historic Places

DIRECTIONS: Take Highway 9 W from Village of Saratoga for 2 mi. Turn left on Sanborn Rd for .9 mi, then right at AYH sign for .4 mi.

- 🏠 Los Altos 25 mi N, Santa Cruz (summer) 25 mi S

TURLOCK 🏠 Accord, 475 W. Main, Turlock, CA 93380
- 🏠 Don & Lynn Padlo
- ☎ (209) 634-2691
- ➞ ♨ 4 ♨ 4
- 🛏 $3 S, $3 W
- SN $1/day use
- 🚰 Hot & cold
- 🎵 Safeway 2 blks
- 🚺 yes
- 🚌 Turlock ½ mi
- 🚂 Riverbank 25 mi
- 🚲 ½ mi
- ⛺ no
- ✳ Yosemite 70 mi, Motherlode Country 50 mi, San Francisco 80 mi, Sacramento 80 mi, California State College-Stanislaus 2 mi. Rivers: Taolumne (15 mi), Merced (5 mi). Lakes: Don Pedro (35 mi), Merced Lake (45 mi). Industry: Wine, almond, dairy (Riverbank Cheese Plant 25 mi)
- ✳✳ Swimming pool
- ★ no
- 🚐 yes
- 🛏 50¢
- ➞ Turlock is turkey production capital of the world.

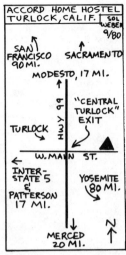

DIRECTIONS: Approx. ½ mi from Hwy 99 overpass (towards downtown).
- 🏠 Sacramento 80 mi N, San Francisco 80 mi NW

WATERFORD 🏠 Nut Haven Ranch, 13972 Yosemite Blvd (Hwy 132), Waterford, CA 95386
- 🏠 Mary Ann & Mark Hite
- ☎ (209) 874-1343
- ➞ 4
- 🛏 $3
- 🎵 100 yds
- ✳ Swimming in Toulomne River on property, 20-acre ranch, on route to Yosemite.

DIRECTIONS: 1.2 mi E of A&W Root Beer.
- 🏠 Turlock 15 mi SW, San Francisco 70 mi W

COLORADO
Rocky Mountain Council, 1107 12th St., P.O. Box 2370, Boulder, CO 80306

ASPEN, Highlands Inn (SA, rates) P.O. Box 4708, Aspen, CO 81611, 1650 Maroon, Creek Rd.
- 🏠 Joe Cooper, Steve Peer
- ☎ 303-925-5050
- ➞ 18
- 🏠 Jan 1-April 14, June 1-Sept 14, Nov 23-Dec 31
- ♨ July, Aug & Winter season

- 🛏 $7.50 S, $10 W
- 🚰 Hot & cold
- 🎵 Clark's Market 3 mi
- 🚌 Aspen 3 mi
- 🚺 yes
- 🚂 Glenwood Spring
- 🚲 3 mi in Aspen
- 🚗 At Inn
- ✈ Aspen Airport 3 mi
- ✳ Aspen Ski ride (summer

chair lift), Maroon Bell Wilderness bus, horse back riding, swimming, whirlpool, sauna, tennis, all located at Inn

** Free bus runs to Aspen every 30 minutes

✱ Room with private bath

→ Inn is located at the base of Aspen Highlands Ski Area

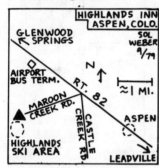

DIRECTIONS: 1½ miles W of Aspen on Hwy 82, turn on Maroon Creek Rd at the Prince of Peace Chapel, then 1½ mi to Inn.

🏠 Crested Butte 30 mi S, Breckenridge 50 mi E, Steamboat Spring 100 mi N

BOULDER 🏠 Boulder International Youth Hostel, 1107 12th St, Boulder, CO 80302

🏠 Mrs. Ruth Barkley

☏ (303) 442-9304 or 442-0522

▬ ♂ 33 ♀ 33

♂ 50 ♀ 50

● $4.25 S

♨ Hot & cold

🍴 modern food supply nearby

🚌 2 short blks

🚲 Denver 30 mi

🚲 The Spoke 2 blks

✈ Denver 30 mi

✱ University of Co. 2 blks, International Alpine School, Eldorado Springs 5 mi

★ 20 min walk to mountains

🅿 yes

🗝 $2 charge, $5 deposit

→ Water fountain fed by a glacier

DIRECTIONS: 2 blks W of Colorado bookstore

🏠 Estes Park 36 mi N, Neder-

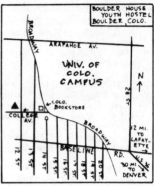

land 20 mi W, Lafayette 15 mi E, Denver 30 mi SE

BRECKENRIDGE, Galbreath's Fireside Inn (SA no kitchen/rates) 114 N French St, Breckenridge, CO 80424

🏠 Gale Galbreath

☏ (303) 453-6456

▬ 24 ♂ 12 ♀ 12

🗝 No, but advisable July & Aug

● Jan 1-April 30 $13 or $21.50 with 2 meals. May 1-Nov 25 $8 or $12 with 2 meals; Nov 26-Dec 31 $15 or $23.50 with 2 meals

♨ Hot & cold

🍴 Grocery Store 3 blks S

🍽 We provide breakfast & dinner

🚌 Frisco 12 mi

🚲 Denver 86 mi

🚲 Norway Haus 3 blks

🚲 across the street

✈ Denver

✱ Sailing on Dillon Lake, 12 mi; horseback riding 6 blks; hiking from door, trans-America

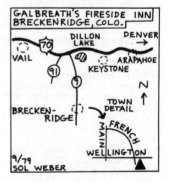

bike trail, backstage theatre
3 blks; Alpine slike 1 mi
** books, magazines, t.v., record player
✗ some bedrooms
➡ Victorian mining town—many mines in area

DIRECTIONS: Corner of French
& Wellington. N end of town,
turn E on Wellington, 2 blks
🏠 Denver 86 mi

COLORADO SPRINGS 🏨 Colorado Springs Hostel (Farragut Hall (SA Student Dormitory) 17 Farragut Ave.,
Colorado Springs, CO 80909
🏠 Mrs. Merle Williams, Mrs.
Connie Halley
📞 (303) 471-2938, (303)
634-9657
🛏 ♂ 20 ♀ 20
💲 $4.25 S, $4.25 W
SN Some private & semi-private
rooms (twin beds). Sleeping
bags permitted.
♨ Hot & cold
🍴 7-11 Convenience Center 2
blks, major supermarkets 1
mi
🍳 Complete kitchens, laundry
facilities
🚌 Greyhound & Trailways, 12
blks, city bus ½ blk
🚂 Amtrack, Denver, 60 mi
🚲 Bicycles for rent on premises (Schwinn's)
🚗 On premises
✈ Colorado Springs Airport, 5
mi
✳ Pikes Peak & Garden of the

Gods, Manitou Springs,
Monument Park & Prospect
Lake, ¼ mi. Indian territory
(Inter-Tribal Village) 10 mi.
🏕 yes
ℹ 75¢

DIRECTIONS: Motorists on I-25
take Exit no. 142 to Pikes
Peak Ave. 15 blks E to Farragut Ave. Motorists on U.S.
24, turn S on Faragut. City
bus passengers take Eastbo-
rough no. 8 bus, get off at
end of 1500 blk on Pikes
Peak Ave, walk ½ blk N.
🏠 Pueblo 40 mi S, Denver 60
mi

CRESTED BUTTE 🏠 Crested
Butte, (SA, other uses), 108
Maroon, Crested Butte, CO
81224
🏠 Clay Bridgford
📞 303-349-5118
🛏 ♂ 6 ♀ 6
SN Group basis only
💲 $100/night for 10 persons
▲ Colorado Institute, Box 875,
Crested Butte, 81224
♨ Hot & cold
🍴 Stefanics 1 blk
🍳 yes
🚌 Gunnison 30 mi
🚂 Denver 200 mi
🚲 Neals 2 blks
🚗 On street
✈ Crested Butte 2 mi
✳ Ski area 3 mi
➡ Located in National Historic
District
🏕 yes

🏠 Aspen 150 mi, Silverton 150
mi

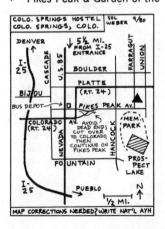

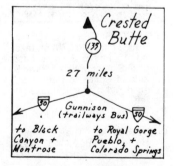

DENVER ⌂ Denver, 1452 Detroit St, Denver, CO 80206

⚫ Ann Ketcham, Mark Coan
🐝 303-333-7672
⛵ 50 ♪ 25 ♪ 25
🔥 June-September
⊝ $3.75 S, $4.25 W
SN Curfew at 11:00 PM
▲ Holy Order of MANS
⌒ Safeway 3 blks W
⚑ yes
🚌 Greyhound & Continental 2 mi, 3 km
🚃 Denver Union Sta. 2 mi
🚲 Collins Bicycle Shop
✈ Stapleton Airport 4 mi
✻ Bike Rental, coffee 10 cents, t.v., parks and free swimming pool nearby. Hostel is halfway between downtown and the airport, 2 blks south of City Park, 45 minutes to mountains, tennis close by.
⌂ yes
🛏 $1

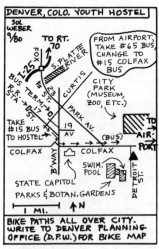

DIRECTIONS: From Bus Depot walk 2 blks S to 17th St, take no. 15 bus E 2 mi to East High School, walk 2 blks on S side of Colfax to Detroit St. Turn right, fourth house on left.
⌂ Boulder 30 mi

DURANGO, ⌂ The Durango Hostel, P.O. Box 1445, 543 E 2nd Ave, Durango, CO 81301.

⚫ Lucy & Art Olson
🐝 (303) 247-5477 or 247-9905
⛵ 60
🔥 Encouraged
⊝ $6.25 S, $7 W
SN Group accommodations usually available.
⌒ Hot & cold
⌒ Safeway 6 blks
⚑ yes
🚌 6 blks E, 3 blks S
🚃 ½ blk SW
🚲 'Outdoorsman' 5 blks N on Main
🏠 Hostel—no charge
✈ Animas Air Park 5 mi, Durango La Plata Field 16 mi
✻ Mesa Verde National Park, Purgatory Ski Area, Narrow Gauge Steam RR, hunting, fishing, mountaineering, Saturday night nightlife all week long.
✻✻ Arrivals on late-night buses call hostel for transportation. Rental cars available. Communal areas open all day 7 AM-11 PM. Hostel vegetable garden. Special discounts, theater, river raft trips, horses, alpine slide, others.
✻ yes
⌂ yes
🛏 $1
➡ Victorian rooming house for railroad workers, miners & cowboys.

DIRECTIONS: From bus station:

go N on 8th Ave. 3 blks to 6th St, then W on 6th St. 6 blks to 2nd Ave, then S on 2nd Ave. ½ blk to hostel. From train station (well known local landmark), go ½ block E and ½ blk N.

🏠 Holbrook 160 mi SW; Flagstaff 300 mi SW; Silverton 50 mi N; Cuba, NM 125 mi S; Pueblo 300 mi E

ESTES PARK 🏠 H-Bar-G Ranch Hostel, 3500 H-Bar-G Rd, Box 1260, Estes Park, CO 80517.

🏠 Anne & Lou Livingston
🐝 303-586-3688
🛏 130
🏠 May 22-Sept 12
⚒ July 15-Aug 15
◑ 700 Flagstaff Star Route, Boulder, CO 80302, 303-442-7296
● $3.75 S with pass
SN During peak season, membership required, AYH or IYHA
♨ Hot & cold
🏪 Brodie's Mkt. 5½ mi
🚻 yes
🚌 Estes Park 6 mi
🚗 Denver 65 mi
🚴 Cosmic Cyclery 6 mi
🚗 At hostel
✈ Denver 65 mi
✳ Rocky Mountain Nat'l Park 3 mi. Hiking trails, tennis court, volleyball, recreation room, piano at hostel. Daily transportation from Estes Park Chamber of Commerce at 5 PM.

** Superb view of "Front Range"
✳ By reservation
🆔 yes
🛏 $1
↦ The Hostel is a former dude ranch.

DIRECTIONS 6 mi NE of town off of Devil's Gulch & Dry Gulch Rds, see map.
🏠 Grand Lake 50 mi W, Boulder 30 mi SE, Nederland 47 mi S, Denver 65 mi SE

GRAND LAKE (A) 🏠 Shadowcliff, Box 658, Grand Lake, CO 80447

🏠 Warren & Patt Rempel
🐝 303-627-9966
🛏 ♂ 20 ♀ 12
🏠 June 1-Oct 15
◑ 1151 Colorado Blvd. no. 106 Denver 80206
● $4 S
🚻 yes
🚌 16 mi
🚗 16 mi
🚴 10 min. away
✳ Backpacking in Nat'l park & forest. Fishing, boating, sailing. Golfing, horses, summer theater, ranger, naturalist talks. Museums, bird watching.
** Spectacular cliffside setting — with stream, rapids, & lake view.
✳ yes
🆔 yes
🛏 50¢

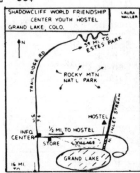

DIRECTIONS: From Grand Lake Village, take Tunnel Rd. ¾ mi. Hostel is 300 yds before

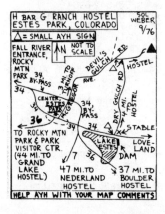

bridge on left.
🏠 Estes Park 49 mi E, Winter Park 40 mi S, Steamboat Springs 100 mi W

GRAND LAKE (B) Dougal's Mountain Inn, P.O. Box 1, 612 Grand Ave, Grand Lake, CO 80442
🏠 David McDougal
☎ (303) 627-3385
🛏 18
🚪 Nov 15-April 15
● $4 S, $5 W
🚰 Hot & cold
🍴 Circle D 1 blk
ⓕ yes
🚌 Granby 17 mi
🚆 Granby 17 mi
✈ Winter Park 34 mi
🚗 on premises
🚕 Denver 100 mi
* Rocky Mountain National Park 1 mi
🚗 yes
🔦 50¢
➡ Hostel constructed entirely of log, very authentic
🏠 Estes Park 50 mi E, Grand Lake (summer only), Winter Park 40 mi

LAFAYETTE (SA, economic), 409 East Oak, Lafayette, CO 80026
🏠 Mr. & Mrs. Richard Mitchell
☎ (303) 665-5997
🛏 14 ⚥ 7 ⚥ 7
● $3.75 S
SN Call before coming to hostel
🚰 Hot & cold
🍴 5 blks S
ⓕ yes
🚌 Regional Transport (RTD)
🚆 Denver 15 mi
✈ Spoke 10 mi
🚗 At hostel
🚕 Denver 15 mi
* Rural farm community

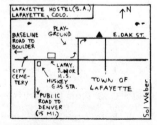

✶ yes
🚗 yes
🔦 $1.75
🏠 Boulder 11 mi

NEDERLAND 1005 Jackson, P.O. Box 391, Nederland, CO 80466
🏠 M/M Richard W. Mitchell
☎ (303) 258-9925
🛏 9
● $3.50
🍴 Nederland Grocery 3 blks
ⓕ yes
🚌 Boulder 17 mi
🚆 Denver 60 mi
✈ Boulder
🚗 On premises
🚕 Denver Int'l 45 mi
🔦 $2 charge $5 deposit
➡ "In the heart of the Colorado Mining Towns"

🏠 Boulder 17 mi E

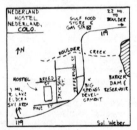

PUEBLO 🏛 Pueblo YWCA, 801 N. Santa Fe Ave, Pueblo, CO 81003
🏠 Phyllis Jackson
☎ (303) 542-6904
🛏 10 bunk beds ⚥ flexible
● $3.75 S, $3.75 W
▲ YWCA
ⓕ yes
🚌 4 blks
🚆 Amtrak, La Junta, 50 mi
✈ 4 blks S
🚗 2 blks W
🚕 Memorial Airport 5 mi E
* Beulah Mountain Park, 25 mi W, Sangre de Cristo & Arts Center, 5 blks S, Rosemount Museum, 10 blks N.
➡ Indoor swimming pool
🔦 75¢

🏠 Colorado Springs 40 mi

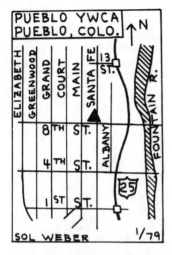

PUEBLO YWCA
PUEBLO, COLO.
SOL WEBER 1/79

SILVERTON Teller House Youth Hostel, (SA) Box 457, Silverton, CO 81433

🏠 Tom Galbraith & Janet Sharp
☎ (303) 387-5423
💲 $5 S, $5 W
SN Rate includes American style breakfast.
▲ Early Riser West
⌂ Swanson (directly behind)
🚌 Cont. Trailways 2 blks
🚂 Silverton-Durango Narrow Gauge 1 blk
🚲 Four Faces S to Durango 50 mi

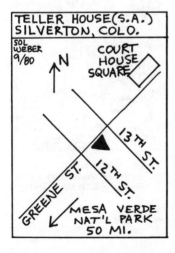

TELLER HOUSE (S.A.)
SILVERTON, COLO.
SOL WEBER 9/80
COURT HOUSE SQUARE
13TH ST.
12TH ST.
GREENE ST.
MESA VERDE NAT'L PARK 50 MI.

🚲 At hostel
Durango & Montrose 60 mi
⛺ Down the street at Nat'l Forest
* Recreation facilities include piano, skiing, horseback riding, hiking, swimming. Silverton is excellent base camp for trail head to wilderness areas and National Forests in summer & winter. Local mining festivities, community theater.

DIRECTIONS: Located in center of the 4 blk business district—across street from Newspaper Office in the center of the town of Silverton.
🚲 Durango 50 mi S

STEAMBOAT SPRINGS Haystack Lodge, (SA, no kitchen, rates) 2030 Walton Creek Rd, P.O. Box 1356, Steamboat Springs, CO 80499

🏠 Michael Lavery
☎ 303-879-0587
🛏 200
🚪 From Dec-March
💲 $5 S, $10 W
🚿 Hot & cold
⌂ 3 blks
🚌 1 mi
🚲 5 blks
🚍 On site
🚗 5 mi
** Ski lodge in winter.
🏕 yes

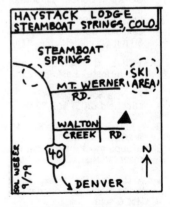

HAYSTACK LODGE
STEAMBOAT SPRINGS, COLO.
STEAMBOAT SPRINGS
SKI AREA
MT. WERNER RD.
WALTON CREEK RD.
40
SOL WEBER 9/79
DENVER

DIRECTIONS: Turn up towards mountain on Walton Creek Rd. (which is 2 mi S of town on US 40) Haystack is first building on left.

WINTER PARK 🏠 Winter Park Hostel, Box 255, Winter Park, CO 80450
🏠 Polly Crook
☎ (303) 726-5356
🍴 👤 15   15
🚪 Recommended Dec 15-April 15
⬤ $4 S, $7 W
🚰 Hot & cold
⌂ ¼ mi
🍴 yes
🚌 200 ft
🚲 70 mi
🚗 2 mi in Fraser
✈ 70 mi (Denver)
🚐 At hostel
* Winter Park, Mary Jane Ski area, 2 mi (shuttle bus in winter) Rocky Mt. Majesty at 9,000 ft. Cross-country skiing right from hostel. Excellent hiking, fishing & summer horseback riding. Historical Corona Pass RR. Summer alpine slide.
✱ By reservation
🏠 yes
🛈 $2

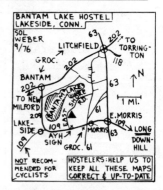

DIRECTIONS: Directly behind Rainbow Mt. Inn in Winter Park. 2 mi N of Winter Park ski area on US 40. 72 mi W of Denver, just over Berthoud Pass
🏠 Grand Lake 29 mi N, Boulder 80 mi E

CONNECTICUT
Yankee Council, P.O. Box 10392, West Hartford, CT 06110
(203) 247-6356

BOLTON 🏠 Home Hostel, 42 Clark Rd. Bolton, CT 06040
🏠 Mr. & Mrs. H.W. Baker
☎ (203) 649-3905
🏠 Lakeside 55 mi; Dudley, MA 50 mi; Springfield, MA 30 mi

LAKESIDE 🏠 Bantam Lake Youth Hostel, East Shore Rd. Lakeside, CT 06758
🏠 Patricia Sobolewski
☎ Litchfield (203) 567-9258
🛏 22
⬤ $3.50 S (May 1-Oct 31), $5 W (Nov 1-April 30)
SN Groups must make advance reservations. (Check-in 5-7 PM).
▲ AYH, Inc./By lease from White Memorial Foundation
🚰 Hot & cold
⌂ Country Foods 1½ mi
🍴 yes
🚌 Litchfield 7 mi; Greyhound,

Bantam 5 mi
🚲 NY-NH&H Waterbury 17 mi
🚗 Tommy's, 40 E Main, Torrington
🚐 on site
✈ Bradley 40 mi
⛺ yes

** Outdoor fireplace, basement recreation area w/fireplace & ping pong.

* Near lake, hiking trails. Excellent spot for summer & winter sports. Historic area of great natural beauty.

✸ yes

🏕 yes
🛈 $1

DIRECTIONS: E side of Bantam Lake, 1 mi N off Rt. 109 between Lakeside & Morris.
🏠 Granville 40 mi NE, Sheffield 34 mi NW

DISTRICT OF COLUMBIA
Potomac Area Council, 1520 16th St., NW, Suite A, Washington, DC 20036 (202) 462-5780

WASHINGTON Washington International YH, (SA Rates) 1332 ''I'' St. NW Washington, DC 20005
🏠 Ronald A. & Yohko Lee Mitchell
☏ (202) 347-3125
🛏 ⚲ 200 ⚲ 200 (4, 6 & 8 per dorm)

⊖ See schedule below
SN Reservation requests must contain a non-returnable deposit of the first night's fee and a stamped self-addressed envelope for confirmation.
🚰 Hot & cold
🛒 Safeway 4 blks on 12th St

Category	Rate	10/Sales Tax	Occpncy Tax	Total
AYH or IYHF Adult Member (Senior)	$6.00	$ .60	$ .15	$6.75
Junior Member (Individuals Only)	3.00	.30	.15	3.45
Member Couple in Private Family Room	18.00	1.80	.80	20.60
Introductory Membership	1.00	—	—	—
Adult Introductory Member	9.00	.90	.15	10.05
Junior Introductory Member (Individual)	5.00	.50	.15	5.65
Linen Packet Rental (in lieu of sheet sack)	4.00	—	—	—
Introductory Member Couple in Private family room	22.00	2.20	.80	25.00
Key Deposit (Refundable)	5.00	—	—	—
Linen Deposit (Refundable) (Senior)	5.00	—	—	—
Total Deposit	10.00			

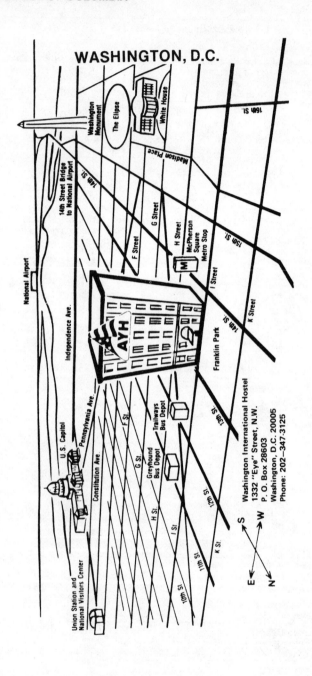

WASHINGTON, D.C.

Washington International Hostel
1332 "Eye" Street, N.W.
P. O. Box 28603
Washington, D.C. 20005
Phone: 202-347-3125

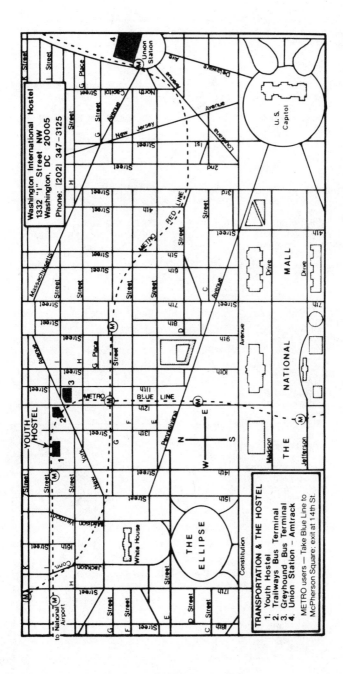

Washington International Hostel
1332 "I" Street NW
Washington, DC 20005
Phone: (202) 347-3125

TRANSPORTATION & THE HOSTEL
1. Youth Hostel
2. Trailways Bus Terminal
3. Greyhound Bus Terminal
4. Union Station – Amtrack

METRO users — Take Blue Line to McPherson Square; exit at 14th St.

121

between E St & F St
♂ yes, no utensils provided
🚌 Greyhound & Trailways 1 blk
🚃 Amtrak 1 mi via subway or bus
✈ Washington National 6 mi, Dulles International 1 hour
DIRECTIONS: 1 blk W of Greyhound & Trailways bus depots on "I" Street NW between 13th & 14th Sts opposite Franklin Park. One-

half blk E of McPherson Square Metro Subway stop. Hostel is 15 minute ride on the metro subway from Washington Nat'l Airport & 1 hr. ride from Dulles Int'l Airport on bus which stops 3 blks W of the hotel at the Capitol Hilton Hotel.
🏠 Knoxville, MD 60 mi
See Maps Following

FLORIDA

MIAMI BEACH Haddon Hall Hostel, (SA, rates), 1500 Collins Ave, Miami Beach, FL 33139
🏠 Max Berger & Anita Krieger
☎ (305) 531-1251
🛏 ⚥ 30 ⚥ 30
● $20-$35 (1 or 2 to a room Dec 15-Apr 15); $12-$18 (1 or 2 to a room Apr 15-May-June-Sept, Oct-Nov, Dec 15); $15-$20 (1 or 2 to a room July & Aug)
▲ Haddon Hall Hotel
🚰 Hot & cold
🔌 within 1 blk
♂ Yes. Stove, oven. Must furnish own utensils, pots, pans, refrigs, kitchenette.
🚌 MTA local at front door; Greyhound 1 blk N
🚃 Amtrak 15 mins by car or bus
✈ Miami International 18 mins by cab
* TV room, Bass Art Museum, Zoo, Parrot & Monkey Jungle, Seaquarium, Theater, Convention Center, maid service & linens, color T.V.s, pool, across from Atlantic Ocean.
✱ By reservation
DIRECTIONS: 1 block S of Greyhound Bus Station on 16th Street; 1 blk S from Lincoln Road located at 15th & Collins Ave.; 2 blks from lifeguarded beach on Atlantic Ocean.

ORLANDO Young Women's Community Club, Inc. (SA, no kitchen), 107 E. Hillcrest St, Orlando, FL 32801
🏠 Mrs. Carol Cheek, Executive

Director
☎ (305) 425-2502
🛏 10
● $5 S
SN Young women only 16-37 years of age
▲ Mrs. Carol Cheek, Ex. Director
🚰 Hot & cold
🔌 7-11 3 blks
🚌 7 blks
🚃 Amtrak 1½ mi
🏍 1 mi
🚲 on site
✈ 15 mi
* Walt Disney World 20 mi, Sea World 15 mi, Circus World 30 mi, Kennedy Space Center 50 mi, Atlantic Ocean beaches 50 mi
** Security Guard, Recreation

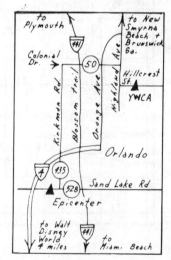

122

Center, Swimming Pool
🔧 I-$1 III-$2
🛏 Linens provided

🏠 Plymouth 18 mi

PANAMA CITY 🏠 Sangraal By-
the-Sea #2 Myrtlewood
Lodge (SA), 226 College Ave,
Panama City, FL 32401
🏠 Mrs. Myrtle Wiggin
☎ (904) 785-6226
🛏 12 ⚡ 6 ⚡ 6
▬ up to 12
🛁 yes
⬤ $4.50
▲ Sangraal By-the-Sea, Inc.
🚿 Hot & cold
🛒 Piggly Wiggly Market 4 blks
🚩 yes
🚌 ½ blk
🚲 Bay Line, St. Andrews
🚴 Downtown Panama City 1 mi

🛫 yes
* Pure white sand beaches,
sea aquarium, amusement
park, deep sea fishing & sail-
ing-windsurfing.
** Located across from City
Dark
★ yes, private rooms
🚐 no
🔧 I $1.50 II $2 III $2.50 I-III $5
🛏 $2 per night
➥ Known as "The Miracle Strip
— 100 Miles of Year Round
Beautiful White Sand
Beach."
DIRECTIONS: From downtown
City Bus or car to Millville
area of town near paper mill.
Just off Hwy 98, College
Ave. next to Immanuel Bap-
tist Church.
🏠 Orlando 150 mi; Brunswick,
GA 150 mi

ATLANTA Georgian Terrace Hotel
(SA, no kitchen) 659 Peachtree St. NE, Atlanta, GA
30308
🏠 Joanna Claire Leifer
☎ (404) 872-6671
🛏 All - 166 Units
▬ 166 Units
🛁 Yes, if possible

HOTEL GEORGIAN TERRACE
ATLANTA, GA.
SOL WEBER 1/79

⬤ $6 in quad; $7 in triple;
$8.50 in double; $14 in
single
▲ Dr. M. Goldstein
🚿 Hot & cold
🛒 Howell House Groceries 1
blk
🚌 8 blks
🚲 10 blks
🚴 at hostel
🚴 8 mi
* Buses direct to all main attractions
➥ 3 restaurants in building

DIRECTIONS: Peachtree at
Ponce de Leon
🏠 Wesser, NC

BRUNSWICK Hostel in the
Forest, P.O. Box 1496,
Brunswick, GA 31520
🏠 Thomas E. Dennard, Jr.
☎ 912/264-9676, 912/265-
0220, 912/638-2623
🛏 36 ⚡ 20 ⚡ 18 (4 private
rooms)
⬤ $4 S, $4 W
▲ Thomas E. Dennard, Jr.
SN Call for rides to hostel ($2
per trip).
🚿 Hot & cold
🛒 Gary's ½ mi E
🚩 yes

GEORGIA

🚌 Trailways & Greyhound 9 mi
🚆 Amtrak 10 mi
🚲 Griffin's 10 mi N in Brunswick
🚗 Parking at Hostel
🚕 St. Simons Island, GA 20 mi
⛺ yes
* Hostel facilities are housed in 2 geodesic domes situated in 90 acres of virgin Georgia forest. We are located close to the Golden Isles, Okeefenokee Swamp, Cumberland Island.
✱ Yes, 4 private rooms
🏠 yes
🔋 $1

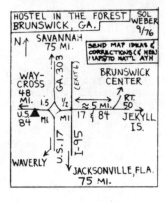

HONOLULU Honolulu International Youth Hostel, 2323A Sea View Ave Honolulu, HI 96822
🏠 Thelma I. Akau
☎ (808) 946-0591
🛏 ⚊ 24 ⚊ 16
🔋 Open all year. Send self addressed, stamped envelope & one night deposit for reservations.
● $4 inc. tax
SN City bus will not accept people with backpacks.
♨ Hot and cold
🍴 Star Super Mkt. 10 min walk SE, E-W Center Cafeteria at Univ. of Hawaii 6 min walk E
⚐ yes
DIRECTIONS: 50¢ Bus fare, 6 mi

from Airport. Bus 8, transfer Bus 4 to Metcalf-University intersection. 50¢ Bus fare includes transfer.

ILLINOIS
Metropolitan Chicago Council, 3712 N. Clark St., Chicago, IL 60613 (321) 217-8114

CAMPBELL HILL 🏠 Ruebke Youth Hostel (SA), Hwy 4 at Taggart 300 mi SW of Chicago, Campbell Hill, IL 62916
🏠 Raymond & Genevieve Ruebke
☎ (618) 426-3136
🛏 3
🍴 At least 5 hrs in advance if evening meal is expected.
● $3 S, $3 W

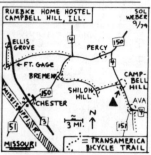

⌂ Hot & cold
🏠 MidTown 1 blk, Farmers Store 1 blk
🚻 yes
🍴 30 mi
🚲 30 mi
🚗 30 mi

DIRECTIONS: Right on the Trans America Bicycle trail

CHICAGO Chicago International House (SA, no kitchen), 1414 E. 59th St., Chicago, IL 60637
⌂ Joyce Penner
☎ (312) 753-2280
🏠 June 1-Sept 7
🛏 yes, June 1-Sept 7
● $11 S
SN no family accommodations
▲ University of Chicago
🚻 no; cafeteria: breakfast, lunch Mon-Fri
🚌 2 blks
🚲 1 blk

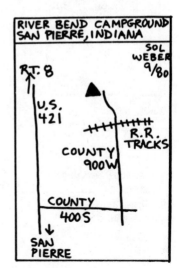

* Lake Michigan shore 4 blks, Museum of Science & Industry 3 blks. Bicycle bikeway thru Burnham paralleling Lake Shore Dr.
** clothes washing facilities
★ no
DIRECTIONS: Lake Shore Drive to 59th Street Exit, 1 blk W

INDIANA
Northwest Indiana Council, 8231 Lake Shore Dr., Gary In 46403 (219) 938-1312
Tri State Council, 5400 Lanius Lane, Cincinnati, OH 45224 (513) 542-2909
Friars, 65 W. McMillan, Cincinnati, OH 45219 (513) 381-5432

SAN PIERRE River Bend Camp Ground. (SA no bedding or dishes), San Pierre, IN 46374
⌂ Eddie & Jane Miller
☎ 219-896-3339
🏠 May 1-Sept 30
● $2 S
⌂ Hot & cold
🏠 Some nearby or 5 mi
🚌 7 mi S
🚲 At hostel
🚗 50 to 60 mi S
⛺ yes
* Jasper Puloski Game Reserve. 20 mi S on Rt 421 (snow geese, wild duck, etc). Canoes to rent
** We have pool & pond
🏕 I-$1.25 II-$1.50 III-$1.50
DIRECTIONS: 8 MI S of La Cross, 8 mi N of San Pierre on 421 to CR 400 N to CR 900 W.

IOWA
Northeast Iowa Council, 139 West Greene Street, P.O. Box 10,
Postville, IA 52162, (319) 864-7421

IOWA CITY Wesley House, 120 N Dubuque St. Iowa City, Iowa 52240
- 🏠 David Schuldt
- ☎ 319-338-1179
- 🛏 2 for family + crib ⚥ 4 ⚥ 4
- 🛏 30 roll-away cost ⚥ & ⚥
- ● $3 S, $6 w/intro pass
- SN Registration is between 7-9 PM daily, no reservations required.
- 🍴 Hot & cold
- ♫ John's 2 blks E
- ⚥ yes
- 🚌 Greyhound, Continental, 4 blks
- 🚲 Novotny's 6 blks on Clinton St.
- 🚃 Cedar Rapids, 25 mi N
- ✳ Amana Colonies 20 mi NW

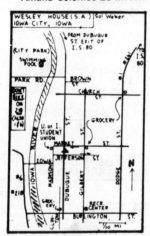

DIRECTIONS: 2 mi S of I-80, off Dubuque St. exit, No. 60
- 🏠 Sioux City 200 mi W

SIOUX CITY (SA no kitchen), 722 Nebraska St. Sioux City, IA 51101
- 🏠 Jon Springer, Y Director
- ☎ (712) 252-3276
- 🛏 61 ⚥
- ● $3 S
- ▲ YMCA of Siouxland
- 🍴 Hot & cold
- ♫ Hinky-Dinky 8 blks
- 🚌 6th & Douglas 6 bks
- 🚲 Omaha 90 mi
- 🚲 6th & Water 1 mi
- 🚌 we have parking lot
- 🚐 Sioux City Airport 7 mi
- ** Complete use of YMCA facilities (pool, gym, track, etc.)

DIRECTIONS: 8 blocks N of I-29 Business District Exit - 8 blks N of Gordon Dr. (Hwy 12) & Nebraska St.
- 🏠 Iowa City 200 mi SE; Lincoln, NB 115 mi SW; Rapid City, SD 400 mi NW

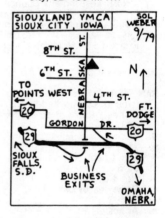

KANSAS
Ozark Area Council, 5400 A Southwest, St. Louis, MO 63139
(314) 644-3560

MARION Stone Prairie, (SA, no kitchen), Rt 1, Marion, KS 66861
- 🏠 Julie and Robert Fischer
- ☎ (316) 382-2057 or (316) 382-2308 (if no answer)
- 🛏 ⚥ 10 ⚥ 10
- 🛏 ⚥ 10 ⚥ 10
- 🏠 March-Nov
- ⚓ Advance booking required
- ● $4.50
- 🍴 Hot & cold

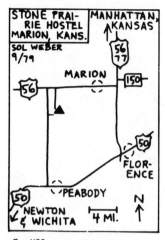

Marion 7 mi
Newton 25 mi
Newton 25 mi
on grounds
Wichita 55 mi S
yes
* Mennonite Museum 7 mi, Large Marion Lake 3 mi
** Well stocked library
private rooms
yes
I-.75 II-$1.50 III-$2.50
$2

DIRECTIONS: **From Peabody:** at W edge of town go 9 mi on blacktop. Turn E, go 1 mi. Hostel on left. **From Marion:** Go W out of Marion 5 mi to Marion Reservoir Rd. Turn S & go 2½ mi on upward road. **From Hillsboro:** Drive E 4 mi to a blacktop. Turn S 3 mi. Then turn left (E) & go 1 mi.

yes
Marion 7 mi

KENTUCKY
Tri State Council, 5400 Lanius Lane, Cincinnati, OH 45224
(513) 542-2909

PIPPA PASSES Old Knott County High School (SA, no kitchen), Box 15, Pippa Passes, KY 48144
Ed & Charlotte Madden
(606) 368-2753
10 &
40 &
Open all year
$2.50 S, $2.50 W
Hot & cold
Country Store 1 mi
yes
Hazard 30 mi
on premises

* Numerous hiking trails. Hills, rock formations, wildlife, streams, nature preserves (all within 20 mi). Music events: Appalachian Music Festival, second week in Sept. Various weekend Country & Bluegrass Shows throughout the year. Summer theatre throughout July and August.
★ By reservation
With reservation
DIRECTIONS: At junction of State Route 899 & 1697

MAINE

BLANCHARD Crossroads Inn, Blanchard, ME 04406
M/M Charles Nute
(207) 848-3781
20 10 10
May 15-Oct 15
RFD 2, Box 235, Carmel, ME 04419
$2 S
Thomas R. Poole
Hot & cold
Poole's Market 4 mi E

yes
Newport 50 mi
Greenville 25 mi
Bicycles Unlimited 4 mi
no
* Swimming 3 mi, canoeing 50 mi, Appalachian Trail at door, skiing 30 mi, Summer theatre at Skowhegan ($6).
** Fireplace, radio, piano, quiet games.
DIRECTIONS: Located at the

crossroads in Blanchard.
🏠 Lincoln 65 mi E

LINCOLN, Big Lake Hostel, Stanhope Mill Rd., Lincoln, ME 04457
🏠 Barbara & Ed Coan
☎ 207-794-8200
🛏 ⌡ 8 ⌡ 8
🏠 June 15-Labor Day Weekend
● $3.50 S
SN sleeping bags required
🚰 Hot & cold
🍴 on premises
🚩 yes
🚌 5 mi
🚃 5 mi
🔧 Western Auto, Lincoln
⛽ on premises
✈ Bangor 50 mi
＊ Recreation room w/wood stove, games, radio-TV. Outside recreation includes badminton, boating, swimming, horseshoes, fishing & miles of logging trails for hikers. Day trips can cover Mt. Katahdin, Maine Coast at Bar Harbor-Mt. Desert Is. region.
＊＊ swimming, boating, fishing
✴ yes

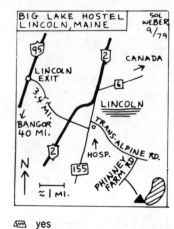

🚗 yes
➡ site of 165-yr-old sawmill, sm. hydro-electric plant now.

DIRECTIONS: From Lincoln, 1 mi S to Hospital, left 2.3 mi on Transalpine Rd, right 0.9 mi on Phinney Farm Rd, left 0.8 mi. Total 5 mi all paved road.
🏠 Fredericton, N.B., Canada, 90 mi N

MARYLAND
Potomac Area Council, 1520 16th St., NW, Suite A, Washington, DC 20036 (202) 462-5780

CAMBRIDGE Cambridge Home Hostel, 1311 Race St, Cambridge, MD 21613
🏠 Albert B. & Annette R. Atkinson
☎ (301) 228-7445
🛏 10
● $4.50
🚌 10 blks
🚃 1 mi
🚰 Hot & cold
🍴 Quick Shop, 4 blks
＊ Sailing on chesapeake Bay, swimming pool
🖊 On request

GRANTSVILLE National Hotel, Box 224, Grantsville, MD 21536
🏠 Judith Miller & Mark Silberstein
☎ (301) 895-5052
🛏 20 ⌡ & ⌡
● $3 S

🚰 Hot & cold
🍴 Durst Dairy Mart
🚩 yes
🚌 Greyhound at hotel
🚃 Amtrak, Cumberland 30 mi
🔧 Cumberland 30 mi
✈ Garrett County Air. 15 mi
＊ Recreation room w/radio, piano & TV. Volleyball field. Sailing (15 mi) canoeing (15 mi), horseback riding. Hiking and biking trails, skiing (3 mi) Savage River State Park; Laurel Highlands of So. Pennsylvania.
＊＊ Reasonably priced restaurant on premises
🚗 yes
DIRECTIONS: At the only traffic light in Grantsville, cor. of US Rt. 40 (Main St) and St. Rt 495; The Hostel is 30 mi W of Cumberland
🏠 Morgantown, WV

KNOXVILLE ♠ Kiwanis Hostel, Rt 2, Box 304, Knoxville, MD 21758
- ⌂ Dave Gilbert
- ☎ 301-834-7652
- ⊨ 31 ↕ 15 ↕ 16
- ⓝ open April 1-Nov 1 only
- ⦿ $3 S
- SN groups accepted Nov 1-Apr 1 by advance reservation
- ▲ Potomac Area Council
- ⌂ Hot & cold
- ⌂ Sandy Hook .5 mi
- ⚑ yes
- 🚂 Frederick 16 mi
- 🚌 Harpers Ferry, WV, 1.5 mi
- 🚲 Frederick 16 mi
- 🚗 at hostel
- ✈ Dulles International 40 mi
- ✳ C&O Canal .5 mi, Harpers Ferry NHP 1.5 mi, Appalachian Trail .5 mi, Potomac & Shenandoah Rivers .5-1.5 mi, Antietam Battlefield 10 mi.

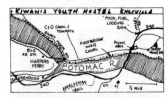

DIRECTIONS: 16 mi W of Frederick on US 340. Left on Rt 180 at blinking yellow light. Right on Sandy Hook Rd. Hostel is first bldg on left.
- ⓕ Washington, DC, 60 mi E; Williamsport, 34 mi W

OAKLAND Camp Minnetoska YH, P.O. Box 26, Oakland, MD 21550
- ⌂ Mr. Fred Learey
- ☎ (301) 334-8292
- ⊨ ↕ 50 ↕ 50
- ⓝ Winter camping Nov 1-April 1
- ⦿ $1.50
- ⌂ cold
- ⌂ Oakland 7 mi E
- 🚂 Grantsville 35 mi, Red House 15 mi
- 🚲 Oakland 7 mi
- 🚗 Western Auto, Oakland 7 mi
- ✈ 20 mi at Garrett Cnty Airport
- ✳ Recreation room with fireplace, record player & quiet

games. Badminton, outdoor fireplace & tennis. Swimming ¼ mi, sailing. Hiking trails. Skiing 15 & 8 mi. Herrington Manor State Park 1 mi, Swallow Falls State Park 7 mi, Deep Creek Lake 10 mi, Cheat River 20 mi.

DIRECTIONS: From Oakland, 7 mi W. On Hutton Rd. right at the end of Sanders Ln. Watch for camp signs. It is 10 mi E of Terra Alta, WV.
- ⓕ Morgantown, WV 40 mi NW; Grantsville 35 mi NE

WILLIAMSPORT ♠ Falling Waters Farm Hostel, Rural Rt. 1, Box 238-B, Williamsport, MD 21795
- ⌂ Richard & Cathy Bean
- ☎ (301) 223-9208
- ⊨ 20 ↕ 10 ↕ 10
- ⦿ $3 S, $3 W

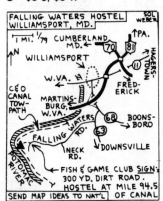

▲ Trancare, Inc.
⌂ Hot & cold
♫ 5 mi on C & O Canal
♥ yes
🚌 Hagerstown 15 mi
🚋 Hagerstown 15 mi
🚲 Hagerstown 15 mi
🍴 at hostel
✈ Hagerstown 15 mi
✱ Recreation Room with fireplace, hiking & biking on C &

O Canal, canoeing on Potomac River, small farm with farm animals, demonstrations on country skills.
✶ yes

DIRECTIONS: 300 yds. E of C & O Canal. Outside of Williamsport off Rt 63, take Falling Waters Rd. to its end. 5 mi.
⬕ Knoxville 25 mi SE

MASSACHUSETTS
Greater Boston Council, 251 Harvard Street, Brookline, MA 02146 (617) 731-6692

AMHERST 🏠 Hampshire College, Office of Summer Programs, Hampshire College, Amherst, MA 01002
⬕ Paul & Victoria Bushey
☎ (413) 549-4600 Ext. 288
🛏 40 ⇃ 20 ⇃ 20
➡ 10 ⇃ 5 ⇃ 5
🕐 June 4-August 25
● $4.75 S
SN Curfew 11 PM
▲ Hampshire College
⌂ Hot & cold
♫ 1 mi
♥ yes
🚌 Peter Pan bus 3 mi, Amherst
🚋 Amtrak 7 mi, Northampton
🚲 Peloton 3 mi, Amherst
✈ LaFleur 7 mi, Northampton
✱ Recreation Room, badminton, pool, basketball, hiking trails, bike path.
✶ yes
△ yes

➥ Modern campus
DIRECTIONS: Located in Enfield House, Apt. 42. 3 mi S of Amherst on Rt 116 and intersection of Bay Rd.
⬕ Springfield 20 mi S; Keene, NH 60 mi N

BOSTON Armed Services YMCA (SA, no kitchen), 32 City Sq, Boston, MA 02129
⬕ Reggie Holland
☎ (617) 242-2660
🛏 ⇃ 15 ⇃ 10
● $6
SN The Y is open 24 hours a day, so a member may check in at any time & must check out by 11 am. Blankets are furnished. No one under 18 can stay unless part of a chaperoned group or letter from parents or guardians. Proof of marriage required

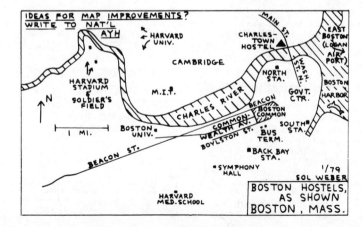

for couples wishing to stay together.

▲ Armed Services YMCA
🛏 Hot & cold
🚌 400 feet
🚲 4 blks
🛴 Bicycle Exchange 2 mi
✈ 4 blks
✗ yes

DIRECTIONS: 1 mi N of downtown Boston, 1 blk from transit system

🏠 Littleton 35 mi W

CEDARVILLE Camp Massasoit, (SA) Sandy Point Rd, RFD 5, Box 636, Plymouth, MA 02360

🏠 Terry & Frank McKenna
☎ (617) 888-2624
🛏 17 ♂ & ♀
🚪 June 15-Labor Day
👆 yes
● $3.50 S

SN No late hours after 10 pm; arrive between 4:30 pm & 7 pm. Hostel closed between 10 am & 4:30 pm. Early arrivals will be charged day fee. Flashlights necessary. No crockery. Bring mess kits...or paper service provided for a fee.

▲ Boston Council, AYH
🛏 Hot & cold
🏪 Cedarville Mkt. 2 mi
♨ Stove, refrig & hot water
🚌 6 mi to Plymouth & Brockton-Sagamore Circle to Hyannis, Plymouth, Boston, New York
🛴 7 mi

🏕 Yes, excellent. $1.50 per night
✳ Boating, swimming, volleyball

DIRECTIONS: From Cedarville Store, Herring Pond Rd to first right, follow to 2nd right. Stay on paved road. Look for red A's on poles & trees.

🏠 Hyannis S; East Bridgewater N

DUDLEY 🏠 Home Hostel
☎ (617) 943-6520
🧍 Bolton, CN 50 mi; Littleton 45 mi; Boston 55 mi; Bridgewater 70 mi; Springfield 45 mi

EAST BRIDGEWATER 🏠 Train Hostel 234 Central St, E. Bridgewater, MA 02333

🏠 Ruth C. Thayer
☎ (617) 378-4046
🛏 40 ♂ & ♀
● $4.50 S, $5.75 W

SN Groups & loners please, call or write ahead.

🛏 Hot & cold
🏪 Ferrandes Supermarket
♨ yes
🚌 Brockton 4 mi
🚲 Boston 22 mi
🛴 at Hostel, bike mechanic on duty daily; Lester Peterson, Satucket Cycle
✳ Art gallery, restored historic buildings. Canoes, nature

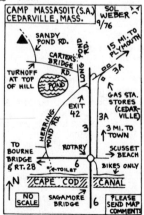

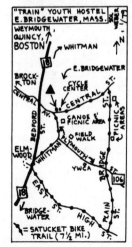

preserve
** The Train Hostel—an authentic Canadian Pacific Pullman Railroad Car. Over 50 years old—an historic 1723 church sanctuary. Church holds services every Sunday at 11 AM. Outdoor fireplace.

DIRECTIONS: In Unitarian Church facing East Bridge-water Town Common just off Rt. 18 & 106, 32 mi from Boston/Brookline/Charlestown

🏠 Boston 30 mi N; Cedarville 20 mi S

EASTHAM 🏠 Starfish Hostel (SA, other use in summer), Rt. 6, RR #1, Box 140, Eastham, MA 02642

🏠 Hoby & Nancy Van Deusen

🐞 (617) 255-1441

ID ⚥ 8 ⚥ 8

🏠 May 1-June 26; Sept 8-Nov 9; hostel opens at 5 PM

advisable

$4.55 W

▲ Hoby & Nancy Van Deusen

Hot & cold

yes

🚌 New York City & Boston via bus at Orleans 1½ mi

🚲 Brewster Bicycle, Cove Rd, 1 blk from 6A Orleans

🚗 on hostel premises

Hyannis

no

* 2 mi from Cape Cod national seashore, bike trails nearby

yes, call in advance

no

DIRECTIONS: 1 mi E of Orleans Rotary Circle (Jct. of Rtes 6 & 6A). On Rt 6 at corner of Hay Rd, cemetery across from hostel.

🏠 Orleans 2 mi W, Truro 17 mi E, Hyannis 26 mi W

GRANVILLE 🏠 Home Hostel

🐞 (413) 357-6637

SN no motor vehicles

HYANNIS 🏠 HyLand Youth Hostel, 465 Falmouth Rd, Hyannis, MA 02601

HY-LAND HOSTEL

Operated by AYH National

🏠 Mr. & Mrs. Harold Wennberg, Rick Charboneau

🐞 Hostel, (617) 775-2970; Members, (617) 771-1585

Summer ⚥ 20 ⚥ 20

Winter ⚥ 10 ⚥ 10

$4.50

▲ National AYH

Hot & cold

🎵 Star Market ½ mi wkdays, Farmland ¾ mi Sun 9-3 PM

fully equipped

🚌 Greyhound Bus, Boston & Providence to Hyannis, Cape Cod Bus Line, Hyannis to Provinceton

🚲 Bicycle Central, Hyannis

* Family up to 6

DIRECTIONS: Rt 28, ¾ mi W of Airport Rotary. Walk to shops, beaches, Island ferry.

🏠 Orleans 25 mi E, Cedarville

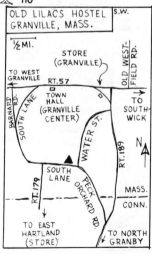

OLD LILACS HOSTEL S.W.
GRANVILLE, MASS.

½ MI.

STORE
(GRANVILLE)

OLD WEST-FIELD RD.

TO WEST GRANVILLE RT. 57

BARNARD RD.

SOUTH LANE

TOWN HALL (GRANVILLE CENTER)

TO SOUTH-WICK

WATER ST.

RT. 189

SOUTH LANE

RT. 179

PECK ORCHARD RD.

N

MASS.

CONN.

TO EAST HARTLAND (STORE)

TO NORTH GRANBY

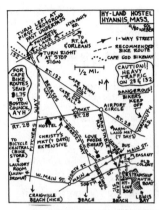

18 mi W, Nantucket and Martha's Vineyard 2 hrs by ferry

LITTLETON Friendly Cross—ways, Whitcomb Ave, Littleton, MA 01460
- Martin & Anne Vesenka
- (617) 456-3649
- 🛏 30 🛏 30
- 🛏 20 🛏 20
- Yes, Groups 3 or more
- $5 S, $7.50 W
- SN Groups with reservation only Dec, Jan, Feb; minimum 20 persons
- Hot & cold
- Johnsons 2.2 mi
- yes
- Ayer or Littleton 6 mi
- Acton 7 mi E
- Littleton 6 mi; Concord 13 mi
- Premises, with reservations
- Boston 35 mi

Yes, large groups only
- Historic Fruitlands Harvard 5 mi; Walden Pond, Concord 13 mi; National Park, Lowell 15 mi; swimming, skating pond.
- yes
- $3.50, 2 sheets, pillowcase, towel

DIRECTIONS: 2.3 mi from RR station; 3.3 mi from Harvard Village; 3.3 mi from 495 exits and Rt. 2
- Peterboro, NH 30 mi N; Boston 30 mi E

MARTHA'S VINEYARD (West Tisbury) Manter Memorial, Edgartown Road, West Tisbury, MA 02575
- M/M Richard Cohen
- (617) 693-2665
- 85 🛏 40 🛏 45
- April 1-Nov 30
- yes
- $4.75 S
- Hot & cold
- Alley's 1 mi
- yes
- Woods Hole 7 mi by ferry
- Vineyard Haven 7 mi
- Woods Hole 7 mi by ferry
- 3 mi E
- Gay Head Cliffs 13 mi; excelent beaches & sailing
- $1
- First Hostel designed & built as a hostel in USA
- Hyannis by ferry NE 20 mi, Nantucket by ferry SW 20 mi

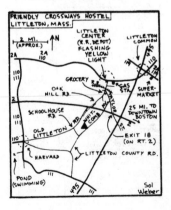

NANTUCKET ⌂ Star of the Sea YH Surfside, Nantucket, MA 02554

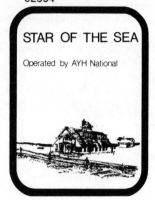

STAR OF THE SEA

Operated by AYH National

⚫ (617) 228-0433
🛏 ⚑ 42 ⚑ 30
🏠 Apr 1, 1981, all year thereafter; hostel opens at 5 PM
⚐ yes
⬤ $4.50
SN No camping permitted on island; Boat transport from Woods Hole & Hyannis; spec. reduction for AYH groups, write in advance.
▲ National AYH
⌀ Hot & cold

⌐ A & P 3 mi; Finast 2.5 mi; buy food before cycling to hostel
⚐ yes
🚲 Young's Bike Shop
🛬 Nantucket 4 mi
🚐 yes
➡ Building listed on National Register of Historic Places; original structure was life-saving station, dating from 1873.

DIRECTIONS: 3 mi from Nantucket on Southside of island at end of Atlantic Ave & Surfside Rd
⌂ Martha's Vineyard, Hyannis

NEWBURYPORT YMCA Civic Center Hostel, 96 State St, Newburyport, MA 01950
⚑ Michael W. Pavesi
⚫ (617) 462-6711 or 462-8811
🛏 ⚑ 20 ⚑ 20 Total accom. 65 ⚑ & ⚑
🏠 June 15-Labor Day (Off season for groups over 20 people by reservation only)
⚐ yes
⬤ $3.50 S
▲ Newburyport YMCA, Inc.
⌀ Hot & cold
⌐ Richdale 2 blks N, Finast ¼ mi, IGA ½ mi
⚐ yes
🚌 Greyhound 3 mi
🚂 B & M, Ipswich Sta., 10 mi
🚲 Elan Ski & Bike Shop, ½ mi S; Open all year/weekends; Emerg. service, call Ken Bass 462-9024

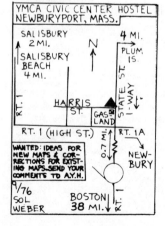

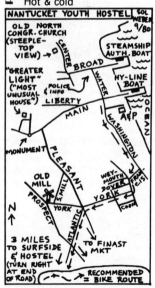

🚗 Municipal parking down-town 2 blks E

🛬 Logan, Boston, 35 mi

✳ Salisbury Beach, (Amusement Park), Hampton & Rye Beaches; Plum Island (Wildlife Refuge). Local art & craft shops, horseback riding, sailing, canoeing, indoor swimming close by; gym; Caterer's Kitchen, catering service for any size group

✱✱ Have Sauna

✗ Yes, prior notice before arrival

🏠 yes

↦ Expected to be listed on National Register of Historic Places

NORTHFIELD 🏠 Monroe Smith Memorial, Daly House, Highland & Pine Sts, Northfield, MA 01360

🏠 Nan & Bruce Brown

☎ (413) 498-5311, ext. 502

🛏 21

🛏 11

🏠 June 21-Aug 22

⛽ no

◑ c/o Northfield/Mt. Hermon School, Northfield, MA 01360

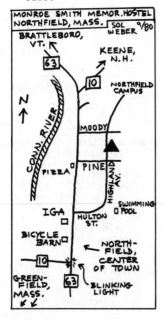

💲 $4.50 S

SN No smoking in hostel

▲ Northfield Mt. Hermon School

♨ Hot & cold

🍴 IGA 1 mi S

🚩 yes

🚌 Links Bus

🚂 Brattle Boro, VT 15 mi

✳ Tennis, swimming, golf, hiking, on campus. Canoeing on Conn River, boat launch 1/8 mi. New England's largest flea markets nearby.

🏠 yes

🔑 I $1.50 II $2.25 III $2.75 I-III $6.50

🛏 $1

DIRECTIONS: 1 mi N of Northfield Center on Rt 10.

ORLEANS 🏠 Mid-Cape YH, Box 140-H Bridge Road, Eastham, MA 02642

MID CAPE HOSTEL

Operated by AYH National

☎ Hostel, (617) 255-2785; Members, (617) 255-9762

🛏 Accommodations for sleeping 60 in cabins 6 & 8 🛏 & 🛏

🏠 May 15-Sept 15; Hostel opens 5 PM (for reservations contact AYH National Office, Delaplane, VA 22025 until June 1)

💲 $4.50 S

SN Family accommodations can not be reserved in advance; only available when space permits

▲ National AYH

♨ Hot & cold

🛒 Stop & Shop Supermarket, 1 mi on Rt 6A S of Rotary; open 9-9 except Sunday

🔥 Yes, 2 gas stoves, refrig, fireplace in rec room

🚌 NYC & Boston via Cape Cod, bus at Orleans

🚲 Brewster Bicycle, Cove Rd, ½ blk E of 6A in Orleans

🏠 yes

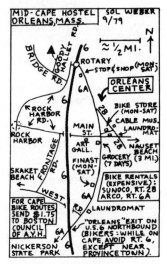

DIRECTIONS: From Rt 6 traffic rotary (just north of Orleans Center), left on Rock Harbor Rd for ¼ mi, then right on Bridge Rd for ½ mi to Goody Hallet Rd.

🏠 Truro 18 mi N, Hyannis 25 mi W

SHEFFIELD Mount Everett YH, Rt 1, Box 161, Sheffield, MA 01257

🏠 Bill & Judy Perry

🌐 (413) 229-2043

🛏 ♂ 20 ♀ 20

🚪 May 15-Sept 5

💲 $3

🚰 Hot & cold

🛒 Sheffield Market 4 mi E, closes at 5 PM; cans & staples at Hostel

🔥 yes

🚌 Arrow, Sheffield 4 mi

🚂 Hudson, NY 25 mi

🚲 HB Fosters, Inc.; GT Barrington 10 mi

🚗 on site, $1 charge

✈ Pittsfield 25 mi

⛺ yes, $2.75

✳ Bash Bish Falls 10 mi; Tanglewood 20 mi; Great Barrington Fair Sept 12-23, 10 mi; Mt. Everett, Appalachian Trail 2 mi; swimming 6 mi; boating, horseback riding, 5 mi.

➡ Oldest continuous Youth Hostel in USA (Chartered 1936)

DIRECTIONS: Under Mt. Road; Turn from Rt 7 at Sheffield Library onto Berkshire School Rd. Go 3 miles W; then 1 mi S on Rt 141.

🏠 Lakeside 34 mi S, Washington 35 mi N, Granville 50 mi E

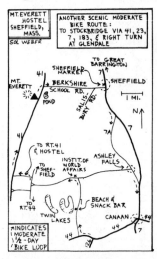

SPRINGFIELD 🏠 Springfield College Camp (SA, no kitchen), 701 Wilbraham Rd. Springfield, MA 01109

🏠 M/M Charles T. Wilson, Box 1733, Springfield College, 253 Alden St, Springfield, MA 01109

🌐 (413) 782-0461

🛏 In cabins ♂ 20 ♀ 20

🚪 July 1-Aug 1

💲 $1.50 S

SN Check in after 4:30 PM & prior to 8 PM. Meals can be furnished upon application

▲ Springfield College

🛁 Hot & cold
🛒 Big Y Market
🚌 Vt. Transit, Springfield 3 mi, local, ¼ mi
🚆 B & M, Penn Central, Springfield, 4 mi

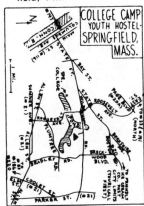

🚲 Bros. Bike Shop 1 mi; Victors ½ mi
DIRECTIONS: 3 mi from center of town; from Main St. take State St. E to Wilbraham Rd.
🏠 Granville 25 mi W

TRURO 🏠 Little America YH, P.O. Box 402, Truro, MA 02666

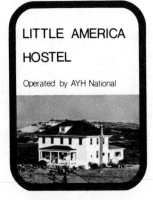

LITTLE AMERICA HOSTEL

Operated by AYH National

🏠 Contact AYH, Delaplane, VA 22025
☎ (617) 349-3889
🛏 ♂ 21 ♀ 21
🗓 June 22-Sept 7
Yes, during closed period, contact AYH National Office,

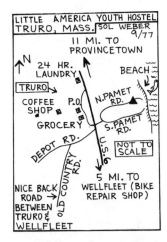

Delaplane, VA 22025
💲 $4.50 S
SN No late hours (after 10 PM). No camping. No sleeping on beaches or dunes. Specify males/females when reserving
▲ Operated by National AYH on permit from National Parks Service
🛁 Hot & cold
🛒 Buy food before coming to Hostel; Truro Center 1½ mi; First National 8 mi in Wellfleet
♂ yes
🚲 Wellfleet Multi-Speed 5½ mi S; Bike Rental 2½ mi; Arnold's Provincetown 10 mi N
** In Cape Cod National Seashore
⛺ yes
🏠 $1

DIRECTIONS: 10 mi S of Provincetown in the Cape Cod National Seashore Park, 1½ mi E or Rt 6 at Truro North Pamet Road
🏠 Orleans 18 mi S, Boston via Provincetown Ferry

WASHINGTON (Pittsfield) Camp Karu, Bucksteep Manor, Washington, MA 01223
🏠 Mrs. Rudolph A. Sacco & Domenick F. Sacco
☎ (413) 623-5535 or 445-5536

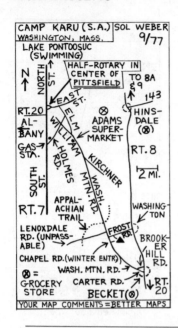

CAMP KARU (S.A.) SOL WEBER
WASHINGTON, MASS. 9/77
LAKE PONTOOSUC (SWIMMING)
HALF-ROTARY IN CENTER OF PITTSFIELD
TO 8A 89
NORTH ST. EAST ST. 143
RT.20 HINSDALE (⊗)
AL-BANY ADAMS SUPER-MARKET
WILLIAM
GAS STA. ELM
RT.8
HOLMES RD. KIRCHNER
2 MI.
SOUTH ST. WASH. MTN. RD.
APPAL-ACHIAN TRAIL WASHINGTON
RT.7
LENOXDALE RD. (UNPASS-ABLE) FROST RD.
BROOK-ER HILL RD.
CHAPEL RD. (WINTER ENTR)
WASH. MTN. RD.
⊗ = GROCERY STORE CARTER RD. RT.20
BECKET (⊗)
YOUR MAP COMMENTS = BETTER MAPS

🛏 ♂ 35 ♀ 28
🏠 Yes, in winter, groups only by reservation
SN Manor House $15 per person. Also rustic cabins, wood stove, no water or electricity.
● $3.50 S
🚰 Hot & cold
🏪 Becket Village 6 mi; Adams Supermarket, Pittsfield, 10 mi
🍴 Yes, in summer; meals can be catered in winter
🚂 Pittsfield 10 mi
⛺ yes
✳ Swimming pool & tennis courts, badminton, volleyball & softball; ski touring rentals; Appalachian Trail, Tanglewood, bird sanctuaries, Hancock Shaker Village, summer theater; lakes nearby.
⚓ Sheffield 35 mi S

MICHIGAN

Metropolitan Detroit Council, 3024 Collidge, Berkley, MI 48072 (313) 545-0511
Western Michigan Council, 1013 West Burton, Grand Rapids, MI 49509 (616) 361-7106

BAY CITY 🏠 Home Hostel, 1121 N. Birney, Bay City, MI 48706
🛏 4 ♂ & ♀
● $2.50 S, $2.50 W
⚓ Saginaw 18 mi S, Flint 60 mi S

BESSEMER Bessemer Indianhead YH (SA, no kitchen), Eli Ave., Yale Location, Bessemer, MI 49911
🏠 M/M Eugene Cocco (Dolores & Gene), 1110 E Iron St., Bessemer, MI 49911
☎ (906) 667-0915; Residence: 663-4456
🛏 ♂ 64 ♀ 64
🏠 Nov-April-Summer for groups of 15 or more only
● $8 S
▲ Bessemer Ind. Hostel & Chicago Council AYH
🚰 Hot & cold
🏪 1 blk away; Supermarket in downtown Bessemer

🚂 Ironwood
🚌 Ironwood
✈ Ironwood

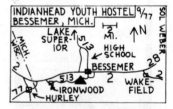

INDIANHEAD YOUTH HOSTEL 9/77
BESSEMER, MICH. SOL WEBER
LAKE SUPER-IOR
MICH. 3 MI.
HIGH SCHOOL
BESSEMER
28
513 WAKE-FIELD
IRONWOOD
HURLEY

DIRECTIONS: About a mile S of US2, turn at 4-way stop near Bessemer High School, Hwy 513; Hostel is on small hill on S side of road, brick bldg.
⚓ Hurley 30 mi W; Cable, WI

CENTER LINE 🏠 Home Hostel, 8585 Harding Ave, Center Line, MI 48015
🏠 Harold & Gloria Gatewood
☎ 313-756-2676
🛏 3 ♂ & ♀

▬ 2 ♀ & ♂
⬤ $2 S
⌂ Hot & cold
⊓ Chatham/Farmer Jack
☞ yes
🚌 VanDyke/Engleman ¼ mi
🚃 Detroit 10 mi
🚲 Joe's Bike Shop ½ mi
🚗 Front of House
✈ Metropolitan Airport 20 mi
✱ Berkley/Detroit Office General Motors Technical Center ½ mi, Greenfield Village 15 mi, Ford Motor Co. Rouge Plant 15 mi, Cadillac Tour Plant 12 mi, Detroit Renaissance Center 10 mi
⌂ Detroit, 2 Hostels

CHARLEVOIX ⌂ Home Hostel, 541 N. Mercer, Charlevoix, MI 49720
⌂ Frances Durance
☎ 616-574-2937
▬ 3 double-2 single ♀ & ♂
⬤ $2 S, $2.50 W
⌂ Hot & cold
⊓ Edwards IGA
☞ 50¢ charge
🚌 Corner Antrim & State Sts. Charlevoix
🚃 Traverse City
🚲 Harbor Springs
🚗 1½ mi
✈ Charlesvoix 1½ mi
⚒ yes
➡ Sand Dunes & beach ¼ mi
✱ yes
🛏 50¢/bed
DIRECTIONS: 1 mi N of Charlevoix on US 31 to Mercer, then left ½ mi. Corner of Mercer & Waller
⌂ Kalkaska 45 mi

COLOMA Camp Warren, 2456 Maple Ave, Coloma, MI 49038
⌂ Harold & Marge Wilbur
☎ 616-849-1433
▬ ♀ 80 ♂ 80
⚒ yes
⬤ $3 S, $4 W
⌂ Hot & cold
⊓ IGA, 5 mi N on 33
☞ yes
🚌 Benton Harbor 7 mi, Coloma Bus Station 7 mi
🚲 Wegner's Schwinn Cyclery 2621 Niles Ave, St. Joseph, 9 mi S
🚗 on site

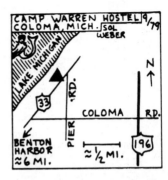

⚒ $2
✈ Kerry Lodge recreation room, retreat center & porch, w/fireplace, piano, fire circle, hiking trails, biking trails, cross country skiing. Points of Natural Interest: Sarett Nature Center; Warren Dunes; Municipal Band Concerts, Summer Theatre.

DIRECTIONS: 7 mi N of Benton Harbor/St. Joseph on US Rt 33. 20 mi S of South Haven; 5 mi W of Coloma, 3 mi W of Gerald Ford Hwy (196).
⌂ Holland 60 mi N

DELTON Circle Pines Ctr., Delton, MI 49046
⌂ Don Shall, Barbara Hofer
☎ (616) 623-5555
▬ 36
▬ 70
⚒ Advance booking required
⬤ $4 S, $5 W
SN 2 nights & 5 meals $30
⌂ Hot & cold
☞ yes
🚌 Kalamazoo 25 mi
🚃 Kalamazoo 25 mi
🚲 Hastings
✈ Grand Rapids 20 mi
✱ Recreation room w/fireplace, piano, record player, ping-pong, quiet games. Volleyball field, swimming, softball & outdoor fireplace. Sailing, canoeing, horseback riding nearby. Hiking Trails, Barry State Canoe Area, 5 mi, biking trails, skiing. $2 fee for day use of all facilities.
🛏 50¢
DIRECTIONS: The Hostel is 5 mi

N of Prairieville. From Delton on M-43, left at school on Delton Rd; 2 mi right at stop sign in Prairieville, onto Norris Rd; 5 mi N turn right Mullen Rd.

DETROIT (A) YMCA, 2020 Witherell, Detroit, MI 48226
🏠 Paul Davis
📞 (313) 962-6126
🔑 Advance booking recommended for individuals.
● $2.25 per person + 4% tax. Dormitories.
DIRECTIONS: 1 blk from Grand Circus Park at heart of city.

DETROIT (B) YWCA, (SA, no kitchen) 2230 Witherell, Detroit, MI 48226
🏠 Esther Hill, Director
📞 (313) 961-9220
🛏 ♀ women only
🚪 open all year
🔑 for groups & recommended for individuals
● $2.25 per person +4% tax. Dormitories-girls & women only
DIRECTIONS: 2 blks from Grand Circus Park at heart of city.

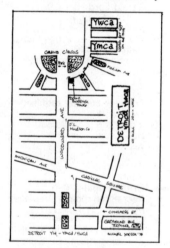

DETROIT (C) 🏠 Home Hostel, (Contact Metropolitan Detroit Council
📞 (313) 545-0511

EAST LANSING MSU Student Housing Co-Ops, (SA, limited kitchen use), 311-B Student Services Bldg, East Lansing, MI 48823
🏠 Jacob Wind
📞 (517) 355-8313, 10 AM-5 PM
🛏 ♂ 10 ♀ 10
🚪 open all year
● $2 S, $3 W
▲ Northern American Student Cooperative Organization, 4312 Michigan Union, Ann Arbor, MI 48104
🚰 Hot & cold
🚽 7-11 2-6 blks
🗝 Available in summer any time; in winter when reserving, ask about cooking
🚌 Greyhound 6 blks
🚆 Amtrak 3 mi
🚲 Community bike co-op 4 blks
✈ Capitol City Airport 4 mi
✱ 9 unique cooperatives situated throughout E. Lansing. A good chance to discover the co-op movement.
DIRECTIONS: Central Office is on Campus, 3rd floor, second bldg. on right of Collingwood, entrance S of Grand River Ave. (Maps available upon reservation)
🏠 Milford 50 mi E, Grand Rapids 60 mi W

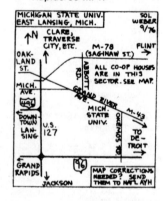

FLINT 🏠 Mott Lake Hostel, G-6511 N. Genesee Rd, Flint, MI 48506
🏠 Jimmy & Kathi Sabin
📞 313-736-5760
🛏 20 in 3 bunkrooms ♂ & ♀
🔑 Advance booking helpful
● $3.50 Junior, $4 Senior,

(deduct $1 per night for advance payment)

SN No smoking inside any building. $10 deposit ($5.00 youth) required for each guest pass holder.

▲ Metro Detroit Council
⌂ Hot & cold
⌂ Sunshine, 24 hrs, 1 mi S
☞ yes, laundry facilities
🚌 Greyhound, Flint, 11 mi
🚃 Amtrak, Flint, 12 mi
🚲 Twisted Rim, 7 mi in Burton
🚗 Hostel parking lot
✈ Bishop-Flint 17 mi
⚲ $2
* Historical Village with steam railroad, Stepping Stone Falls, canoeing, bicycling, hiking, sailing & cross country skiing (rentals available on all), General Motors plant tours,
** Fenced Children's Playground.
✹ 1 room
☂ yes
⚲ $1/night.
→ This hostel made available through the cooperation of the Genesee County Parks & Recreation Commission

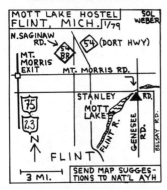

DIRECTIONS: Bicyclists may write for route planning help. From I-75, (US 23) take Mt. Morris Rd exit & go E for 7.5 mi. Turn right onto Genesee Rd & go S 1 mi to the Hostel. Hostel is 4 mi NE of Flint in Genesee Rec area. From I-69 (M-21), take Belsay Rd exit & go N for 6 mi. Turn left onto Stanley Rd & go 1 mi W to the hostel.

⚑ Milford 45 mi S, Williamston 65 mi W, Lansing 70 mi E, Bay City 48 mi N

FRANKFORT ⌂ Home Hostel, 538 Thomas Rd, Frankfort, MI 49635
⚲ Marjorie Pearsall
☎ 616-352-4296
🛏 7 (2 are doubles) ♂ & ♀
⚲ June 15-Sept 5
🔑 Advance booking required
◑ Howard & Ruth Pearsall, 324 Parker Ct., Frankfort 49635
● $2.50 S
☞ yes
🚌 1½ mi (2 km)
🚲 Beulah
✈ Traverse City 35 mi
⚲ camping on grounds
* Sleeping Bear Dunes (30 mi), Canoe the Platte & Betsie Rivers, Interlochen National Music Camp (25 mi), Point Betsie Lighthouse (6 mi), Beautiful Crystal Lake, swimming & sailing (¼ mi).

GRAND RAPIDS (A) ⌂ Home Hostel 3702 Auburn NE, Grand Rapids, MI 49505
⚲ Kay Hislop
☎ 616-361-7106
🛏 4 ♂ & ♀
🛏 4 ♂ & ♀
🔑 year round
● $2 S, $2.50 W
⌂ Hot & cold
⌂ 3 blks
☞ limited
🚌 Grand Rapids 5 mi
🚃 Grand Rapids 8 mi
✈ Grand Rapids 12 mi
DIRECTIONS: 1 blk N of 4 mi W of Plainfield Ave. Take Bus #2 or #7 6 AM to 6 PM.
⚑ Holland 40 mi SW, Twin Lake 45 mi NW

GRAND RAPIDS (B) ⌂ Home Hostel, 1117 Paradise Lake, SE, Grand Rapids, MI 49506
⚲ Charles & Elizabeth French
☎ (616) 676-9247
🛏 4
⚲ open all year
🔑 always
⌂ Hot & cold
⌂ Shop Rite ¾ mi
☞ yes
🚌 Grand Rapids 10 mi

MICHIGAN

sailing · backpack · canoeing · mackinac
cross-country skiing · bicycle tours
dunes · hike · swim · camping
island · hang gliders
mountains · sleeping
bicycle tou
im · can
ng glic
ountai
aver
ang g
ckpa
oe:
co
wi

For current hostel addresses
send a S.A.S.E. to
Metropolitan Detroit Council A Y H
3024 Coolidge, Berkley 48072
(313) 545-0511
West Michigan Council A Y H
1013 W. Burton, Grand Rapids 49509
(616) 451-8077

For general info
Michigan Travel Bureau
Box 30226, Lansing 48909

For 3 free county maps or a set
of county biking maps ($9.95)
Dept. of Natural Resources
Box 30034, Lansing 48909

⚏ Kalamazoo 50 mi
🏃 4 mi
🚐 4 mi
⚲ yes
DIRECTIONS: I-96 to Cacade E exit. 2 mi E to Hall St. Left on Hall, ¾ mi to Paradise Lake to 4th house on left.

HART ⌂ Hart Home Hostel, 19 Courtland, Hart, MI 49420
🏠 William & Leola Hanna
☎ 616-873-4565
⚏ 🍴 3 🛏 3
🍽 🛏 3
🏠 open all year
📞 Call or send reservations
● $2.50 S, $2.50 W
⚱ Hot & cold
🍴 Hart Thriftway 1 blk
⚲ yes
🚌 North Star 6 blks
🏃 Muskegon-Gambles, Hart
🚕 across the street
🚐 Muskegon 45 mi
✱ Sand Dunes 13 mi; Lake Michigan-beaches & parks 13 mi; Cross Country Skiing
✖ yes
DIRECTIONS: 1 blk W of Courthouse
🏠 Twin Lake 45 mi

HOLLAND ⌂ Home Hostel, 602 Lawn, Holland, MI 49423
🏠 Sue Hainsworth
☎ 616-392-1311
⚏ 🍴 1 🛏 1
🍽 🍴 2 🛏 2
🏠 open all year
● $2.50 S, $2.50 W
DIRECTIONS: W on Howard, S on Oak to Lawn.

KALKASKA 🏚 Blue Lake, Rt 1, Box 157, Kalkaska, MI 49646
☎ 616-587-8298 or 587-8871
⚏ 🍴 20 🛏 20
🏠 Dec 1-March 21
📞 entire year
● $5.50 S, $7.50 W
🍴 4 mi
⚲ yes
🚌 20 mi
⚏ Traverse City
🏃 Gaylord
🚕 across the road
🚐 Traverse City
⚐ camping available
✱ Swimming, canoeing, boating, sailing, skiing, hiking, badminton, ping pong, at

the hostel & tennis or golf in town.
✱ Arrangements can be made for some
⚐ yes
🔑 I-$1.25 II-$1.50 III-$3 I-III-$5.75
🛏 $1.50 for bed linens. $1 sheet sack
➡ Meals are provided for groups only unless special arrangements have been made.
🏠 Charlevoix Home Hostel, 50 mi (616) 547-2937

LAKEVIEW ⌂ Home Hostel, 10350 Orchard Lane, Lakeview, MI 48850
🏠 Robert & Phyllis Painter
☎ 517-352-6351
⚏ 3 🍴 & 🛏
🍽 3 🍴 & 🛏
🏠 open all year
📞 Advance booking required
⚱ Hot & cold
🍴 2½ mi
🚌 Howard City 13 mi
⚏ Grand Rapids 45 mi
⚐ yes
🏃 19 mi
🚐 Grand Rapids 50 mi
✱ Tamarack Lake, 200 ft; canoeing on Tamarack Lake in front of Home Hostel; Sm. Ski Area 4 mi; Tennis Court in front of hostel; cross country skiing in winter.
🔑 I-free
DIRECTIONS: Lakeview, located off M-46, 10 mi E from No. 131. Turn at blinker off No. 46. Go toward town. Turn right at 1st rd. Tamarack Rd. Go E to next rd.. Bale Rd. Turn N on Bale Rd. Go to 3rd sm. rd. Turn W toward lake (private rd) Hostel at end.

LUDINGTON ⌂ Home Hostel,

201 S. Washington St., Ludington, MI 49431
🏠 George & Lois Von Drak
☎ (616) 845-7404
🛏 4 ♂ & ♀
💦 yes
● $2.50
🚰 Hot & cold
🚌 ¾ mi
🚍 Muskegon

MILFORD (A) 🏠 Foote Hostel, 1845 Dawson Rd, Milford, MI 48042
🏠 Kevin & Linda Lundquist
☎ 313-684-9775
🛏 50 ♂ & ♀
🚪 April 16-Oct 14
💦 advance booking required
● $2.50 (students), $3 (adults)
▲ Detroit Council AYH
🚰 Hot & cold
🍴 3 supermarkets in Milford 3 mi, two open 24 hrs.
🔥 Gas stove w/ oven, h/c water, elec. refrig.
🚌 Brighten 10 mi
🚆 Pontiac 35 mi
🚲 Milford 4 mi
🚗 parking at hostel
✈ Detroit Metro Airport 45 mi
⛺ camping on hostel grounds
* Kensington Metro Park 1 mi
** meals served occasionally
✦ special accommodations available for families
🖥 yes
🛏 $2

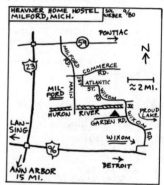

➝ this hostel built by volunteer hostelers

DIRECTIONS: 30 mi NW of Detroit on I-96. Use Milford exit (No. 155), take Milford Rd. to Dawson Rd. (turn left) to Hostel (first left driveway past paved bridge)
🏠 Detroit YMCA & YWCA; Flint, Mott Lake

MILFORD (B) 🏠 Heavner Home Hostel, 2775 Garden Rd, Milford, MI 48040
🏠 Alan Heavner
☎ (313) 685-9603 or 685-7974
🛏 4
💦 yes
● $2 S
🚰 Hot & cold
🍴 Milford 3 mi
🚲 yes
🚆 Pontiac 25 mi

🚆 Ann Arbor 30 mi
🚲 Union Lake 10 mi
🚗 Here
🚍 Detroit Metro 40 mi
* Canoe rental, cross country, ski rental next door, state park surrounding hostel, Detroit 45 min away, horseback, sailing all close.
** Surrounded by state park, all wilderness
DIRECTIONS: 6 mi N of I-96 exit at Wixom Rd. (exit 159). Follow Proud Lake Rec Area signs to Garden Rd. Left to 1st house.
🏠 Foote 7 mi

READING Kimball YMCA Center, Long Lake Road, Reading,

MI 49274
🏠 Len & Ruth Conner
☎ (517) 283-2427
🛏 ⚹ 15 ⚹ 15
🏚 Sept 1-May 31 (During summer some arrangements may be possible-in any season advance reservations are required)
⚑ advance booking required
● $3 S, $4 W
▲ Leonard Conner
⌂ Hot & cold
⌒ Bakers Acres 2½ mi SE
⚐ yes
🚴 Spoke Shop 12 mi E
✻ Fireplace, piano, ping pong,

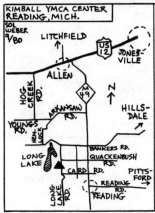

volleyball, badminton, lake, swimming, fire circle, obstacle course, nature trail, canoeing.
DIRECTIONS: Go 1 mi N on M-49 from Reading. Turn W (left) on Card Rd & go 2 mi. Turn N (right) on Long Lake Rd & go ½ mi. Camp is on the left.
🏠 White Pigeon 60 mi SW

SAGINAW, (University Ctr) (SA, no kitchen) Saginaw Valley, Dept. of Residence Halls, Saginaw Valley College, 2250 Pierce Rd, Saginaw, MI 48710
🏠 Brian & Rhonda Gano, Great Lakes Hall, Saginaw College
☎ (517) 790-4255
🛏 ⚹ 10 ⚹ 10 can be adapted for use by groups
🏚 May 1-Aug
⚑ yes

● $3 S
▲ Metro. Detroit Council AYH & Tri City AYH Club
⌂ Hot & cold
⌒ 2 mi N
🚌 Bay City Midland & Saginaw
🚴 The Bike Shoppe, 7 mi on Salzburg Rd in Bay City
✈ Tri-City 12 mi
DIRECTIONS: M-84 exit from I-75, 3 mi W & S to turn off to Saginaw Valley College (SVC). Follow Fox Rd & Collins Dr to Great Lakes Hall. Register at Doan Center.
🏠 Blue Lake 125 mi NW, Foote 90 mi SE, Bay City 20 mi N

SAULT STE. MARIE Lake Superior State College (SA, no kitchen) Sault Ste. Marie, MI 49783
🏠 Fern Spencer
☎ (906) 632-6841, ext. 411
🏚 June 15-Aug 15
⚑ advance booking preferred
● $4.85 + tax
⌂ Hot & cold
⌒ .25 mi
🚌 1.5 mi
🚴 Adjacent to SA
✈ 18 mi
✻ Soo Locks 1.5 mi
✖ advance booking required

DIRECTIONS: Exit 394 — I-75

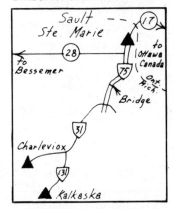

TWIN LAKE 🏠 Home Hostel, 3175 First St, Twin Lake, MI 49457
🏠 Mary C. Payne
☎ (616) 828-6675
🛏 ⚹ 2 ⚹ 3

🏠 open all year
⚓ advance booking required
🛁 (tub), Hot & cold
🎵 John's 3 blks
🍴 yes
🚌 Muskegon 13 mi
🚲 Muskegon 11 mi
🚗 on site
✈ Muskegon 20 mi
⛺ camping on hostel grounds
* Canoeing 6 mi, hiking trail 20 mi, cross country skiing 15 mi, fine arts camp 5 mi, Lake Michigan 12 mi
** swimming, sailing, 1 blk
✴ Special accommodations available for families
DIRECTIONS: From Muskegon Causeway, 9 mi on M-120. From blinker light in Twin Lake, go 1 blk N, turn left for 2 blks.
🏚 Hart 35 mi NW, Grand Rapids 45 mi SE

WHITE PIGEON 🏠 Home Hostel, White Pigeon, MI 49099
🏠 Edith Hostetter
☎ 616-483-7236
🛏 1 double
🛏 floor
🏠 open all year
● $2 S
SN Please call for availability
🎵 Troyers 1 mi
🍴 yes
🚌 Greyhound in front daily
🚲 Niles 20 mi
🚗 Sturgis, Three Rivers Cycle Shops, 10 mi
🚗 at Hostel & all around
✈ Kalamazoo & South Bend, 38 mi each
* Covered bridge 10 mi, historic Centreville 10 mi, Constantine & Three Rivers area, State Forest & game area, lakes & fishing nearby.
DIRECTIONS: On US 12, ½ mi E of US 131.
🏚 Reading 55 mi E

WILLIAMSTON 🏠 Home Hostel, 115 E. Riverside, Williamston, MI 48895
🏠 Ed & Lynnae Ruttledge
☎ 517-655-2830
🛏 1 1 1
🛏 1 10 1 10
🏠 open all year
⚓ advance booking required
🛁 Hot & cold

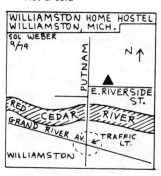

WILLIAMSTON HOME HOSTEL
WILLIAMSTON, MICH.
SOL WEBER 9/79

🎵 Felpausch's 4 blks
🍴 yes
🚌 Local party store, 3 blks
🚲 E. Lansing 16 km
🚗 E. Lansing 16 km
✈ Lansing (capitol Area AP), 30 km
⛺ camping on hostel grounds

DIRECTIONS: From downtown Williamston go N on Putnam. Riverside is first street going E after crossing the river.
🏚 Foote Hostel approx. 72 km E, Grand Rapids 175 km W

MINNESOTA
Minnesota Council, 475 Cedar St., St. Paul, MN 55101
(612) 292-4126

BARNUM Camp Wanakawin (SA), Barnum, MN 55707
🏠 Ann Biron
☎ 218-389-6981 or 722-7425
🛏 75 1 & 1
🏠 Labor Day-May 31

⚓ advance booking required
◑ 202 W 2nd St., Duluth
▲ YWCA, Duluth, MN
✴ By reservation only
🏚 Duluth 40 mi N

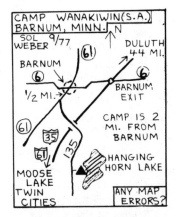

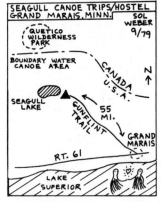

DULUTH YWCA (SA), 202 West 2nd St., Duluth, MN 55802
- 🏠 Joyce M. Greeno
- ☎ (218) 722-7425
- ⚊ ♂ 6 ♀ 6
- ⚊ ♂ 6 ♀ 6
- 🚪 open all year
- ● $3.50 S
- ⚱ Hot & cold
- 🍴 Ideal Market 1 blk
- 🚲 yes
- 🚌 1 mi
- ✈ by reservation
- 🚐 yes
- 🏠 Barnum, MN 50 mi S, Grand Marais 160 mi N

GRAND MARAIS Seagull Canoe Trips/Hostel (SA, no kitchen) Box 119-H, Grand Marais, MN 55604
- 🏠 Lynn Palrud
- ☎ (218) 388-2271
- ⚊ 54 ♂ & ♀
- 🚪 May 15-Sept 15
- 🔼 season

- ◐ Lynn Palrud, 1009 Ravine Trail, Minneapolis, MN, 55416
- ● $2 S
- SN Hostel is 55 mi from Grand Marais
- ⚱ Hot & cold
- 🍴 Seagull Resort, adjacent
- 🚌 Grand Marais 55 mi
- 🚲 Duluth 160 mi
- 🚶 Duluth 160 mi
- 🚗 at hostel
- 🚐 Devil's Track 45 mi
- ✳ Wilderness canoe trips in Boundary Waters canoe area & Quetico National Park; complete or partial outfitting & expert routing available at hostel. Write for free brochure.
- 🏠 $1.50

DIRECTIONS: 55 mi N of Grand Marais on the (paved) Gunflint Trail, several distance signs, sign at entrance.
- 🏠 Duluth 160 mi SW; Thunder Bay, Canada.

HAMEL Pinewood YH, 4535 Willow Drive, MN 55340
- 🏠 Rev. & Mrs. Arthur G. Emerson
- ☎ (612) 478-6930
- ⚊ ♂ 5 ♀ 8
- 🚪 June 1 to Labor Day
- 🔼 1 wk advance reservation requested
- ● $2.50 S
- ⚱ Hot & cold
- 🍴 Hamel 2½ mi
- 🚲 Stove w/4 burners, oven; re-

147

MINNESOTA

frig., cooking utensils
🚍 Zephyr Lines ¼ mi, Medicine Lake Bus leaves downtown Minneapolis 4:30 & 5 PM.
🚂 Burlington-Northern 17 mi
🚲 Bikeways 7 mi
✈ International 25 mi

DIRECTIONS: (suburban Minneapolis), 2½ mi W of Hamel, MN. Turn N on Willow Drive (opposite Wright-Hennepin Electric Bldg.) 1st Farm on W side. (17 mi W of Minneapolis on State Hwy 55)

NIMROD Crow Wing Trails YH, Nimrod, MN 56478
🏠 Mr. & Mrs. George Gloege Crow Wing Trails, Assoc. Sebeka, RR No. 2, 56477
☎ (218) 472-3250
🛏 ♂ 10 ♀ 10
🕐 June 10-Sept 15
● $2 S
▲ Association of Outfitters to Crow Wing Trails Association

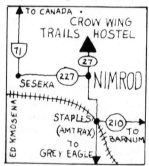

🚰 Hot & cold
🏪 Nimrod Co-op 1 mi S
🚻 Modern
🔧 Johnson Hardware, Sebeka, 11 mi
🏕 permissable

DIRECTIONS: 1 mi N of Nimrod on Country Hwy 27
🏠 Grey Eagle 75 mi S

WABASHA The Anderson House YH, 333 Main St, Wabasha, MN 55981
🏠 Jeanne Hall, John & Gayla Hall
☎ (612) 565-4525 or 4524
🛏 ♂ 16 ♀ 16
● $5
▲ Anderson House Hostel
🚍 Greyhound 1 mi to depot
🚂 Amtrak, 30 mi in Winona
🚲 Andy's Hardware, 2 blks on Main St
✈ Rochester 45 mi
* Recreation room w/TV, organ. Outside patio; tennis, beach campground, swimming, sailing & canoeing 3 blks. Hiking Trails 3 mi. Skiing 1 mi. 90 mi of cross-country skiing within 15 miles through many state parks.
🍴 I-$1.50 II-$1.75 III-$2.50

DIRECTIONS: 1 mi into town from Hwy 61 & 3 blks from Hwy 60. In the residential section of town. The Hostel is ½ mi E off Hwy 61.
🏠 Turtle Lake, WI 80 mi N; Hamel 75 mi NW

MISSOURI
Ozark Area Council, 5400 A Southwest, St. Louis, MO 63139
(314) 644-3560

FREMONT Ozark Wilderness Hostel, P.O. Box 278, Fremont, MO 63941
🏠 Mark Grimmer, Derrick Grimmer, Bob Schmidt, Linda Kloessner
☎ (314) 251-3549
🛏 ♂ 15 ♀ 15
🕐 Apr 1-Dec 1
▲ Environmentally Appropriate Technology, Inc.
🚰 Hot & cold
🏪 Fremont Store ¼ mi

🚻 yes
🚍 at front of hostel
🚂 Poplar Bluff 65 mi
🚲 B & H Bikes at hostel
🚗 at hostel
✈ Poplar Bluff 65 mi
* Recreation room, books & magazines, quiet games, billard table. Badminton & equipment, pool, outdoor fireplace, swimming in the Current River, canoeing, hiking & biking trails. Ozark Na-

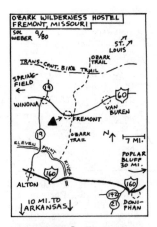

tional Scenic Riverway.
DIRECTIONS: Intersection of US
60 & Highway Y 10 mi W of
Van Buren.

KANSAS CITY The Martinique
(SA, apartment house),
3014-16 Harrison St., Kansas City, MO 64109
🏠 Bob & Janet Dutton
🕾 (816) 561-2044
⊨ ↕ 5 ↕ 5
⊨ ↕ 20 ↕ 20
⤒ no
◉ $5 S, $5 W
⌓ Hot & cold
♫ Bob's Grocery ¼ blk
🚲 39th & Main 1 mi
⚲ no
✳ Worlds of Fun Amusement
Park
★ yes, private room
🚗 no
DIRECTIONS: Catch Troost bus
at Bus Depot to 30th St.
Walk 1 blk W to Harrison St.
Hostel is 1½ mi from downtown KC.
🏠 St. Louis 250 mi E

ST. LOUIS (A) Huckleberry Finn
Youth Hostel (complete facilities),
1904-1906 S. 12th St, St. Louis,
MO 63104
🏠 Tom & Sheela Cochran
🕾 (314) 241-0076
⊨ ↕ 15 ↕ 15
⤒ yes, during Apr-Sept
◉ $4 S, $4 W
SN Hours: 6 PM-8 AM
⚑ yes
🚌 1⅓ mi, local in front of bldg
🚲 1½ mi
🚲 5 mi
🚗 at hostel 10 spaces, $1 extra
per auto per day
✈ 20 mi
⚲ no
✳ Gateway Arch 1 mi
★ no
🚗 yes
🏠 50¢/night
⤝ Located in 1870s brick bldg
in Soulard National Historic
District
DIRECTIONS: 1 blk S of intersection of I-55 & I-44; between
Geyer & Allen Aves on S.
12th St.; Caron-Delet or

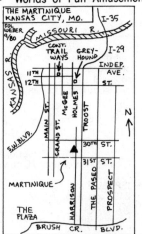

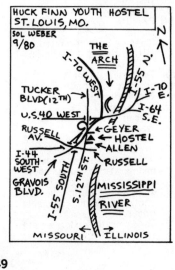

MISSOURI

Gravois (city) bus to Geyer Ave or S on Broadway to Geyer & W 70 12th St.

ST. LOUIS (B), The Tripper, Portage, De Sioux, MO 63373

- ⌂ Stephen C. Banton
- ☏ (314) 725-1616 Day; (314) 872-7570 Night
- ⊢ 10 ♀ & ♂
- ⌂ Summer only
- ⚑ Advance booking required
- ◑ 172 Forest Brook Lane, St. Louis, MO 63141
- ⊜ $55 2-day trip; $75 3-day trip
- ▲ Stephen & William Banton, 172 Forest Brook Ln., St. Louis, MO 63141
- ⌂ Hot & cold
- ☇ yes
- ⛟ 12 mi S
- 🚃 37 mi SE
- 🚲 12 mi S in St. Charles
- ⛴ at harbor
- 🚗 19 mi SE

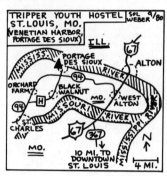

* Mississippi & Missouri Rivers Elsah, Portage, De Sioux, Alton, St. Louis, Piasa Bird, St. Charles, Clarksville, Skylift, Kimswick, Jefferson Barrack, Hannibal, St. Generie

** Hostel is a houseboat for river trips. Call or write for itinerary packages.

MONTANA

EAST GLACIER PARK Bear Creek Ranch (SA, other users), P.O. Box 151, East Glacier Park, MT 59434

- ⌂ Jennifer Knoch & Rollie Stenson
- ☏ (406) 226-5962
- ⊨ 14 ♀ 10 ♂ 4
- ⚑ yes
- ⊜ $4 S, $4 W
- SN Private & semi-private rooms can be provided. Sleeping bags permitted.
- ▲ Montana Land & Cattle Co.
- ⌂ Hot & cold
- ⌢ Timberline 13 mi W
- ☇ yes, not equipped
- 🚃 Brown Bus Line
- 🚲 E. Glacier 17 mi E
- 🚲 Glacier International 65 mi W

* Glacier National Park & Great Bear Wilderness, adjacent. Extensive trails for hiking, backpacking, snowshoeing, cross country skiing, fishing, rafting, wildlife photography all available from ranch.

** Ranch located on former site of McCarthysville, historic

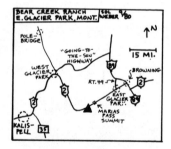

railroad town. Historic log structure.

- ★ rooms & suites
- ☇ on request, varies with menu
- ⓪ 50¢

DIRECTIONS: 17 mi W of E. Glacier Park, MT on US Hwy 2.

- 🚂 Cutbank 61 mi E, Polebridge 60 mi NW, Kalispell 75 mi W

KALISPELL Rocky Mountain YH, 845 First Ave., E., Kalispell, MT 59901

- ⌂ Dana & Rhonda Huschle
- ☏ (406) 257-2937

🛏 12 ♿ & ♿
🏠 June 1-Sept 25
🛗 reservations advised
⬤ $3 S
🔺 Fred Mandl
🚰 Hot & cold
🛒 Rosavers ½ mi S on Rt 93
🍴 Utensils provided
🚌 Brown Bus Line 9 blks
🚃 In Whitefish 15 mi
🚲 Wheaton's 6 blks at 214 First Ave. W
🚗 On premises
* Fireplace, radio, record player, rubber horseshoes, books & magazines. Volleyball, badminton, ring toss, softball & tennis court nearby. Swimming 2 mi. Sailing 7 mi S. Horseback riding, hiking trails, biking & skiing 15 mi. Glacier National Park 35 mi N of Kalispell. Summer Theatre.
✯ by reservation
DIRECTIONS: Come into Kalispell on 93N. Just before Court House, take Rt onto 9th St. E at stop sign. You will be looking across at the hostel. The Hostel is 35 mi S of Glacier Park or 120 mi N

of Missoula
🏠 Missoula 120 mi

MISSOULA The BirchWood (SA, single mixed dormitory), 600 S. Orange St., Missoula, MT 59801
🏠 Italo E.L. Franceschi
☎ (406) 728-9799
🛏 6 ♿ & ♿
🛏 16 ♿ & ♿
🏠 Jan 1-Dec 14
🛗 June-Aug
⬤ $3.50 S, $4 W
🚰 Hot & cold
🛒 SuperSave 1 blk
🍴 kitchen available
🚌 Greyhound ½ mi
🚃 Amtrak, Whitefish 129 mi
🚲 4 blks
🚗 limited
✈ 6 mi W of city
* Junction of TransAm & Great Parks Bike Trails. Swimming, hiking, hot springs, downhill & cross country skiing nearby. Univ. of Montana.
** laundromat; common room with wood stove; bike storage
🚗 yes
🏠 50¢
→ Gateway hostel for Bikecentennial Great Parks Bicycle Trail

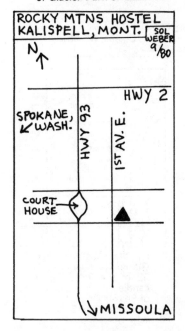

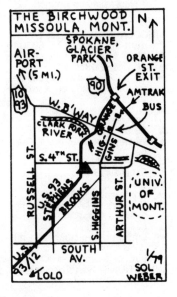

MONTANA

DIRECTIONS: SE corner of Orange St. & S 4th St. W
🏠 Kalispell 115 mi N, Polebridge 167 mi N

POLEBRIDGE North Fork Hostel, Polebridge, MT 59928
🏠 John Frederick
🛏 5 🛏 5
🏚 June 1-Oct 1. In winter for groups by reservation only
🍴 Yes, in winter for groups only with reservations
◐ Star Route, Kila, MT 59920
⦿ $4
🚰 Hot & cold
🍴 Polebridge Mercantile, ¼ mi NW of Hostel
🏴 yes
🚌 Brown Lines 52 mi
🚂 Amtrak 30 mi
🛒 3 stores in Kalispell, 52 mi S
🍳 at hostel
✈ Glacier International 42 mi
✳ Float trips 1/8 mi; canoeing 1/8 mi; horseback riding; hiking trails 1 mi; skiing 50 mi.
✳✳ Old-fashioned atmosphere with wood heaters, kerosene & propane lights (no electricity).

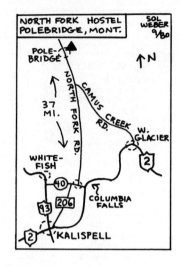

🅿 yes
🛏 50¢
↦ Original log structure was located on homesteaded land in Glacier National Park.
🏠 E. Glacier Park 68 mi SE, Kalispell 52 mi S

NEBRASKA
Nebraskaland Council, 12637 N Street, Omaha, NE 68137
(402) 435-6664

LINCOLN Wesley House, 640 N 16th St., Lincoln, NE 68503
🏠 Mr. & Mrs. Mel Luetchens
☎ (402) 432-0355
🛏 22 🛏 & 🛏 , buns available for boys & girls on a group basis
🍴 Groups only; individuals not accepted
⦿ $2 S
▲ Wesley House Student Chapel
🚰 Hot & cold
🍴 Safeway 13 blks
🏴 yes
🚌 Continental Trailways
🚂 Burlington-Northern 2½ mi (4 km)
🛒 Lawlors 10 blks
✈ Lincoln Municipal 18 mi (12.8 km)
🛏 25¢ for sleeping sack
DIRECTIONS: Hostel is located

on the Western edge of Glacier National Park; ¼ mi SE of the Polebridge Mercantile (follow signs) at end of Beaver Drive.
🏠 Kalispell 52 mi S

NEW HAMPSHIRE
Greater Boston Council, 251 Harvard Street, Brookline, MA 02146
(617) 731-6692

ALTON 🏠 Green Tops, RDI Roberts Cove Rd., Alton, NH 03809
🏠 Mary & Willard Kempton
☎ 603-569-9878
🛏 ⚥ 20 ⚥ 21
🛏 Separate Family Cabin, 5 persons
🌙 June 1-Sept 8
🔑 advance booking prefer
◐ 1160 NW 15th St., Ft. Lauderdale, FL 33311
● $5 S
🚰 Hot & cold
🍴 Kitchen available
🚍 Alton 6½ mi
🚂 Concord 45 mi
🚴 Nordic, Wolfeboro
🚲 on premises, $1/day
🛥 Laconia 23 mi
* White Mountains, Lake Winnipesaukee, Water Ski, Sailing, near mountain climbing. Island owned by house parents. Pool on premises.
** Wildlife trail. Dormitory & kitchens in large, renovated barn
✶ Special accommodations available for families
🅿 yes

DIRECTIONS: 5 mi from Alton/Alton Bay to AYH symbol & flashing yellow light . . . left on Roberts Cove Rd, 1 mi to

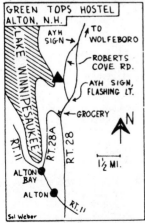

hostel
🏠 Belmont 25 mi W, Durham 35 mi S

BELMONT 🏠 Lakes Region YH, Rt 106, Box 342, Belmont, NH 03220
🏠 Ike Gardner
☎ (603) 524-2880
🛏 ⚥ 8 ⚥ 8
🌙 June 30-Aug 15
🔑 Aug 16-June 30
● $4.75 S
🚰 Hot & cold
🛒 IGA 2½ mi in Laconia
🍴 yes
🚍 Laconia Trailways 2½ mi
🚴 Boot & Wheel, 598 Union Ave., Laconia 2½ mi
🛥 Gilford 7 mi
DIRECTIONS: 3 mi N of Belmont,

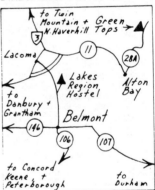

on Rt 106, 2nd right past Belknap Trailer Park. Obscure gradual right past a group of billboards
🏠 Danbury 40 mi W, Alton Bay 20 mi E

DANBURY Ragged Edge at Ragged Mt (SA, Limited to Reservations only) Ragged Edge Rd., Danbury, NH 03230
🏠 Georgette/Bill Garamella
☎ 603-622-0685 or 768-9980
🛏 ⚥ 5 ⚥ 5
🛏 ⚥ 5 ⚥ 3
🌙 open all year

⬧ Advance reservations required all year round

⬤ $3.75 S, $4.50 W, $5 Ski Season

SN please, reservations only

⌂ Hot & cold

⊓ Danbury Gen. Store 4 mi

⚑ yes

🚌 New London 15 mi

🚆 White River Junction 26 mi

🚲 Danbury 4 mi, Franklin 25 mi W

🚥 at hostel

✈ Manchester 50 mi S, Lebanon 25 mi W

* Ragged Mt Ski Area. AMC Trail, hiking, cross country skiing & snow shoeing Mt. Cardigan State Park10 mi, New Found Lake 10 mi. Ruggles Mine10 mi, Lake Sunapee 17 mi, Dartmouth Hopkins Ctr., Hanover 26 mi.

** Rec. room, piano, fireplace, bathing

✹ on limited basis. inquiries welcomed

➟ Hostel established/maintained/Financed by Garamella family toward a continuous growing AYH

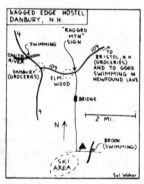

DIRECTIONS: Go 1¼ mi from Rt 4 in Danbury on Rt 104 to Ragged Mt. Ski Area sign, then go right 3 mi & turn left at ski area.

🏠 Grantham 35 mi W; Alton 45 mi E

DURHAM University Hostel, Randall Hall, UNH, Durham, NH 03824

🏠 Barbara A. Paiton

📞 (603) 862-2120

🛏 40 ♂ & ♀

▬ as needed

🏠 June 1-Aug 13

⬤ $3 S

▲ Univ. of New Hampshire

⌂ Hot & cold

⊓ Shop & Save 200 yds

⚑ need individual utensils

🚌 ½ mi

🚲 ½ mi downtown

🚥 Adjacent to hostel

✈ Logan, Boston, 1½ hrs

* Historic Portsmouth 12 mins, UNH Rec. Area w/lake 4 mi, NH seacoast 30 mins, NH lakes & mountains 40 mins.

** Full use of Univ. facilities (some w/fees)

🏠 $2.50/bundle

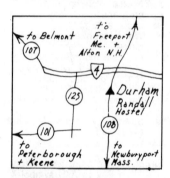

GRANTHAM Ledges Farm (SA, rates, no kitchen), Grantham, NH 03755

🏠 M.J. Martin

📞 603-863-1002

🛏 120 ♂ & ♀

⬤ $5

⊓ Remeys

🚌 N. London 5 mi

🚆 30 mi

🚲 Newport

🚥 on site

✈ Lebanon 20 mi

* 1000 acres, groomed ski trails

** Hereford Farm

✹ yes

DIRECTIONS: 9/10 mi up asphalt road W of Grantham, by bridge off Rt. 10

🏠 Danbury

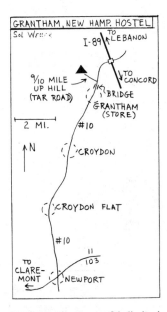

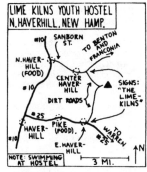

- ⚐ preferred
- ◑ Loomis St, Southwick, MA 01077
- ◉ $3
- ⌂ Hot & cold
- ♫ Aldrich 4 mi
- ⚐ yes
- 🚍 Walls River, VT 8 mi
- 🚃 White River Junction 40 mi
- 🚲 Simple-N. Haverhill; Complicated-Franconia
- 🚲 At hostel, 50¢
- ✈ Lebanon 40 mi
- ⚐ yes
- ✳ Swimming, hiking, AMC trails & Natl. Forest. Black Mt. Fire Tower, horseback riding $5; Conn. River 6 mi.
- ⬧ 50¢

DIRECTIONS: Rt 116 off Rt 10 N. Haverhill, 3 mi to Lime Kiln Rd, then 1¼ mi to Hostel. 3 mi W off Rt. 25 at E. Haverhill

- ⚑ Waterville Valley 70 mi E

KEENE Doyle House (SA, limited kitchen), Keene State College, Keene, NH 03431
- ⌂ College Staff Person
- ☏ (603) 352-1909 ext. 230. Residential Life Office hours are 8 AM-4:30 PM, weekdays only.
- ━ 25 ♂ & ♀
- ⬧ June 24-Aug 14
- ◉ $4
- SN Send mail to Residential Life Office & identify "AYH"
- ▲ Keene State College
- ⌂ Hot & cold
- ⚐ Limited facilities, eating places nearby (do not supply pots & pans)
- 🚍 nearby
- 🚲 Bicycle storage, nearby
DIRECTIONS: 289 Main St. on the college campus.
- ⚑ Amherst, MA 60 mi S, Peterborough 25 mi SE

NORTH HAVERHILL ⚑ The Lime Kilns, Lime Kiln Rd, North Haverhill, NH 03774
- ⌂ Keith & John O'Shaughnessy
- ☏ 603-989-5656
- ━ 26 ♂ & ♀
- ━ 30-also with blankets ♂ & ♀
- ⬧ Memorial Day to Columbus Day

PETERBOROUGH ⚑ Sharon Studio Barn Hostel, Sharon Cross Rd, (Sharon) Peterborough, NH 03458
- ⌂ Carl & Gena Shapley
- ☏ 603-924-6928
- ━ 26 ♂ & ♀
- ━ 15 ♂ & ♀
- ⬧ May 15-Oct 15
- ◑ Boston Council
- ◉ $3.75 S
- SN "rainy" day stay, $1
- ▲ Shapley Schools, Inc. Box 310, RFD #2, Peterborough
- ⌂ Hot & cold
- ♫ A&P, Grand Union 3 mi
- ⚐ yes
- 🚍 Peterborough 3 mi
- 🚃 Brattleboro, VT 40 mi

NEW HAMPSHIRE

Jaffrey 5 mi
on location, $1/day
Keene 25 mi
camping on hostel grounds
** provision for extended stays, meditation house, Yoga, New Age disciplines
✶ family accommodations available
meals upon request only. III-$2
$1
DIRECTIONS: Off Rt 123, 1st left 1½ mi after Sharon Art Ctr, left on Cross Rd & left into hostel. From Peterborough intersection 101 & 202 S 1½ mi, left on Sharon Rd 1½ mi to hostel turn off to left.
Friendly Crossways, Littleton, MA 30 mi S; Keene 25 mi W

RANDOLPH Bowman Base Camp, US Rt 2, Randolph, NH 03570
Marguerite Bean & John Sullivan
(603) 466-9487
25
25
June 1-Sept 15
not essential but desirable
$5.50 S
Hot & cold
Country Store 1000 ft E, Supermarkets 5 mi
yes
Gorham 5 mi
Milan 10 mi
yes
✶ Hostel at foot of Lowes Path up Mt. Adams beyond to entire Presidential Range of

White Mtns.
★ yes
no
Unique location by White Mtns. Presidential Range.
DIRECTIONS: 1000 ft W of Mobile Station, the one & only service station in town. Large "Bowman Base Camp" sign S of Hwy in front of camp.

TWIN MOUNTAIN Ammonoosuc Campground Hostel (SA, no kitchen), Box 178, Twin Mountain, NH 03595
George & Kathleen Saffian
(603) 846-5527
maximum 10 persons ✶ & ✶
open all year
$4.50 S, $5.50 W
SN Lodge Camping Rate $1.50 per person (for winter hostlers there must be at least 4 people or Hostel will not open) By reservation only. Groups must send one nights fee as deposit, not refundable if not cancelled two weeks prior to trip. (Dec-Apr Lodge will honor paid reservations of AYH groups)
Hot & cold
Broks Gen. Store 1/8 mi N, in winter; in summer store at hostel.
4 burner gas stove w/oven, elec. refrig, h/c water
Whitefield 10 mi
Littleton 13 mi
Twin Mtn. 1/8 mi
✶ Ideal for hikers, cyclists, downhill skiers & ski tours
DIRECTIONS: 1/10 mi S of the Intersection of Rt 3 & Rt 302; 13 mi N of Franconia

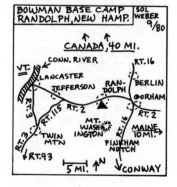

BOWMAN BASE CAMP
RANDOLPH, NEW HAMP. SOL WEBER 9/80
CANADA, 40 MI.
CONN. RIVER
VT. RT. 16
LANCASTER
JEFFERSON RAN-DOLPH BERLIN
GORHAM
RT. 115 RT. 2 RT. 2
MT. WASHINGTON RT. 16 MAINE 10 MI.
TWIN MTN PINKHAM NOTCH
RT. 93 5 MI. N CONWAY

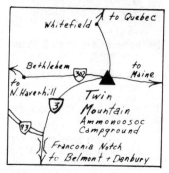

to Quebec
Whitefield
Bethlehem to Maine
to N. Haverhill 302
Twin Mountain Ammonoosuc Campground
93
Franconia Notch
to Belmont + Danbury

156

Notch
♠ N. Haverhill 37 mi SW; Waterville Valley 60 mi S

WATERVILLE VALLEY Waterville Valley Bunkhouse (SA, rates), Waterville Valley, NH 03223
⬧ Gloria Duhaime & Manuel Silva
☎ (603) 236-8326
⬌ ♂ 80 ♀ 80
⬧ Thanksgiving to April 30, May 29-Oct 16 w/advance reservation
● $6/night (before Dec 17, after March); $7/night regular season; $9/night Holidays
⌂ Hot & cold
⬧ Mobile Sta. ½ mi W

🍴 yes
🚌 Trailways, Plymouth 18 mi
🚲 Waterville Valley Pro Shop, 100 yds
🚤 Laconia 40 mi
✱ Recreation room w/fireplace, piano, & pinball. Swimming pool, outdoor fireplace, tennis courts & golf course. Sailing, canoeing, hiking trails, skiing & ice skating. White Mtn. Park, Osceloa Tower, Cascades, Kettles, & Mt. Tecumseh.
🗝 I-$2.95 III-$4.50
DIRECTIONS: From I-93, Campton-Waterville exit, Rt. 49, 10 mi to sign for Waterville Valley Bunkhouse
♠ Twin Mountain 60 mi N

NEW JERSEY
Delaware Valley Council,
35 South 3rd, Philadelphia, PA 19106
(215) 925-6004
Metropolitan New York Council, 132 Spring Street, NY, NY 10012
(212) 431-7100

LAYTON Old Mine Road YH, Box 172, Layton, NJ 07851

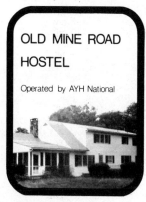

OLD MINE ROAD HOSTEL

Operated by AYH National

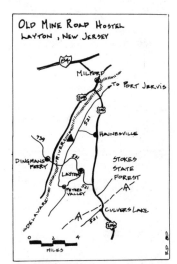

⬧ Rob Dorival
☎ (201) 948-6750
⬌ Flexible ♂ 10 ♀ 10
⬧ Closed Christmas Eve (Reg. Hrs: 5 PM to 9 AM
● $3.50
▲ Natl. AYH by permit from Natl Park Service

⌂ Hot & cold
⬧ Hainesville or Layton 2½ mi
🍴 yes; no personal eating utensils provided
🚌 Short Line 6 mi

NEW JERSEY

🚲 John Schwinn Cyclery, 105 Water St, Newton

* Nordic/downhill skiing, snowshoeing, canoeing, waterfalls. East Coast bicycle trail, Appalachian Trail, Peters Valley Crafts Village.

** In the Delaware Water Gap Natl. Recreational Area

DIRECTIONS: 2.2 mi N of Dingman's Ferry Bridge on Sussex Rt 521

🏠 LaAnna 55 mi SE, Kingston 75 mi N

MILBROOK A 24-bed, summer only, hostel, will open in June 1981. Contact AYH National Office for details.

OCEAN CITY Sassafras Lodge Hostel, (SA, rates) 1145 Central\ Ave, Ocean City, NJ 08226

🏠 Nelson & Joan Dice

📞 609-399-4555

🛏 40 ⚏ & ⚏

🌓 Closed all Saturdays. Memorial Day thru Labor Day weekends. Closed Memorial Day & Labor Day weekends. Open Sat. during rest of year & all other days.

🔑 Advance booking required

💰 $4.50 S, $5 W ($3.50 spring or fall)

🚿 Hot & cold

🍴 Wawa, 1200 blk W. Ave

✓ yes

🚌 ½ mi

🚂 ½ mi

🚲 hostel grounds

✈ Ocean City 2 mi

* Piano, shuffleboard, air hockey. Volleyball, swimming, tennis, sailing, fishing, surfing. Ocean City Music Pier

✗ yes

🏛 Philadelphia (Chamounix Mansion) 85 mi NW; Media, PA 95 mi NW

NEW MEXICO

Rocky Mountain Council, 1107 12th Street, P.O. Box 2370, Boulder, CO 80306 (303) 442-9304

ALBUQUERQUE Canterbury YH, (SA, 2 univ. students in residence), 1906 Central, SE, Albuquerque, NM 87106

🛏 ⚏ 2 ⚏ 2
⚏ 2 ⚏ 4

🌓 open all year

🔑 Summer

💰 $4 S

▲ St. Thomas of Canterbury Episcopal Church, 425 Univ.

🍴 Foodway 4 blks

✓ yes

🚌 2 mi
🚂 2 mi
🚲 1 blk
🚶 street
✈ 2 mi
🚗 yes
⛽ $1

CUBA 🏠 Circle "A" Ranch, P.O. Box 382, Cuba, NM 87013

🏠 Susan Schulte

📞 (505) 289-3350

🛏 34 ⚏ 17 ⚏ 17
6 ⚏ 3 ⚏ 3

🌓 full-time June 1-Sept 30; weekends winter

🔑 no

💰 $5.50 S

SN Uses country customs

▲ Alice Woolf, owner

🚿 Hot & cold

🍴 Town & Country 6 mi

✓ yes

🚌 Cuba 6 mi

🚂 Albuquerque 80 mi

✓ yes

🚲 on grounds

✈ Albquerque 80 mi

⚓ no

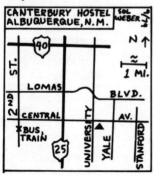

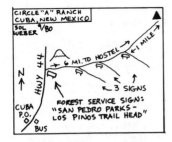

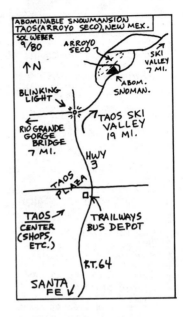

* Navajo Reservation 20 mi, Chaco Canyon Indian ruin 40 mi. Many Indian pueblos 40-50 mi. Sante Fe 2 hrs by car, Hot Springs 40 mi, Continental Divide 20 mi, San Pedro National park Wildlife Refuge 2 hr walk. Numerous Spanish & Indian historic buildings & sites.

** Extremely beautiful, peaceful & friendly.

★ yes

🏠 yes

⚷ I-$1 II-$1.50 III-$2 I-III-$4.50

🚪 $1

⇠ Lodge in style of houses built in Mexico mountain country in late 1800 by English miners.

DIRECTIONS: From Cuba Post Office go N on Hwy 44. Before hwy goes uphill note Forest Service signs that point to road leading right. Turn & follow Forest Service signs that say San Pedro Parks & Los Pinos Trail Head. At 3rd sign go left 1 mi.

🏠 Albuquerque 80 mi S, Durango 100 mi N

TAOS (Arroyo Seco) The Abominable Snowmansion (SA, no kitchen), P.O. Box 3271, Taos, NM 87571

🏠 R.C. Stoney & T.L. Root

☎ (505) 776-8298

🛏 55 ♂ 27 ♀ 28

🚪 closed only Easter-May 31 & Oct 1-Thanksgiving

⬆ Suggested during ski season

● $6 S, $8 W

▲ R.C. Stoney, Box 3271, Taos, NM 87571

🚰 Hot & cold

🍴 L & B Gen. Mdse. ½ blk

🚲 no

🚌 Taos 10 mi

🚂 Santa Fe 100 mi

🚴 Repair at hostel, parts in Taos

🚗 at hostel

✈ Santa Fe 100 mi

⚓ no, 2 mi

* Carson National Forest 2 mi (trout fishing & hiking), Taos Ski Valley 9 mi, Taos Indian Pueblo 10 mi (900 yr. old high-rise adobe), Rio Grande Gorge 12 mi (650 ft gorge on #1 US Wild & Scenic River), Hondo Hot Springs 10 mi, 55 art galleries in Taos 10 mi.

** Circular fire place & game tables

★ no

🏠 yes

⚷ I-$2 II-$2.50 III-$5 I-III-$9

🚪 $1.50

⇠ Hostel is an historic 2-story adobe.

DIRECTIONS: From Taos Plaza, 5 mi N on State Hwy 3. Turn right (E) on State Hwy 150 (toward Ski Valley & Arroyo Seco) at blinking light. Proceed 5 mi. Just after Casa Cordova Restaurant on left.

🏠 Durango 200 mi SW, Cuba 150 mi

NEW YORK

Metropolitan New York Council, 132 Spring St., NY, NY 10012
(212) 431-7100
Northern New York Council, 65 Park Street, Malone, NY 12953
(518) 483-7334
Syracuse Council, 459 Westcott Street, Syracuse, NY 13210
(315) 472-5788

AUBURN Auburn YMCA-WEIU (SA, YMCA), 27-29 William St, NY 13021
- 🏠 Nancy Carreiro & Dorothea Duke
- ☎ (315) 253-5304
- ▬ ♦ 12 ♦ 12
- ▬ ♦ 12 ♦ 12
- ⬆ advance notice appreciated
- ● $4 S, $4 W
- ⌂ Hot & cold
- ⌒ Wogman's Grocery ¼ mi
- ♥ yes
- 🚌 Auburn 2 blks
- 🚂 Syracuse 35 mi
- 🚲 Lake Country Sports ¼ mi
- 🚗 Parking garage across street
- ✈ Syracuse 35 mi
- * Professional baseball team in Auburn (Class A) at Falcon Park, Finger Lakes Mall 1 mi, Emerson Park 1 mi, Seward House 1/10 mi, various museums within walking distance.
- ** 2 gyms, pool, racquetball courts, sauna
- 🔃 yes
- 🚩 $1

DIRECTIONS: Near center of Auburn, 1 blk S of W Genesee St on William St.
- 📍 Syracuse 29 mi E, Owasco 9 mi S, Jack's Reef 17 mi N, Geneva 25 mi W

BATAVIA 🏠 139 Tracy Ave., Batavia, NY 14020
- 🏠 Chester Andrews
- ☎ (716) 343-3763
- ▬ 2
- ⬆ yes
- ● $2
- ⌂ Hot & cold
- ♥ no
- 🚌 Batavia 1 mi
- 🚂 Buffalo (Depew Sta) 30 mi
- 🚲 1½ mi
- 🚗 At hostel
- ✈ 35 mi
- 📍 Buffalo YWCA 35 mi W; Geneva 16 mi E; Springville 54 mi SW; Niagara Falls, Ontario 50 mi NW

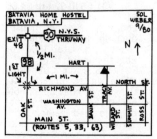

BLUE MT. LAKE The Steamboat Landing (SA, no kitchen), Blue Mt. Lake, NY 12812
- 🏠 Mr. & Mrs Fletcher Clark
- ☎ (518) 352-7323
- ▬ Variable ♦ 6 ♦ 6
- 🌙 May 31-Oct 1
- ◐ P.O. Box 458, Old Forge, NY 13420
- ● $4 (3 to a room), $5 (2 to a room)
- ⌂ Hot & cold
- ⌒ Lakeview Groceries ¼ mi S
- 🚌 At Hostel (Jun 30-Labor Day)
- 🚂 Adirondack 40 mi
- 🚗 At Hostel
- ✈ Albany-Seaplanes land on Blue Mt. Lake
- * Swimming, sailing, canoeing ($8 per day, $48 per week,

$80 for 2 weeks); many hiking trails; bike trails from Indian Lake to Blue Mt. Lake
✖ By reservation
DIRECTIONS: Blue Mt. Lake on Rt. 30 & 28N, 50 yards N at Intersection with Rt. 28
🏠 Old Forge 35 mi W, Paul Smith's 65 mi N, Warrensburg approx. 60 mi SE

BUFFALO YWCA Residence (SA) 245 North St, Buffalo, NY 14201
🏠 Ms. Jeanette Hess
☎ (716) 884-4761
▬ Females Only ⚹ 8
◕ $3.25 S
SN Hostel does not provide blankets
▲ Metropolitan YWCA
♨ Hot & cold
⌂ Bells 200 ft N
✆ yes
🚌 Greyhound 6 blks
🚃 Amtrak, Erie; Lackawana 3 mi
🚲 Allen Hardware at Elmwood & Allen Sts 1 blk
✈ Buffalo 10 mi
✳ Only 1 hour's drive from Niagra Falls, boutiques, antiques, art galleries. Buffalo Zoo, Albright-Knox Gallery.
DIRECTIONS: Downtown Buffalo, corner of Elmwood & North Streets, turn W on North St. off Main, cross Linwood/Franklin, Delaware, Elmwood, Hostel is 1 mi N of Center of Buffalo
🏠 Jamestown 80 mi S

CANTON 🏠 St. Lawrence (SA) St. Lawrence University, Canton, NY 13617
☎ 379-5757
▬ 8 ⚹ 4 ⚹ 4 larger groups accommodated with advance notification
🏠 June 1-Aug 10 only
◕ $2.50 S
♨ Hot & cold
⌂ P & C Grocery 2 blks
🚌 Court Street, Canton 2 blks
🚲 Ray's Bicycle Shop, 62 Miner St, Canton
🚗 On campus
✈ Ogdensburg 18 mi
✆ I-$1.50 II-$2 III-$3.25

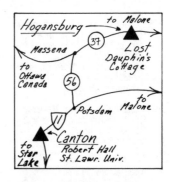

CLYDE 🏠 Honey Farm Home Hostel, RD 1, Kelsey Rd E, Clyde, NY 14433
🏠 Pat Campbell & Jim Taylor
☎ (315) 923-7102
▬ ⚹ 3 ⚹ 3
▬ ⚹ 3 ⚹ 3
✆ yes, by telephone
◕ $2.50 S, $2.50 W
SN No smoking in hostel
♨ Cold only
⌂ Some food available at hostel; Midstate, Clyde 3 mi
✆ yes
🚌 Clyde 3 mi
🚃 Syracuse 45 mi
🚲 Clyde
🚗 At hostel
✈ Syracuse 45 mi
⚓ yes
✳ Chimney Bluffs State Park 12 mi N, Horse & buggy at hostel, Fireman's Fireworks Aug 15 in Clyde, Horseback riding at hostel).
✳✳ Russian stove, wood stove cooking only. Natural foods sold at hostel. Hostel is farmhouse undergoing renovations.
★ no

![HONEY FARM HOME HOSTEL CLYDE, N.Y. map: SOL WEBER 9/80; KELSEY RD.; CLYDE-HUNTS RD.; ROCHESTER 31; 414 CLYDE; 89 SAVANNAH; SYRACUSE; EXIT 41, N.Y. STATE THRUWAY]

🏕 no

DIRECTIONS: 2 mi N of Clyde on Rt 414, turn right on Kelsey Rd, 1¼ mi to last house on left (on top of hill).

🏠 Geneva 24 mi S, Auburn 29 mi E, Jack's Reef 34 mi E, Syracuse 45 mi E

DRESDEN 🏠 Camp Whitman, RD 1, Penn Yan, NY 14527

🏠 Camp Manager

☎ (315) 536-8391

🛏 10

⊢ R

🕯 April 1-Oct 31

🔥 April 1-May 31 & Sept 1-Oct 31

◑ Presbytery of Geneva, 72 Castle St, P.O. Box 164, Geneva, NY 14456

⊖ $3 S, $3 W

▲ Presbytery of Geneva, 72 Castle St, P.O. Box 164, Geneva, NY 14456 (315) 789-7416

🚰 Hot & cold

🍴 Dresden 3 mi

🚩 yes

🚍 Dresden 3 mi

🚌 Rochester or Syracuse 60 mi

🚴 Penn Yan

🛶 At the camp

✈ Rochester or Syracuse 60 mi

⛺ yes

* Wineries at Hammondsport 45 mi; Corning Glass Manufacturing Center & Museum, Corning 45 mi; Watkins Glen George & Grand Prix Auto Racing Track, Watkins Glen 20 mi.

** Over 100 acres of woods, ravines, meadows & trails. Includes wildlife, pond, lake shore, swimming pool, recreation field & equipment.

★ yes

🏕 yes

🔑 I-$1   II-$1.75   III-$2.50 I-III-$5.25

🏠 not available

→ A beautiful modern camp & conference center located in a rustic setting on the longest of the Finger Lakes.

DIRECTIONS: Off Rt 14 on Seneca Lake either S of Dresden 3.2 mi or N of Himrod 3.2 mi.

🏠 Dundee (Wayne) 6 mi S, Geneva 15 mi N

DUNDEE The Household Center YH, Old Bath Rd., RD-1, Dundee, NY 14837

🏠 Thomas & Janet Hayes

☎ 607/292-3842

🛏 ♀ 10 ♂ 10

🕯 March 15-Nov 15

⊖ $3.50 S

🍴 2 stores 1 mi S

🚩 yes

🚍 Dundee 10 mi

🚌 Rochester 80 mi

🚴 Wayne 1 mi S

✈ Chemung 30 mi

* Radio, books & magazines, tether ball, swimming 8 mi; Finger Lakes Trail, located near winemaking areas, several scenic state parks within 50 mi, an extensive network of back roads ideal

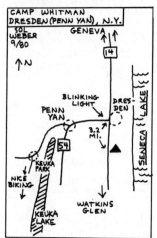

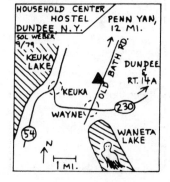

for bicycling throughout the Finger Lakes
✻ With reservations

DIRECTIONS: 13 mi S of Penn Yan Pass Airport, 1 mi N of Wayne (Rt 230); 8 mi N of Hammondsport on Bath Rd
⬦ Vestal 60 mi SE

GENEVA ⌂ Baker Home Hostel, 53 Garden Apts, Geneva, NY 14456
⬦ Paul Baker
☏ (315) 789-9564
⬌ floor
● $2.50 S, $2.50 W
⌂ Hot & cold
⚑ yes

GILBERTSVILLE The Major's Inn (SA, has not yet met all hostel requirements), Box 136, Gilbertsville, NY 13776
⬦ Deborah Schwabach
☏ (607) 783-2412
⬌ ⬦ 6 ⬦ 6
⬌ ⬦ 20 ⬦ 20, floor space
⬦ May 15-Oct 1 (no heat in bldg)
⬦ suggested
● $2.50 S
SN Somewhat primitive but interesting
⌂ Tubs, hot & cold
⬠ Valueway
⚑ yes
🚌 Oneonta 15 mi
🚂 Utica 50 mi (Amtrak)
🚲 Oneonta
🚗 At hostel
✈ Oneonta 15 mi
⛰ yes
✳ Cooperstown 30 mi, Baseball Hall of Fame, Farmers Museum.

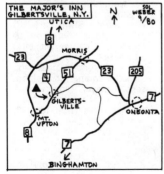

✱✱ Moser Gilbert's Ghost
★ no
⬛ yes, intro only
➡ 1895 Victorian mansion
DIRECTIONS: On NY Rt 51 between Mt Upton & Morris, in center of town.
⬦ Willet 48 mi W, Vestal 59 mi SW, Sharon Springs 55 mi NE, Syracuse 87 mi NW

HOGANSBURG Lost Dauphin's Cottage, P.O. Box 366, Hogansburg, NY 13655
⬦ Doris Eckroph
☏ (518) 358-2829
⬌ ⬦ 7 ⬦ 7
● $3.50 S, $4.50 W
⌂ Hot & cold
⬠ Harry's Mkt. 2 blks
⚑ yes
🚌 Massena 15 mi
🚂 Plattsburgh 55 mi
🚲 Massena 13 mi
🚗 in driveway
✈ Massena 13 mi
⛰ yes
✳ Akwesasne Mohawk Reservation (hostel is surrounded by reservation); St. Lawrence Seaway-Eisenhower Locks 7 mi; Barnhardt Park 7 mi
✱✱ Hostel is historic architectural A-frame house, lived in by son of France's Louis XVI & Marie Antoinette
⬛ yes
DIRECTIONS: W along Rt 37 25 mi from Malone; E along Rt 37 13 mi from Massena
⬦ Paul Smith's Rotary Hostel 55 mi S, Ottawa 60 mi NW

JACK'S REEF ⌂ Whitman Home Hostel, 7213 Kingdom Rd, Memphis, NY 13112
⬦ Frank & Shirley Whitmore
☏ (315) 689-9064
⬌ 10 ⬦ 5 ⬦ 5
⬌ 10 ⬦ 5 ⬦ 5
⬦ yes
⌂ Hot & cold
⬠ Williams Supermarket 2 mi
⚑ yes
🚌 Ionia 2 mi
🚂 Syracuse 25 mi
🚲 Bikery, Baldwinsville
🚗 At hostel
✈ Syracuse 25 mi
⛰ yes
✳ Beaver Lake Nature Center,

NEW YORK

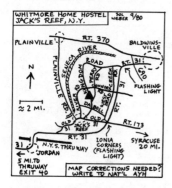

Plainville Turkey Farm 7 mi, Weedsport Old Erie Canal Lock restoration 10 mi

** Swimming pool, garden. Located on a working farm.

★ no

⛺ no

DIRECTIONS: From junction of Rtes 173 & 31 (flashing light) W on Old Rt 31 1½ mi to Kingdom Rd, turn right (N) on Kingdom Rd for 1½ mi to hostel on left.

🚂 Syracuse 20 mi E, Geneva 35 mi W

JAMESTOWN Jamestown YMCA, 101 E. Fourth St, Jamestown, NY 14701

🏠 John C. Wheeler

☎ 716-664-2802

🛏 ⚲ 30, men only

● $3 S

SN Sleeping bags required

🚰 Hot & cold

🍴 Quality Markets 2 blks W

🚌 Greyhound, D & F, & Bluebird Bus Lines in city

🚃 Amtrak, Buffalo 75 mi

🚶 5 blks S

🚗 city lot adjacent

✈ Allegheny Commuter

** **No registrations Sundays**

DIRECTIONS: Center location Jamestown downtown area; 2 mi S of Southern Tier Expressway, NY Rt 17; 30 mi S of I-90 (NY Thruway)

KINGSTON Hidden Valley Lake YH, CPO Box 190, Kingston, NY 12401

🏠 Mrs. Mickey Duncan

☎ (914) 338-4616

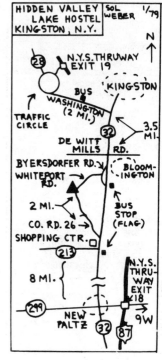

🛏 18 ⚲ & ⚲ flexible

⚑ Preferred

● $4.50 S, $5.75 W

SN Bring sleeping bags; special arrangements for groups of over 20 people

▲ Outdoor Inns, Inc.

🚰 Hot & cold

🍴 Rosendale Shopping Center 2 mi S

⚲ yes

🚌 Trailways, Bloomington 1 mi

🚶 Several in Kingston 4½ mi

* 3 geological faults on site, Minnewaska State Park, 15 mi; Historic Kingston & mushroom center on site; Recreation room with fireplace, radio, magazines; volleyball, badminton, piano, record player, ping pong & books; softball; cross country ski trails (trail fee $2, rentals available).

DIRECTIONS: From Kingston take Rt 32, go 4½ mi S of Kingston, then 1 mi W of Rt 32. From South Rosendale,

go Rt 32, top of hill past Rosendale Shopping Center.
🏠 Staatsburg 28 mi E

LACONA (Smartville) Smart House Nature Center, Box 199, Smartville Rd, Lacona, NY 13083
🏠 Alice & John Arneson
☎ (315) 387-5521
🛏 22
⬆ Preferred
● $5 S, $6.75 W
🚿 Hot & cold
🍴 Lacona Supermarket 6 mi
✓ yes
🚌 Sandy Creek 6 mi
🚂 Syracuse 50 mi
🚲 outside Lacona 5 mi
🚗 on premises
✈ Watertown 30 mi
⛺ yes
* Central to over 30,000 acres of State Forest & Wildlife Management lands; wilderness; excellent hiking, biking, cross-country skiing, birding, fishing. 12 mi to Lake Ontario, 8 mi to Salmon River Reservoir for canoeing.
** Trail map; equipment rental, sales; lessons. AYH trail fee $1/day.
✳ yes
🛏 sheet & pillowcase 50¢, sleep sacks 25¢
➡ Historic Victorian house is one of few remaining relics of Tug Hill's lumbering heydays; sawmill remains on Center

DIRECTIONS: 6 mi E of Sandy Creek/Lacona exit off Interstate 81 or Rt 11, on Co. Rt 15 (Smartville Rd); 500 ft E of Intersection of Co. Rt 15 & Rt 50 Northside
🏠 Syracuse International 50 mi S, Old Forge 72 mi E, Star Lake 84 mi N

LAKE GEORGE (Glens Falls) 🏠 Lake George, (mail) c/o Lake George Center, Box 176, Lake George, NY 12845
☎ (518) 793-1627 or 793-3878 (7/1-8/31); after 7/1 (518) 668-2634 or 668-2001
🛏 1 5
🏠 June 12-Aug 31 (June 12-June 30 by advance reservation with deposit only)
⬆ No, but helpful July 1-Aug 31
◑ P.O. Box 176, Lake George, NY 12845
● $3.50 S
SN Strict 9 AM departure
▲ Lake George Center, Inc.
🚿 Hot & cold
✓ yes
🚌 Lake George 7 mi; Trailways, Greyhound
🚂 Fort Edward 16 mi
🚲 Glens Falls 7 mi
🚗 on premises
✈ Glens Falls 10 mi; Albany 60 mi
* Many attractions in Lake George area. For complete listing, write Warren County

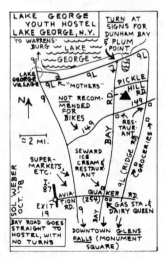

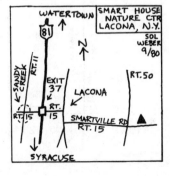

Publicity Dept., Lake George, NY 12845. Transportation to Duck Hole Trail-Head (for High Peaks area) with advance notice at reasonable rates for groups only.

** Swimming on grounds, 12 mi county bike trail

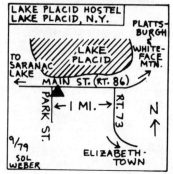 yes

DIRECTIONS: Hostel is on Upper Bay Rd at corner of Pickle Hill Rd. At intersection of Rt 9 & Rt 149 (Exit 20 Northway); 4 mi N of Glens Falls; turn E on 149, 3 mi to Bay Rd, turn N 1 mi; hostel is on right

🏠 Warrensburg 20 mi N

LAKE PLACID Lake Placid Youth Hostel (SA, serves others), 54 Main St, P.O. Box 311, Lake Placid, NY 12946

🏠 Mr. David Book
🕾 518 523-2008
🛏 1 5 1 4
🔒 advance booking required
● $5 S
▲ Adirondack Resort Ministries (Baptist Convention of NY)
🚰 Hot & cold
🔌 2 blks
🍴 yes
🚌 1 blk
🚗 Amtrak in Westport, 45 spur planned into Lake Placid
🚲 2 blks
🏪 1 blk
✈ Saranac Lake 16 mi
⛏ yes
* Swimming, sailing, canoeing. Flat water canoeing 10 mi; White water canoeing down-

hill & cross-country skiing. Backpacking trails 1 mi. Center for music, drama & arts in town.

🔦 I-$1 II-$1.25 III-$1.75

DIRECTIONS: From I-87, take 9N to Rt 73, go W to Lake Placid Center. Enter Hostel from Park St, which crosses Main St.

🏠 Paul Smith's 20 mi N, Blue Mt. Lake 65 mi SW

LITTLE FALLS🏕 Holy Family Renewal Center (SA, no kitchen), 639 E. John St, Little Falls, NY 13365

🏠 Tim & Eum Dorsey
🕾 (315) 823-1548
🛏 34
🔒 Suggested, center may be full with other groups
● $5 S, $5 W
🚰 Hot & cold
🔌 1 blk
🍴 no
🚌 1 blk CNY Coach
🚲 Utica 25 mi
🏪 At hostel
✈ Utica 35 mi
⛏ no
* Gen. Herkimer Home, Moreland Park, city parks, lakes, ski slope, picturesque small

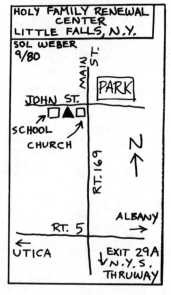

HOLY FAMILY RENEWAL CENTER
LITTLE FALLS, N.Y.
SOL WEBER 9/80

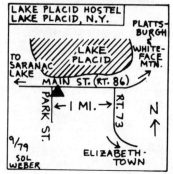

LAKE PLACID HOSTEL
LAKE PLACID, N.Y.
9/79 SOL WEBER

town, band concert in park.
** Hostel is 28 year old stone
structure.
★ yes
🚐 yes
⚲ I-$2 II-$3 III-$3
🔥 $1 (included in overnite fee)
DIRECTIONS: Turn N of Rt 5 onto Rt 169, turn left at the 1st
traffic light onto John. Next
door to St. Mary's.
🏠 Syracuse 72 mi W, Sharon
Springs 31 mi SE, Old Forge
70 mi N, Gilbert 58 mi SW

MALONE 🏠 Home Hostel, 65
Park St, Malone, NY 12953
🏠 Richard & Lorna Giles
☎ (518) 483-7334
🛏 6
🍴 yes
⚫ $3 S, $3 W
🚰 Hot & cold
🗄 George's Fruit Mkt 3 blks
🚩 yes
🚍 2 blks
🚲 ½ mi
🚗 At hostel
** Large yard, easy access to
downtown
🚐 yes
DIRECTIONS: Call for directions.
🏠 Plattsburgh 45 mi E, Canton
50 mi W, Lake Placid 60 mi
SE, Hogansburg 25 mi NW

MEDUSA 🏠 Manice Home Hostel, 41 Farmers Picnic Grove
Rd, Medusa, NY 12120
🏠 Edward A. Manice
☎ (578) 239-6987
🛏 4
🍴 2
🍴 preferred
⚫ $3 S
SN Simple old-fashioned farmhouse
🚰 Hot & cold
🗄 Bellis General Store 3 mi
🚩 yes
🚍 Albany 35 mi
🚕 Albany or Hudson 35 mi
🚲 Albany
🚗 By house
🚌 Albany 38 mi
⛺ yes
* Water-powered grist mill 4
mi
DIRECTIONS: Take Rt 85 SW
from Albany to Rensselaer-
ville (30 mi), thru Co. Rt 353
to Co. Rt 359 to Co. Rt 360 &

then 3 mi to Manice. Family
home on Co. Rt 360 (Far-
mers Picnic Grove Rd) near
Hale Rd.

NEW BALTIMORE 🏠 New Baltimore, S. Main St at Pichler
Rd, Box 205, New Baltimore
12124
🏠 Robert Gaesser
☎ (518) 756-9097
🛏 4
🍴 2
🗄 New Baltimore Mart ¼ mi
🚩 yes
🚍 New Baltimore 1/8 mi
🚕 Albany, Rennslear 15 mi
🚲 Coxsackie 4 mi
🚗 On premises
🚌 Albany 15 mi
⛺ yes
* Catskill Mtn hikes, on Hudson River
** 140 year old house
★ no
🚐 no
DIRECTIONS: 15 mi S of Albany
on Rt 144, 4 mi N of Cox-
sackie via River Rd.
🏠 Medusa 12 mi W, Sharon
Springs 62 mi NW, Warrensburg 75 mi N, Kingston 42
mi S

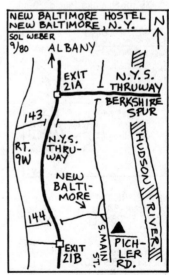

NEWCOMB The House of Grace,
P.O. Box 234, Newcomb, NY

12852
🏠 Tom Kellogg
🛏 10 ⚑ 6 ⚑ 4
🏠 June 1-Oct 30
⛽ no
📍 768 Valley View Pkwy, Webster, NY 14585
● $2.50 S, $2.50 W
▲ Tom Kellogg
♨ Hot & cold
🍴 Bissels 2 mi E
🚲 yes
🚌 Schroon Lake 30 mi SE
🚂 Tupper Lake 37 mi NW
✈ Glensfalls 70 mi Se
🚗 On   p
✈ Saranac Lake 70 mi N
⚓ yes
* Located on lake/river with canoe, good new mountain fire tower 5 mi, beach 1 mi E, Adirondack Ecology Center 4 mi W, miles of hiking trails adjacent, horse carriage rides ½ mi W.
** Old wooden church building
★ no
DIRECTIONS: N side of 28N at the W edge of town next to Santanoni Forest Pres. entrance.
🏠 Warrensburg 50 mi SE, Star Lake 70 mi NW, Paul Smith's 75 mi N, Lake Placid 70 mi NE

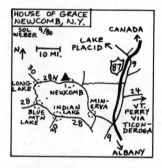

NEW YORK CITY Prince George Hotel (SA, rates, no kitchen) 14 E. 28th St, New York, NY 10016
🏠 Richard Garcia & Mary Naughton
📞 (212) 685-9207
🛏 100 ⚑ & ⚑
● $13-$26 S, $11-$24 W
SN no limit of stay, no reservations

▲ ECOM, Economy Accommodation System Inc.
♨ Hot & cold
🚌 Port Authority 25 blks
🚂 Grand Central Station 14 blks
🚌 19th & 2nd Ave
🚗 27th St & Lexington Ave $6/day
✈ LaGuardia Airport 10 mi
* Empire State Bldg 5 blks, Central Park 30 blks, 5th Ave shopping 20 blks, Radio City 20 blks, all other Manhattan attractions within convenient subway/bus ride
★ 4-bedded rooms

OLD FORGE 🏠 Brooker Family Lodge, Rt 28, Old Forge, NY 13420
🏠 Marlene & Bill Brooker
📞 315-369-6072
🛏 ⚑ 16 ⚑ 16
🛏 ⚑ 5 ⚑ 5
🏠 Dec 15-Mar 15
🚲 yes
🚌 Utica 50 mi
🚂 Utica 50 mi, Old Forge
🚙 Old Forge
🚗 At hostel
✈ Utica 50 mi
⚓ yes
* Fire Tower, Bald Mt. 1 mi to top from Hostel; Cross country ski trails start at Hostel; canoeing; Fulton chain of

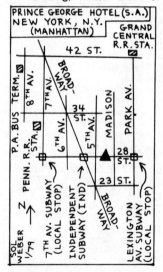

lakes start at hostel.
** Wood burning stove, piano
✱ yes
🏠 yes
🛏 $1 each

DIRECTIONS: 4.5 mi N of Old
    Forge on Rt 28 or 4.5 mi S of
    Eagle Bay on Rt 28.
🏠 Blue Mt. Lake 35 mi NE

OWASCO Camp Y-Owasco (SA,
    no kitchen, YMCA Camp,
    tents), Box 341, Sam Adam
    Lane, Auburn, NY 13021
🏠 Don O'Bren
☎ (315) 784-5451
🛏 Bunks in tents on matbags
    👤 15 👤 15
🛏 May 1-Oct 1
🔑 May 1-15 & Sept 1-Oct 1 only
◑ 27 Williams St, Auburn, NY
    13021
● $2 S
▲ Auburn YMCA-WEIU
🚰 Hot & cold
🎵 Lakeview Grocery 5 mi
⚑ no
🚌 Auburn 11 mi
🚆 Syracuse 50 mi
🚲 Auburn
🚗 At hostel
✈ Syracuse 55 mi
⛺ yes
✳ Riding stables 8 mi, Fillmore
    Glen State Park 7 mi, New
    Hope Grist Mill 12 mi, swim-
    ming in Owesco Lake, athle-
    tic fields, boating & canoeing
    by prior arrangement.

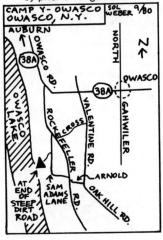

** Lakeside setting
★ yes, separate tents available
🏠 yes
🔑 I-75¢ II-$1.25 III-$2
➡ YMCA camp for 58 years,
    ACA camp
DIRECTIONS: S from Auburn 5
    mi on Rt 38A. Right on Rock-
    efeller Rd 3 mi to Sam
    Adams Lane, ½ mi to dirt
    road on right.
🏠 Syracuse 40 mi NE, Geneva
    34 mi W, Jack's Reef 25 mi
    N, Auburn 9 mi N, Willet 51
    mi SE

PAUL SMITH'S Rotary Youth
    Hostel, Keese Mill School-
    house, Paul Smith's, NY
    12970
🏠 Pete Kick & Ted Halveston
🛏 👤 4 👤 4

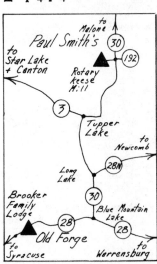

🛏 👤 4 👤 4
🔑 In winter
● $3.50 May-Sept, $4.50 Oct-
    April
▲ The Malone, NY Rotary Club
    & Malone Extension Ctr. of N
    County Community College
🚰 Hot & cold
🎵 Moody's Sunoco, Gabriels 4
    mi
⚑ yes
🚌 Trailways & Greyhound,
    Saranac Lake 13 mi
✈ Alleghney Airlines flies into
    Saranac Airport at Lake

Clear 7 mi S

yes

DIRECTIONS: Hostel is 2 mi W of Paul Smith's College, intersection of Rts 30 & 192, 13 mi N of Saranac Lake. Take the Keese Mill-Otisville Rd 2 mi W thru Keese Mill & past gravel pit to old Keese Mill Schoolhouse. Now Rotary YH.

Lake Placid 20 mi S, Hogansburg 63 mi N

PLATTSBURGH Mountain Air Residence (SA, also a school), 63 Broad St, Plattsburgh, NY 12901

John Mockrey

(518) 561-1620

May 24-Aug 31

$5 S

Mountain Air Development, Inc.

Hot & cold

Many within walking distance

yes

4 blks

5 blks

1 blk

no

Lake Champlain 2 mi, Adirondack Mtns., Valcour Island. Swimming, skiing, canoeing, horseback riding, hiking, biking.

yes

Malone 45 mi W, Lake Placid 60 mi SW

SHARON SPRINGS Sharon Springs International, 181 Union St, Sharon Springs, NY 13459

Seth E. Many

(518) 284-9706 or 284-2460

5 4

July-Aug; all other times through pre-arrangement

$4 S

Sharon Springs Mini Mall ½ mi Rt 20

Greyhound

Amsterdam 30 mi

Western Auto 12 mi N in Fort Plain, Cobles Kill 11 mi S

At hostel

Albany 40 mi, Syracuse 90 mi

Mineral Springs & health

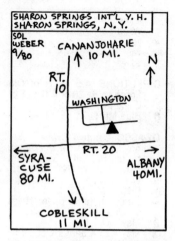

SHARON SPRINGS INT'L Y.H.
SHARON SPRINGS, N.Y.
SOL WEBER 9/80
CANANJOHARIE ↑ 10 MI.
RT. 10
WASHINGTON
N ↑
RT. 20
←SYRACUSE 80 MI.
ALBANY 40 MI. →
COBLESKILL 11 MI.

spa, village pool, hiking, tennis, Otsego Lake 20 mi. Howe Caverns, Cobles Kill, Mohawk River/Erie Canal. Farmers, Baseball & NY Historical Museum at Cooperstown 20 mi.

DIRECTIONS: ¼ mi N of Intersection Rts 10 & 20 E 2 blks on Washington St, S 1 blk on Willow St. to 181 Union St, rear house.

SPRINGVILLE Home (SA), 16 Woodward Ave, Springville, NY 14141

Henry Kvashay

(716) 592-3864

12

May 1-Nov 1

preferred

$4.50 S

Hot & cold

yes

1 blk (Trailways)

Buffalo 30 mi

1 blk

200 ft

Buffalo 30 mi

Near 2 Indian reservations, 60 mi to Niagara Falls, Letchworth Park 40 mi.

no

$1

100 year plus old building, beautiful architecture, artistic plaster work.

DIRECTIONS: In center of town, near junction of Rtes 219 & 39

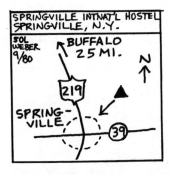

🏠 Buffalo 27 mi N, Dundee 115 mi E, Jamestown 50 mi SW

STAATSBURG (Hyde Park) Club Highview YH (SA, Outdoor Inns, Staatsburg-Hyde Park, NY 12580

- 📞 (914) 266-5667 (if no ans 338-4616)
- 🛏 ⚡ 29 ⚡ 20
- 🚪 May 1-Oct 1
- 💲 $4.50 S
- ▲ Outdoor Inns/Highview
- 🚰 Hot & cold
- 🍴 Clinton Hollow 2 mi S
- 🚻 yes
- 🚌 Hyde Park or Rhinebeck 8 mi
- 🚂 Rhinecliff 10 mi
- ✈ Rhinebeck 8 mi N
- 🛫 Poughkeepsie 20 mi
- * Recreation room with fireplace, radio, piano, record

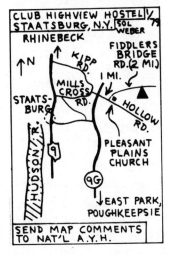

SEND MAP COMMENTS TO NAT'L A.Y.H.

player, ping pong & book & magazines. Volleyball field, badminton, swimming pond, softball, fireplace & tennis court. Roosevelt & Vanderbilt at Hyde Park, Rhinebeck & Aerodome, Norris Park on Hudson

DIRECTIONS: Go 1 mi E of Rt 96 on Hollow Rd (6 mi S of Rt 308, 5 mi N of East Park) to church then left 2 mi on Fiddlers Bridge Rd. The Hostel is 8 mi N of Hyde Park S of Rhinebeck.

🏠 Hidden Valley Lake Kingston 25 mi W

STAR LAKE Star Lake Campus (SA, no kitchen), State University College at Potsdam, Star Lake, NY 13690

- 🏠 Doc & Sue Catana
- 📞 (315) 848-2480, 268-4980
- 🛏 180
- 💲 $3.50 S, $4.50 W
- ▲ Potsdam Auxiliary & College Educational Services, Inc.
- 🚰 Hot & cold
- 🍴 Dolan's 1 mi N
- 🚻 no
- 🚌 Gouverneur 37 mi
- 🛫 Watertown 70 mi
- 🏕 no
- * Recreation room, lake with beach, boats; ski slope; x-country & hiking trails
- 🔑 I-$1.90 II-$2.75 III-$4

DIRECTIONS: Turn S off NY Rt 3 at Shell Station. Take 4th right turn, take 2nd right turn, proceed to Camp office.

🏠 Malone 85 mi N, Canton 32 mi N

SYRACUSE (A) 🏠 Downing International Hostel, 459 Westcott St, Syracuse, NY 13210

- 🏠 Jeffrey Leaman & Becky Buck-Leaman
- 📞 315-472-5788
- 🛏 ⚡ 4 ⚡ 4 W, ⚡ 8 ⚡ 8 S (more space may be available by reservation)
- 💲 $4.50 S, $5.50 W
- ▲ Syracuse Council of American Youth Hostels
- 🚰 Hot & cold
- 🍴 Fifields 1 blk
- 🚻 yes

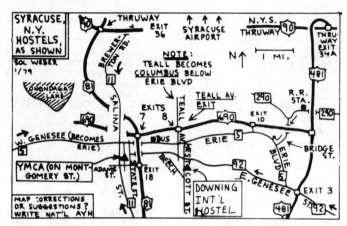

Greyhound 1¼ mi
Amtrak, East Syracuse 4 mi
2 blks (repairs only)
At hostel
Hancock International 9 mi
Green Lakes State Park 11 mi, Canal Museum 2 mi, Everson Art Museum 2 mi, Syracuse University 1 mi, Le Moyre College 1½ mi.
When space permits
yes
1st Council owned city hostel in US.

DIRECTIONS: E Genesee St. (NY Rt 92) from E & W, turn S on Westcott St, 2 blks on left. Teall Ave exit from I-690, S on Teall, cross Erie Blvd onto Columbus, left one blk on E Genesee, right on Westcott, 2 blks to hostel.

Vestal HH 80 mi S, Dundee 85 mi SW, Old Forge 100 mi NE, Lacona 50 mi N; Auburn 25 mi W; Jack's Reef 20 mi W; Vernon Center 30 mi E; Little Falls 75 mi E

SYRACUSE (B) YMCA (SA), 340 Montgomery St, Syracuse, NY 13202

Joseph Stinson, Residence Director
(315) 474-6851
Cannot accommodate males under 18 ₰ 90
$6 a night (half of regular $12 a night fee)
Many groceries nearby
Restaurant in Lobby

Greyhound 4 blks
Amtrak 5 mi
Meltzer's 7 blks S on Salina St
Hancock 8 mi
DIRECTIONS: Downtown Syracuse.

VERNON CENTER ⌂ Conland Home Hostel, Rt 1, Box 61-A-12, Rt 235, South, Vernon Center, NY

Robert & Katrina Conland
(315) 829-2315
2
2
yes
Hot & cold
Bart's, Vernon Center 1 mi
yes
CNY Coach, Vernon
Utica & Rome (Amtrak)
Jerry's, Oneida

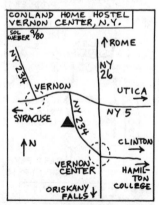

🛶 At hostel
🚰 Oneida County (Utica) 17 mi
⛺ yes
* Oneida Ltd. Factory Store & Mansion House, Vernon Downs, Root Glen at Hamilton College.
★ no
🏧 no
DIRECTIONS: From NY Rt 5 E or W, S on Rt 234 ¾ mi.
🏃 Syracuse 30 mi W, Little Falls 40 mi E, Old Forge 74 mi N, Willet 56 mi SW

VESTAL 🏠 Home Hostel, RD 2, Box 257, Noyes Rd, Vestal, NY 13850
🏠 Craig & Cherryl Smith
☎ 607-748-3529 after 5 PM
🛏 3
🍽 10
🌙 Closed June 10-July 25
🔑 24-hour advance notice required
● $2.50
SN 2 nights maximum stay, closed 8 AM-5 PM
🚿 Hot & cold
🚌 Binghamton 12 mi
🚕 Syracuse 85 mi
🚲 Ted's Bike Shop 6 mi
🛶 At hostel
🚰 Broome County Airport 15 mi
⛺ yes
** Cross-country skiing, swimming pool
🔦 I-$1, III-$2, I-III-$3

DIRECTIONS: 5 mi SW of intersection of Rtes 434 & 26.

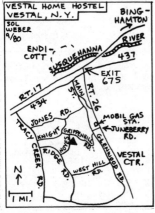

See map for details. A climb from any direction.
🏃 La Anna 90 mi SE, Syracuse 85 mi N, Dundee 85 mi NW, Mt. Tremper 130 mi E

WARRENSBURG The Glen House, The Glen, Route 28, Warrensburg, NY 12885
🏠 M/M Richard Nelson & M/M Timothy Fierle
☎ 518-494-3250 (Reservations, 518-457-8087 9-4 PM)
🛏 (10 2-person rooms most with single beds). Accom. for single hostelers & families.
🔑 Advised but not required
🌐 Res. Add. Student Assoc. cc 116 SUNYA, Albany 12222
● $4 S, $4 W
SN Only money orders or cashiers checks accepted for reservations. No personal checks.
▲ Student Association of SUNY Albany
🚿 Hot & cold
🏪 Grand Union 8 mi
🚌 Warrensburg 8 mi
🚲 yes
🚕 Hudson Falls 30 mi
🛶 On premises
🚰 Glens Falls 25 mi
* Located on 840 wooded acres in the Adirondack Mts. Lounge with fireplace; swimming, fishing, hiking, lake skiing, snowshoeing, volleyball. White water canoeing, Gore Mt. Ski Center, Lake George Village. Excellent fall foliage.
✱ Sandbox, large yard. 7 mi hiking trails.
🌙 $2 per bed

DIRECTIONS: I-87 exit 23, N on Rt 9 through Warrensburg, left Rt 28, 5 mi
🏃 Lake George 22 mi, Blue Mt. Lake 52 mi NW

WILLET 🏠 Home Hostel, Willet Produce Farm, Mooney Hill Rd, Willett, NY 13863
🏠 Jarlath Hamrock
☎ (607) 863-4435
SN Bring own sleeping bags or sheets
🚲 yes
* 350 acre tract, vegetable gardens & crop cultivation,

swimming, horses.
♟ Vestal 50 mi S, Syracuse 50 mi N, Dundee 100 mi W

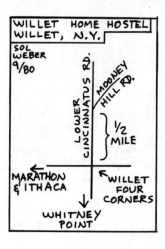

NORTH CAROLINA

BLOWING ROCK 🏠 Blowing Rock Assembly Grounds, P.O. Box 974, Blowing Rock, NC 28605
🏠 Kenneth W. Clapp
☎ 704-295-7813
🛏 86
⬆ Recommended
⬤ $4 S, $6 W
▲ Southern Conference, United Church
🚿 Hot & cold
🎵 Blowing Rock Variety
🚌 Blowing Rock 5 mi
🚲 Post Road Bick Shop 6 mi
🚗 On grounds
✈ Hickory 30 mi
⚱ yes
* Blue Ridge Parkway 1 mi, "Horn in the West" outdoor drama 8 mi, Linville Caverns & Gorge 30 mi, Grandfather Mountain 22 mi. Appalachian State University 9 mi.
** Numerous recreational facilities
✗ yes
🍴 I-$2 II-$2 III-$3
🍶 $1.50

DIRECTIONS: From Blue Ridge Parkway, take 321 S 1.2 mi to traffic light. Turn left onto Sunset Dr & travel .5 mi to golf

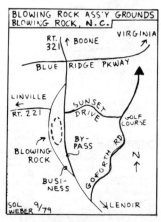

course. Turn left onto Goforth Rd & travel .2 mi to get to gate of Assembly Grounds.

WESSER Nantahala Outdoor Center, Star Rt, Box 68, Bryson City, NC 28713
🏠 Payson & Aurelia Kennedy
☎ 704-488-2175
🛏 6 ♀ & ♂
⬆ Advised during summer
🎵 On premises
⚥ yes

🚌 Continental Trailways passes by us
🚲 Asheville 80 mi
🏇 Asheville 80 mi
🛶 On premises
* Whitewater raft trips on Nantahala River, horseback riding, cross country skiing, whitewater instruction programs, Appalachian Trail, Smokey Mt. 25 mi, Cherokee Indian Reservation 35 mi, Fontana Dam 20 mi.
★ Regular motel rooms
🍴 Available at restaurant
DIRECTIONS: 13 mi SW of Bryson City on US 19, where Appalachian Trail crosses the Nantahala River in Wesser.

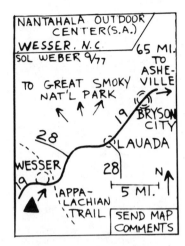

OHIO

Columbus Council, 160 South Dawson Ave., Columbus, OH 43209
(614) 846-3229
Erie-Ana Council, 304 N. Church St., Bowling Green, OH 43402
(419) 352-1252
Lima Council, P.O. Box 173, Lima, OH 45802 (419) 222-7301
Toledo Council, 3440 Lawrin Dr., Toledo, OH 43623
(419) 474-0267
Tri-State Council, 5400 Lanius Lane, Cincinnati, OH 45224
(513) 542-2909, or
Friars, 65 W. McMillan, Cincinnati, OH 45219 (513) 381-5432

BOWLING GREEN ⌂ Wintergarden Youth Hostel, Wintergarden Rd, Bowling Green, OH 43402
🏠 Joan/Robert Beard
☎ (Houseparent 419-352-9349) 419-352-9806
🛏 32 ♂ 16 ♀ 16
🔒 But preferred
● $2 S, $2.50 W
SN Houseparents do not live at hostel. Call for lodging between 5-8 PM only.
▲ City of Bowling Green, 304 N Church St. Bowling Green, 43402
🚿 Hot & cold
🍴 Perkins Market ½ mi
🍷 yes
🚌 Bowling Green 1½ mi
🚲 Toledo 25 mi
🏇 D.J.'s Bike Shop 1½ mi
🛶 At hostel
✈ Toledo 25 mi
* Swimming, Bowling Green City Park, Ft. Meigs, Perrys-

burg 14 mi, Toledo 1½ mi, attractions 25 mi N.

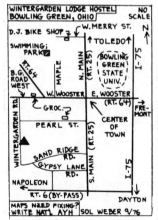

DIRECTIONS: 1 mi SW of downtown. 1.8 mi W from I-75.

Follow Wooster Rd W to Wintergarden Rd, turn left.

🚶 Detroit, Zanesfield 90 mi

CHILLICOTHE 🏠 Home Hostel
- ☎ 614-775-3632, 773-3989
- 🛏 3
- ● $2.50 S, $2.50 W
- 🚰 Hot & cold
- 🛒 McCambridges 3 mi
- 🍴 yes
- 🚌 295 E Main St, 4 mi
- 🚕 404 E Main St, 4 mi
- 🚲 Rivers Bend Sports Co., 74 W. Water St
- ✈ Port Columbus International Columbus 60 mi
- ⛺ yes
- * Mound City National Monument 1 mi, "Tecumseh" at Sugarloaf Mountain Amphitheatre mid-June thru Aug 10 mi, Adena State Memorial 2 mi.
- ** Lake for swimming, fishing.
- ➡ Overlooks "Seal of Ohio." View of Mt. Logan Range.

CINCINNATI 🏠 Bonecutter Home Hostel, 6085 Belleair Place, Cincinnati, OH 45224
- 🏠 Jerry & Monica Bonecutter
- ☎ (513) 541-1972
- 🛏 2
- 🔑 no
- ● $2 S, $2 W
- 🍴 yes
- 🚌 7 mi
- 🚕 6 mi
- ✈ 15 mi
- ⛺ no
- 🔑 50¢
- 🚶 Chillicothe 60 mi

COLUMBUS (A) Columbus YMCA (SA), 40 West Long St, Columbus, OH 43215
- ☎ (614) 224-1131
- ● $4.50 S, $4.50 W
- ▲ Columbus Metropolitan YMCA
- 🚰 Hot & cold
- 🚌 Greyhound 5 blks
- 🚕 other places, $1.75
- ✈ Columbus 10 mi
DIRECTIONS: Downtown Columbus 2 blks N of Geographical Center which is Broad & High Sts.
- 🚶 Lucus 55 mi N, Dresden 65 mi E

COLUMBUS (B) 🏠 Columbus Home, Columbus, OH
- ☎ (614) 235-7669
- 🛏 4
- 🛏 6
- ● $1 S, $1 W
- SN Advance reservation not required; participate in Columbus Council Local Program
- 🍴 yes
DIRECTIONS: 2 blks from US 40, 4 mi E of downtown.
- 🚶 Zaneshield 52 mi NW, Lucas 70 mi NE, Dresden 60 mi E, Chillicothe 55 mi S

DRESDEN 🏠 Home Hostel
- 🏠 Steven & Cynthia Buck
- ☎ (614) 754-1330
- 🛏 10
- 🔑 At all times
- ● $1 S
- 🚰 Hot & cold
- 🛒 ½ blk
- 🍴 As available
- 🚌 Zanesville 16 mi
- 🚕 Columbus 65 mi
- 🚲 Zanesville 16 mi
- 🚗 At the hostel
- ✈ Columbus 60 mi
- * Roscoe Village, Coshocton, 16 mi
DIRECTIONS: Given with reservation confirmation.
- 🚶 Columbus Home Hostel 60 mi W, Malabar Farm (Lucas) 60 mi NW

LIMA 🏠 Home Hostel.
- ☎ (419) 222-7301 or 226-3169
- 🛏 4
- 🔑 48 hour advance advised

LUCAS 🏠 Malabar Farm Youth Hostel, Rt 1, Lucas, OH 44842
- ☎ (419) 526-9336
- 🛏 22
- 🏠 June, July, Aug. All other times by reservation.
- ● $1.50 S, $2.50 W
- ▲ Columbus Council AYH, (614) 846-8229
- 🚰 Hot & cold
- 🛒 Perrysville 5.5 mi E
- 🍴 yes
- 🚌 Mansfield 10 mi
- 🚕 Amtrak, Crestline 17 mi
- 🚲 4 bike shops located in Mansfield 10 mi
- ✈ Mansfield 16.5 mi
- * Swimming, sailing/boating 3.5 mi, canoeing (less than

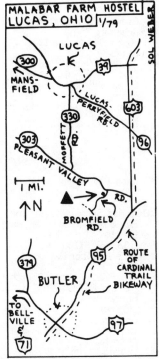

MALABAR FARM HOSTEL
LUCAS, OHIO 1/79

LUCAS

300
MANS-
FIELD

39

LUCAS
PERRYFIELD RD.

603

330

303

PLEASANT VALLEY

96

1 MI.

N

RD.

BROMFIELD RD.

95

ROUTE OF CARDINAL TRAIL BIKEWAY

379

BUTLER

TO BELL-VILLE

97

71

- 1 Double
- 5 Sleeping bag spaces
- Open all year
- Preferred but not necessary
SN No smoking or alcohol (also drug) consumption on premises.
- Hot & cold
- ½ mi
- 1 mi
- ½ mi
- Marietta 6 mi, Parkersburg, WV Airport
- In back yard
- Campus Martins Museum, River Museum, ½ mi. Marietta is oldest city in Ohio. 1st settlement in old Northwest Territory. Many old homes Victorian architecture.

ZANESFIELD Marmon Valley Farm, Rt 1, Zanesfield, OH 43360
- William D. & Phyllis Wiley
- (513) 593-8051
- varies
- Except Dec 15-Jan 15 Thanksgiving & Easter
- Always
- $2 S, $3 W
- Hot & cold
- Bellefontaine 7 mi
- Lima 45 mi
- Bellefontaine 7 mi
- At hostel
- Bellefontaine 7 mi
- Volleyball, softball, outdoor fireplace, horseback riding, swimming . Ohio Caverns 8 mi, Zane Caverns 6 mi, Piatt Castles 8 mi.
DIRECTIONS: From Bellefontaine, go 7 mi SE on US 33, take Country Rd 28 to left which turns onto Country Rd 153, turn right & go several hundred yards to Marmon Valley Farm. Hostel is 7 mi SE of Bellefontaine.
- Columbus 50 mi SW

10 mi), horseback riding, hiking trails, skiing, ice skating, Malabar Farms State Park, Mansfield Art Center, Mohican State Park.
DIRECTIONS: At Malabar State Park (listed on all State Maps) 12.5 mi SE of Mansfield on Bromfield Rd. The Hostel is 12 mi SE of Mansfield.
- Bowling Green 103 mi N, Zanesfield 80 mi W, Dresden 65 mi E, Columbus 75 mi S

MARIETTA Home Hostel
- 614-374-5042, office. 614-373-4667, home

OREGON
Oregon State Council, 4212 SW Primrose St., Portland, OR 97219

ASHLAND The Ashland Hostel, 150 N. Main St, Ashland, OR 97520
- Mark & Nena Ahalt

- (503) 482-9217
- 25
- Jan 1-Nov 30
- Suggested during July & Aug

177

● $3.50 S, $4.50 W
SN Parking limited to 4 vehicles
⌂ Hot & cold
⌂ Quik-Stop 1 blk
🛈 yes
🚌 Greyhound 2 blks
🚲 Klamath Falls 60 mi E
🚴 Cycle Sport 4 blks
🚗 4 spaces on premises
✈ Medford 12 mi
⚓ no
* Shakespeare Festival 5 blks, Feb-Oct. Mt. Ashland Ski Slope open in winter 18 mi.
** Located in historic town area.
★ yes
🏧 yes
🛈 50¢

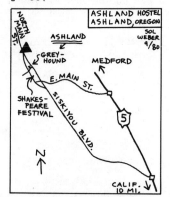

ASHLAND HOSTEL
ASHLAND, OREGON
SOL WEBER 9/80

DIRECTIONS: Three exits from Interstate 5 to the center of town. Hostel located 2 Blocks from bus station on the Main Street across from three historic Victorian houses.
D Bandon, Oregon 170 mi W
Mt. Shasta, CA 90 mi S

BANDON ⌂ SEA Star Traveler's Hostel, 375 2nd St, Bandon, OR 97411
⌂ Jim Kennett, Sue Bristow, Charlie Anderson, Steve Berry, Susan Fitch, Sharon Trompeter
🕿 503-347-9533
🛏 ♀ 15 ♂ 10
🛈 Apr 1-Oct 31
● $3.50
▲ Sea Star Collective
⌂ Hot & cold
⌂ Grain & Goods Coop, next door
🛈 yes
🚌 Greyhound in Bandon
🚲 Roseburg 70 mi
🚴 Mike's Bike Repair ¼ mi
🚗 At hostel
✈ Air West, North Bend 25 mi
* Small town artist community; beautiful ocean beaches; dunes, cliffs & rock formations; horseback riding; beachcombing, museum, historic lighthouse.
🏧 yes
DIRECTIONS: Just off Hwy 101 on 2nd St. in "Old town Bandon."
🏴 Coos Bay 23 mi N, Arcata 170 mi S

COOS BAY Sea Gull, 438 Elrod, P.O. Box 847, Coos Bay, OR 97420
🕿 (503) 267-6114
🛈 June 15-Labor Day
● $3 S
▲ 1st Presbyterian Church, P.O. Box 847, 97420
⌂ Hot & cold
⌂ 1-6 blks
🚌 Greyhound
🚲 This year, a few blks away
🚗 At hostel, $4
✈ Eugene 125 mi
* Coos Bay is a lumber & shipping town. Sand dunes & beaches.
🍴 I-III $4

MITCHELL Oregon Hotel, Main St, Box 12, Mitchell, OR 97750
⌂ Donna Heller & Judy North
🕿 462-3534
🛏 24
🛈 Open all year
● $3 per bunk
▲ Bikecentennial
⌂ Hot & cold
⌂ Norton's ½ blk W
🛈 yes
🚌 Mitchell
🚲 Pineville 47 mi
✈ Redmond 60 mi
* Recreation room with books & magazines, quiet games & TV. Tennis court, outdoor fireplace & park with a playground. Painted Hills Park Fossil Beds.

SISTERS, Santiam Lodge, Star
Rt, Sisters, OR 97759
🏠 Edward & Alice Patterson
☎ Bend, OR Mobile: YJ4-0594
131
🛏 ⚥ 20 ⚥ 23
🍴 May 1-Nov 1
● $3 S
SN This is a Presbyterian Camp.
When there is a group in,
kitchen is not available for
use by hostelers. Can pro-
vide meal with warning
($1.50).
♨ Hot & cold
⌂ Hostel—limited
🚌 At hostel
🚴 Bend 40 mi
🚗 At Hostel
✈ Redmond 40 mi

⚓ yes
* Swimming, horseback
riding, hiking, skiing, Saw-
yers Ice Caves (7 mi), mountain climbing, rivers, waterfalls, Backpacks available for
rent $1 per day.
** Fireplace, ping pong, piano,
quiet games, books, maga-
zines, volleyball field.

DIRECTIONS: 20 mi W of Sisters, on US Hwy 20, right at
Milepost 80. Also: 87 mi E of
Salem, taking Hwy 22 then
Hwy 20 the last 5 mi. Also 80
mi E of Albany on Hwy 20 all
the way.
🏠 Mitchell 100 mi E, Coos Bay
190 mi SW

BOWMANSVILLE 🏠 Bowmansville Youth Hostel, Box 117,
Bowmansville, PA 17507

BOWMANSVILLE
YOUTH HOSTEL

Operated by AYH National

🏠 M/M Roger Lawn
☎ (215) 445-4831
🛏 also groups ⚥ 20 ⚥ 20
🍴 Jan 6-Dec 19
⚑ Sept 15-May 15
● $3.50 S
SN The Hostel is the oldest bldg
in town
▲ Owned/operated by AYH Inc.
♨ Hot & cold
ⓕ yes
🚌 Reading 15 mi or Zinn's

Diner 6 mi
🚆 Reading or Lancaster
🚴 Martin's Bicycle Shop 8 mi
✈ Reading or Lancaster
* Sumptuous Penn Dutch
meals; Phares Hurst,
445-6186. Hiking on Horse-
shoe Trail; Ephrata Cloister,
Green Dragon Farmer's
Market (Fridays)
⚓ yes
DIRECTIONS: In center of town
at intersection of Rt 625 &
Maple Grove Rd. 13 mi S of

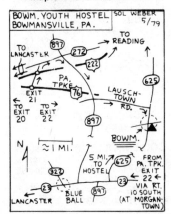

BOWM. YOUTH HOSTEL SOL WEBER
BOWMANSVILLE, PA. 5/79

Reading
🏠 Denver Youth Hostel 10 mi W, Geigertown 11 mi E

BRICKERVILLE 🏠/🏠 Cannon Hill Hostel, Rt 1, Box 687, Fox Rd, Newmanstown, PA 17073
🏠 Mr. & Mrs. Paul Hagel
🕿 (717) 626-6277
🛏 ♦ 20 ♦ 20
🏠 March 1-Dec 1
♦ yes, if large group
● $3.50 S, $3.50 W
♨ Hot & cold
⌂ Buy groceries before you come to hostel. Mountain Trail Groceries 1½ mi N of Spring Lake Park on Rt 501, closed Monday.
♦ yes
🚌 Lititz 6 mi N
🚏 on Sundays, Lancaster 20 mi
🚴 Lititz 6 mi
🚗 At Hostel
✈ Lancaster 18 mi
✳ Landis Valley Farm Museum 10 mi; Lititz Pretzel House 7 mi; Lancaster Farmers Market, Tues & Fri 20 mi; Ephrata Cloisters 10 mi; Middle Creek Wildlife 3 mi; Chocolate Museum Lititz 7 mi; first distillery in America 4 mi; swimming at Spring Lake Park.
🛏 $1

DIRECTIONS: Call hostel for directions.

COLLEGEVILLE 🏠 Evansburg State Park Youth Hostel, 837 Mayhall Rd, Collegeville, PA 19426
🏠 M/M Alan Levitsky
🕿 (215) 489-4326

🛏 ♦ 15 ♦ 15
🏠 Jan 6-Dec 19. Reservations by phone or mail, Sept 15-May 15
● $3.50 S
SN Park gate at Mill Rd is locked at 8 PM; walk or bike ½ mi to hostel.
▲ AYH, Inc. by lease from State of Pennsylvania
♨ Hot & cold
⌂ Keyser's on Germantown Pike in Evansburg 1½ mi
♦ yes, complete
🕿 Norristown 10 mi

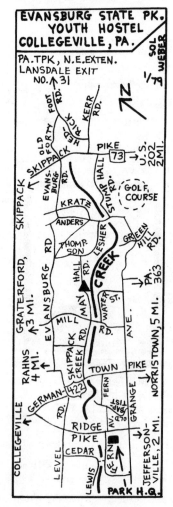

🚲 Norristown 10 mi

🚲 Tailwind Bicycle Shop in Creamery 3 mi

✈ Collegeville

✱ 3,400 acre State Park hiking, biking & fishing in Skippack Creek. Horseback riding. Skiing in Spring Mount 7 mi; Audubon Bird Sanctuary 5 mi; Valley Forge National Park 10 mi.

★ Family rooms available by reservation

⚠ yes

DIRECTIONS: From Collegeville take 422 (Germantown Pike) E 2 mi to Skippack Creek Rd; turn left. Go 1 mi to Mill Rd & turn left. Go 10 yds & turn right on Mayhall Rd. Hostel is first house on left.

🏠 Weisel apprx. 18 mi, Ridley Creek apprx. 20 mi, Chamounix Mansion apprx. 20 mi

DENVER 🏠 Denver, Rt 1, Stevens, PA 17578

🏠 Mr. & Mrs. Alvin Enck

☎ 215-267-5166

🛏 ♂ 20 ♀ 20

🏠 March 1-Dec 1

⬆ Especially if group; self-addressed stamped envelope requested with reservations

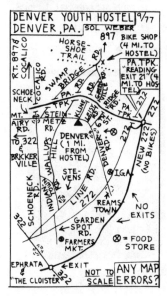

● $3.50 S, $3.50 W

☛ yes

🚌 Lancaster

🚲 Lancaster

🚲 J & J Bike Shop, Reinholds, 4 mi

🚗 At Hostel

✱ Farmers Market 4 mi; Cloister 5 mi; Landis Valley Museum 12 mi; Horseshoe Trail 2 mi; Horses stabled & for rent across street.

DIRECTIONS: 1 mi from Denver on corner of Steinmetz & Kline road.

🏠 Brickerville or Cannon Hill 12 mi W, Bowmansville 12 mi E

DOWNINGTOWN Marah Creek State Park Youth Hostel, N. Reeds Rd, Lyndel, PA. A 30-bed hostel, located on the East Coast Bicycle Trail will open in June 1981. Contact AYH National Office for details.

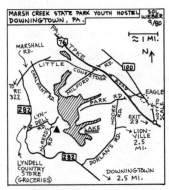

FOMBELL (Zelienople) 🏠 Camp Silver Lake, Box 810, RD 1, Fombell, PA 16123

🏠 Janet Bagnell

☎ (412) 452-6720

🛏 ♂ 22 ♀ 15

⬆ yes

● $2.50 S, $3 W, $1 tenting overnight

SN No smoking in bldgs

▲ Lawrence Nelson, MD, 125 Lute Lane, West Mifflin, PA 15122

🚰 Hot & cold

🛒 General Store 1½ mi W

☛ yes

🚐 Zelienople 3 mi E
🚲 Pittsburgh 40 mi S
🏍 Stefflers 3 mi E in Zelienople
🚗 at camp
✈ Pittsburgh 30 mi S
⚓ yes
* Ski lodge with fireplace, books & magazines; volleyball field; swimming pool; hiking, tobogganing & cross country skiing on hostel grounds; canoeing on Connquenessing Creek bordering hostel. Brush Creek Park 5 mi, McConnell's Hill State Park 10 mi, Moraine State Park 13 mi, Harmony Museum 4 mi, Lake Arthur 13 mi, Wildwood Highlands Si Area 20 mi.
★ yes, by prior arrangement
🚐 no

DIRECTIONS: From Zelienople (at Rt 19 & 68), follow sign for 288 & 588 W, at fork in road follow Rt 588 W (left); watch for camp sign on left, 3 mi from Zelienople. Hostel is 30 mi N of Pittsburgh.

GEIGERTOWN 🏠 Shirey's Hostel, P. O. Box 49, Geigertown, PA 19523
🏠 M/M David O. Shirey
☎ 215/286-9537
🛏 ♂ 24 ♀ 24
🛏 ♂ 10 ♀ 10
🏠 Mar 1-Dec 1; (Dec 1-Mar 1, 20 beds)
🍴 yes
● $4 S, $5 W
⚲ Hot & cold
⊓ At Hostel
⚓ yes
🚐 17 mi
🚲 7 mi
🏍 5 mi
🚗 At Hostel

🚐 yes
📋 Linens $1.25/set
⚑ Bowmansville 15 mi W, Evansburg 25 mi E

HOOVERSVILLE Camp Harmony YH RD 1, Hooversville, PA 15936
🏠 Larry & Barbara Deffenbaugh
☎ (814) 798-8128
🛏 ♂ 40 ♀ 40
● $2.50 S, $3.75 W
▲ Western District Church of the Brethren & Pittsburgh Council
⚲ Hot & cold
⊓ Foodrite 1 mi E in Hooversville
⚑ yes
🚐 Somerset 3 mi W
🚲 Johnstown 15 mi
🏍 City Cycle, 3217 Elton Rd, 9 mi Johnstown
✈ Somerset 16 mi S
* Recreation room with fireplace, piano, shuffleboard, & rubber horseshoes. Volleyball, badminton, swimming pool, softball, outdoor fireplace & tennis. Swimming on site. Canoeing 15 mi, Hiking trail, skiing.

DIRECTIONS: 6 mi to Stoystown N, 1 mi from Hooversville W, 16 mi N of Somerset, 15 mi S of Johnston
⚑ Mt. Pleasant 40 mi W

LaANNA 🏠 LaAnna YH, Rt 2, Box 1026, Cresco, PA 18326

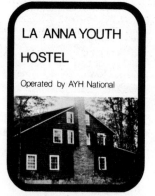

LA ANNA YOUTH HOSTEL

Operated by AYH National

🏠 Mr. & Mrs. Roy L. Walter
☎ (717) 676-9076

■ ♦ 20 ♦ 20
🔼 Nov 1-April 1
🚪 closed Dec 24-25; Dec 31-Jan 1
● $3.50 May 1-Sept 30; $4.50 Oct 1- April 30
SN operated by National AYH
🏠 Hot & cold
⌂ 5 mi, buy groceries before coming to hostel
♂ yes
🚌 Martz or Greyhound, Mt. Pocono
✱ Tobyhanna State Park, hiking trails, swimming, boating, picnic area. Promised Land State Park & Bruce Lake Natural area 12 mi.
🔺 yes

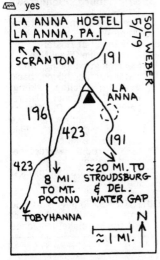

DIRECTIONS: 28 mi E of Scranton, 12 mi N of Mt. Pocono, 5 mi S of Newfoundland, 300 yds S of junction of Rts 191 & 423 on dirt road.
🏠 Quakertown 55 mi S; Bushkill 35 mi E

MEDIA Ridley Creek Park YH, 841 Sycamore Mills Rd, Media, PA 19063
📞 (215) LO6-9846
■ 20 ♦ & ♦
● $3.50 S
🔺 AYH, Inc. by lease from State of Pennsylvania
🏠 Hot & cold
⌂ Media 3.8 mi
🚌 Newtown Square 4.5 mi

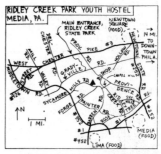

🚲 Media Cycle Center, State & Providence 3.5 mi
✱ Ridley Creek State Park which has a 5 mi bike trail, horseback riding & trout fishing; cross-country skiing; noteworthy fall splendor; birding
★ yes
DIRECTIONS: Located on the bicycle trail in Ridley Creek State Park 3.8 mi N of Media (N on Ridley Creek Rd; W on Sycamore Mills Rd), 4.5 mi SW of Newtown Sq. (SW on Bishop Hollow Rd, W on Sycamore Mills Rd). 10 mi E of West Chester (E on Rt 3 & S on 352; E on Sycamore Mills Rd). There is a wooden gate at each end of Sycamore Mills Rd (speed limit 15 mph).
🏠 Philadelphia 16 mi E, Geigertown 37 mi NW

MOUNT PLEASANT 🏠 Laurelville Mennonite Church Center, (SA No kitchen/rates) Rt 5, Box 145, Mount Pleasant, PA 15666
🏠 Resident Staff
📞 412-423-2056
■ ♦ 15 ♦ 15
🔼 Advance reservations required
● $5.50 S, $6.50 W
🏠 Hot & cold
⌂ Mountain Getaway Grocery
🚌 Greensburg 16 mi
🚃 Greensburg 16 mi
🚲 Youngwood 12 mi
🚴 on premises
✈ Pittsburgh
🔺 yes
★ yes
♦ Meal prices available upon request.

⌂ $2
SN Will close Oct 1, 1981
DIRECTIONS: 3 mi E of Mt. Pleasant on Rt 31, ½ mi N on Rt 982, ½ mi to right on a Co. road
⌂ Ohiopyle 35 mi S

NEWTOWN Tyler State Park Hostel, P.O. Box 94, Newtown, PA 18940
⌂ Doug Maas
☏ (215) 968-0927
⊨ ⚡ 15 ⚡ 15
● $3.50 S
* Theodore Roosevelt State Historical Park 10 mi E; Washington Crossing State Park 10 mi E
AYH yes
DIRECTIONS: From the PA Turnpike Exit 27 follow PA Rt 322 E out of Willow Grove through Richboro. From Exit 28 follow PA Rt 1 N to Interstate Hwy 95. Follow I95 N Newtown Yardly exit. Head W through Newtown to the park on PA Rt 322. By train from New York City, go to Trenton, NJ; then, Newtown is an easy 15 mi bicycle ride. Note: Vehicles not allowed on park roads. Use access &

parking from Swamp Road.
⌂ Quakertown 40 mi NW, Evansburg (Collegeville) 40 mi W, Philadelphia 20 mi S

OHIOPYLE ⌂ P.O. Box 99, Ohiopyle, PA 15470
⌂ Peter Slavic & Robbie Matesic
☏ 412/329-4476
⊨ 24 ⚡ 12 ⚡ 12
● $3 S, $3.50 W
▲ Pgh. Council AYH & Ohiopyle State Park
⌂ Hot & cold
⌂ Falls Market ¼ mi S
⚑ yes
🚌 Uniontown 20 mi W
🚍 Greensburg, Johnstown 50-75 mi N
🚲 The Bike Path, Uniontown, 20 mi W
🚗 parking lot at Hostel
🚐 Connellsville 25 mi NW
* Swimming, canoeing, whitewater rafting, hiking, backpacking, cycling, skiing. Ferncliff National Natural Landmark, Bear Run Nature Reserve, Ohiopyle Falls. See Frank Lloyd Wright's "Fallingwater" 6 mi N.
** Living room w/fireplace, quiet games. Large, very private grounds for picnicking & play
AYH yes
DIRECTIONS: Riding S as you enter town, cross 2 sets of RR tracks, make immediate

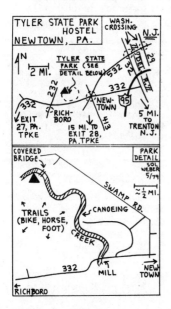

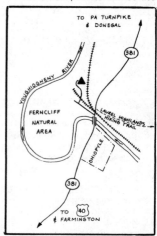

184

right turn before crossing bridge, bear right on gravel.

🏠 Mt. Pleasant 25 mi N; Morgantown, WV 35 mi SW

PALMYRA 🏠 Camp Seltzer (SA, serve other than hostelers & rates not same as regular rates) 651 S. Green St, Palmyra, PA 17078

🏠 Daniel & Mary Alice Herner
🕿 (717) 838-4957
🛏 ♀ 15 ♂ 15
🛏 ♀ 15 ♂ 15
🔧 Open only for organized, chaperoned groups of 10 or more with $15 deposit & advance reservations.
● $5
SN We do not supply pillows or sheets. No mail delivery at camp.
▲ First United Methodist Church, Palmyra
🚰 Hot & cold
🍴 Weis 1 mi
♂ yes
🚌 Lebanon 9 mi
🚆 Harrisburg 20 mi
🚲 Roy's Bike Shop 1 mi
🚗 on site
🚗 Harrisburg-Middletown 22 mi
* Seltzer's Bolonga Factory 2 mi; Hershey Amusement Pk. 4 mi; Chocolate World 4 mi; Founders Hall & M.S. Hershey School 8 mi.

left on Franklin St. Houseparents house is second on right. He will direct you to hostel.

🏠 Brickerville 20 mi SE

PHILADELPHIA 🏛 Chamounix Mansion, Philadelphia Intl. Youth Hostel & Community Meeting Center, West Fairmont Park, Philadelphia, PA 19131

🏠 Bruce & Debby Paige
🕿 (215) 878-3676
🛏 ♀ 20 ♂ 20
🛏 additional 20 in the summer
🏠 Jan 15-Dec 15
🔧 yes, for groups
● $4
▲ City of Philadelphia & Fairmount Park & Friends of Chamounix Mansion
🚰 Hot & cold
🍴 ¾ mi; buy food before coming to hostel
♂ yes
🚌 Greyhound & Trailways 7 mi; City bus stop ¾ mi
🚆 Penn & Reading 6 mi, Philadelphia
🚲 South Street Bicycle, 626 S. 4th St
🚗 available at hostel
🚗 18 mi SE
* Fairmount Park Trolley. Playhouse in the Park summer theatre Center City & In-

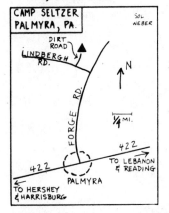

CAMP SELTZER PALMYRA, PA.   SOL WEBER

DIRT ROAD
LINDBERGH RD.
FORGE RD.
¼ MI.
N
422
422
TO LEBANON & READING
PALMYRA
TO HERSHEY & HARRISBURG

DIRECTIONS: Turn S from Rt 422 onto Forge Rd. Ride 5 blks & turn right onto E. Birch St. Ride 2 blks & turn

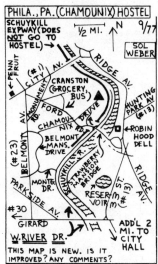

PHILA., PA. (CHAMOUNIX) HOSTEL
SCHUYKILL EXPWAY (DOES NOT GO TO HOSTEL) →   ½ MI.   N   9/77
SOL WEBER
PENN FRUIT   CITY AV. (#1)   RIDGE AV.
CRANSTON GROCERY, BUS)
MONUMENT AV.   FORD RD.
CHAMOU-NIX DRIVE   HUNTING PARK AV (#13)
BELMONT AV. (#23)   BELMONT MANS. DRIVE   ROBIN HOOD DELL
SCHUYLKILL R.   STRAWBERRY MANSION BRIDGE   RIDGE AV.
MONTE DR.   RESERVOIR   ST. (#3)
PARKSIDE AV.   #30   SCHUYLKILL R.   ADD'L 2 MI. TO CITY HALL
GIRARD   W. RIVER DR.
THIS MAP IS NEW. IS IT IMPROVED? ANY COMMENTS?

dependence Hall; Liberty Bell, Phila. Museum of Art, Franklin Institute of Science, & the US Mint.

** Bicycling through Fairmount Park. Ping pong, badminton & piano at hostel.

✗ yes, limited

🔔 yes

🛏 50¢

→ Built in 1802. First city-owned hostel in the U.S.A.

DIRECTIONS: 7½ mi NW of Philadelphia City Hall from Center city, cycle NW on Benjamin Franklin Parkway to Art Museum, follow signs (except 7-9:30 AM) to W. River Dr. Continue up Drive, bearing left just before road passes under Strawberry Mansion Bridge, turn left at Bridge, then every right till you reach mansion. Bus no. 38 from Center city. Pick up on JFK Blvd at 19th St. Get off at Ford & Cranston Rds. ¾ mi to the Hostel.

🏠 Media 16 mi SW; Evansburg 18 mi NW

PITTSBURGH Pt. Park College YH (SA, no kitchen) 201 Wood St, Pittsburg, PA 15222

🏠 Janet D. Evans

☎ 412/391-4100

🛏 30 Sept 1-May 1

🛏 200 May 1-Sept 1

🔔 Sept-May

⊖ $5 S, $5 W

▲ Pt. Park College

🎵 3 blks

🚌 Greyhound/Trailways (8 blks)

🚃 AMTRAK/B&O

🚲 Across st. $3.75/day

✈ Pittsburgh Intern. 15 mi

DIRECTIONS: From AMTRAK & Bus: 4 blks E (downtown) on Liberty Ave., left on Wood St., 5 blks. On Wood St between 3rd Ave. & Blvd of the Allies.

QUAKERTOWN 🏠 Weisel Youth Hostel, RD No. 3, Quakertown, PA 18951

🏠 Mr. & Mrs. Steven Schafer

☎ (215) 536-8749

🛏 ♂ 12 ♀ 12

🛏 closed Feb 13-19 & Sept 14-21

🔔 Advance booking, required for all groups

⊖ $2.50 S, $3 W

▲ Bucks Co. Dept. of Parks & Rec.

🚰 Hot & cold

🎵 Quakertown 4 mi

♀ yes

🚌 Quakertown 4 mi

🚃 Lansdale 10 mi

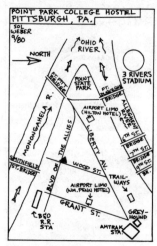

POINT PARK COLLEGE HOSTEL PITTSBURGH, PA.

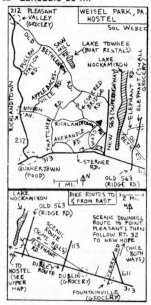

WEISEL PARK, PA. HOSTEL

⚡ Quakertown 4 mi
🚏 at Hostel
🚌 Allentown 15 mi
✲ Winter cross-country skiing, sledding, ice skating; Summer, hiking, fishing, swimming, boating.
✶ yes, by reservation
🚗 yes

DIRECTIONS: 4 mi S of Quakertown. Follow Rt 313 S from Quakertown to Wagon Wheel Inn, turn left on Sterner Mill Rd, turn left at Clymer Rd, to dead end. Turn left on Richlandtown Rd, then right into hostel. Hostelers coming from Phila. go N on Rt 611, turn left on Rt 313 W. Continue about 12 mi, turn right on Rt 563. Go ¾ mi to Sterner Mill Rd. Left on Sterner Mill Rd then a right onto Richlandtown Rd. Hostel is ¼ mi down road on right side.

🏠 Evansburg 25 mi SW, Philadelphia 40 mi S

WILLIAMSPORT YMCA Wayside, (SA) 343 W. 4th St, Williamsport, PA 17701
🏠 Margaretta Bower
☎ (717) 323-7134
🛏 ⚦ 20 ⚦ 20

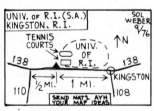

🏠 April 30-Sept 30 (7 PM daily; closing time 9 AM daily)
● $2.50 includes YMCA membership fee
SN Bring sleeping bags
🚰 Hot & cold
🛒 Weiss Market 3 blks W
🍴 yes
🚌 Continental Trailways 4 blks
🚲 Tilly's Bike Shop 2 mi
✈ Williamsport, Lycoming Airport 5 mi
✲ Swimming pool, gyms, bowling lanes, fishing, hunting & hiking.
✶ yes, by reservation
DIRECTIONS: Located on corner of 4th & Elmira Sts, downtown Williamsport.
🏠 Palmyra

RHODE ISLAND
Greater Boston Council, 251 Harvard St., Brookline, MA 02146 (617) 731-6692

KINGSTON University of Rhode Island YH, (SA) University of Rhode Island Memorial Union, Kingston, RI 02881
🏠 James & Kiki Latimer
☎ (401) 789-3929
🛏 ⚦ 8 ⚦ 7
🏠 Closed Dec 21-31. Open rest of year (hours 7:30-11 PM)
● $4
SN No cooking facilities
▲ Kingston Student Services, KSS Inc.
🚰 Hot & cold
🛒 Kingston Hill Store 1 mi
🚌 URI, 1 mi
🚆 West Kingston 1 mi
🚲 "Hi Wheeler" 8 mi in Wakefield
🚗 Lot on site

✈ 22 mi Green State Airport
⚓ yes, $1.50
✲ URI campus 1 mi; stores & restaurants 1 mi; Great Swamp Canoeing 1 mi; Atlantic Ocean beaches 5 mi; quiet games, ping pong, badminton & volleyball; FREE POPCORN AT NIGHT.
✶ 1 room with reservations

RHODE ISLAND

⌂ 50¢
DIRECTIONS: 1 mi W of URI entrance on Rt 138 or 25 mi E of Interstate 95 on Rt 138.
♛ Newport 30 mi E

NEWPORT Newport Armed Services YMCA, 50 Washington Sq. Newport, RI 02840
⌂ Robert L. Johnson
☏ (401) 846-3120
▬ 25 ⚡ 12 ⚡ 13
▬ 25 ⚡ 13 ⚡ 12
⬆ reservations only
● $5.50 S
SN Reservations only
▲ Armed Services YMCA
⌂ Hot & cold
⌂ Almacs ½ mi
🚌 2 blks
🚲 1 blk
🚗 on street
✈ 25 mi
✳ Beaches, ocean drive, mansions, music festivals, sailing

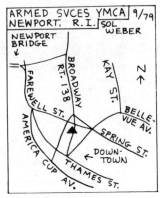

events, sporting events, historical sites.
✳✳ Accommodations for larger groups

♛ Kingston 30 mi W; New London, CT 75 mi W

SOUTH DAKOTA
Minnesota Council, 475 Cedar Street, St. Paul, 55101
(612) 292-4126

RAPID CITY YMCA (SA, no kitchen, mixed dorm) 815 Kansas City St, Rapid City, SD 57701
⌂ Director, George Zeise
☏ (605) 342-8538
▬ 12 cots in 1 room
⌂ June 1-Aug 30
⬆ Call ahead. Building is not always open but arrangements can be made to open if notified ahead.
▲ YMCA
⌂ Hot & cold
⌂ 6 blks
🚌 Jack Rabbit, Trailways 7 blks
🚗 on street (meters during day)
✳ Mt. Rushmore 20 mi; Black Hills outside city; Badlands 60 mi; Wounded Knee 100 mi

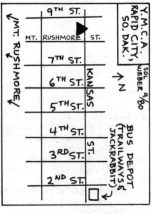

✳✳ Swimming pool, gameroom

TENNESSEE

GATLINBURG Bell's Wa-Floy Retreat Hostel, Box 212, Rt 3, Gatlinburg, TN 37738

⌂ Floy Bell
☏ (615) 436-5575
▬ ⚡ 10 ⚡ 10

188

- $5 S, $6 W
- yes
- Trailways front door
- Asheville or Knoxville
* Recreation room, fireplace, quiet games, volleyball field, swimming pool, softball & equipment, outdoor fireplace, horseback riding 1 mi, hiking, skiing, water slide 3 mi; The Great Smoky Mt. National Park.
- $1
- Only by prior arrangements.

DIRECTIONS: 10 mi E of Gatlinburg on Hwy 73 E; ¼ mi W of Cobbly

- Wesser NC 75 mi E

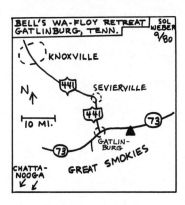

TEXAS

AUSTIN Austin Youth Hostel, 1312 Newning Ave, Austin, TX 78704

- Janette Ingram/David Smith
- 512/442-1584
- ⇥ 10 ⇥ 8
- except first Sunday of every month
- Recommended all year
- $4 S, $4 W

SN Closed first Sunday of each month. Complete laundry facilities.

- Hot & cold
- Safeway 1 mi
- yes
- 1 mi Greyhound
- Amtrak 2 mi
- 2 mi
- on street, free
- Manor Rd 10 mi
* Well-known progressive country & rock groups play regularly at local clubs; swimming at Barton Springs.
* No private rooms, but children welcome
- yes
- $1

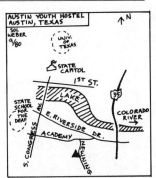

→ See the deep South in its fullest splendor. Spring & autumn are most spectacular.

DIRECTIONS: From downtown Greyhound Bus), S on Congress; cross river; left on Academy; right on Newning 1 blk. Catch No. 14 Travis Heights bus at corner 6th & Colorado. Get off corner Newning & Riverside Dr 3 blks S on Newning.

- Albuquerque 800 mi WNW; Marion, KS 800 mi N

VERMONT

COLCHESTER Mrs. Farrell's Youth Hostel, Williams Rd, RD No. 4, Colchester, VT 05446

- Ms. Nancy Farrell

- 802-878-8222
- 5
- Absolutely!
- $3 S
- Cold

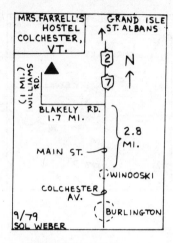

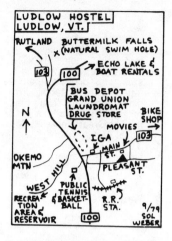

⌂ 2 houses away
☞ yes
🚌 8 mi
🚆 6 mi
🚲 8 mi
🛶 In front of hostel
✈ 8 mi
* Beach, swimming, canoe & sailboat rental.
✶ yes

DIRECTIONS: Rts 2 & 7 (Colchester Ave) to Winooski, straight on Main St. (still Rts 2 & 7) for 2.8 mi. Left on Blakeley Rd 1.7 mi. Right on Williams Rd 1 mi. White cottage, green trim.
⚑ Waterbury 30 mi approx.

LUDLOW Ludlow Youth Hostel, 44 Pleasant St, Ludlow, VT 05149
⌂ Barbara Storrs/Rich Russo
☎ 802-228-5127 or 228-8646
🛏 ⚹ 10 ⚹ 10
     ⚹ 10 ⚹ 10
🏠 May 15-Oct 1
⚑ yes
● $3 S
⚐ Barbara Storrs/Rich Russo
⚑ Hot & cold
⌂ IGA
☞ yes
🚌 1/10 mi
🚆 1/10 mi
🚲 1 mi
🚗 Available at Hostel
✈ North Springfield 18 mi
* Calvin Coolidge Homestead

Plymouth 15 mi. Killington Gondola Rt 100 N, 17 mi. Brumley Alpine Slide Rt 115 25 mi.
✶ yes
DIRECTIONS: Back to back with movie theatre on Main St. (Rt 103).
⚑ Rochester 44 mi N, Grantham, NH

ROCHESTER Schoolhouse Youth Hostel, Main St, Rt 100, Rochester, VT 05767
⌂ David Marmor
☎ (802) 767-9384
🛏 72
🏠 May 15-Oct 15, Nov 15-April 15
🎿 Ski season & weekends
● $2.50 S, $5 W
SN Ski Hostel
▲ Metro. NY Council, AYH
⚑ Hot & cold
⌂ The Arthur Murray Store 150 yds
🚌 Rutland 33 mi
🚆 White River Junction 45 mi
* Cross country skiing, Mt. Cushman, Maple sugaring, organic gardening, Long Trail, Texas Falls, tennis, architectural services. Moss Glen Falls, Bowl Mill.
✶ Family rooms
🔲 Passes sold
� A 150-year-old building
⚑ $1
⚑ Ludlow 44 mi S, Warren 25 mi N

ROCHESTER, VERMONT (POP. 900)
IN THE ♥ OF THE GREEN MTS.

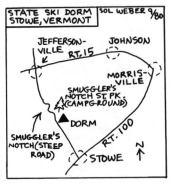

STATE SKI DORM STOWE, VERMONT   SOL WEBER 9/80

Winooski Home Hostel 50 mi W

STOWE ♠ Vermont State Ski Dorm (SA, state requirement), RD 1, Stowe, VT 05672
🏠 Gerry Spaulding
☏ (802) 253-4010 or 253-4014
▬ ↕ 26 ↕ 24
🏠 Dec 1-Apr 30 & June 1-Sept 30 (operates as ski lodge only during winter)
🍴 no
● $3 S, $14.97 W
SN Winter rate includes two meals
▲ Vermont Dept. of Forest, Parks & Recreation
🚰 Hot & cold
🏪 Stowe Country Shop 4 mi
🚚 yes
🚌 Russel's Taxi, Stowe 8 mi
🚂 Amtrak, Waterbury 15 mi
🚲 Stowe Bike Shop 6 mi
🚲 At dorm
✈ Burlington Airport 50 mi
⚜ no
∗ Swimming 1 mi, hiking 1 mi, horseback riding 2 mi, whitewater kayaking 15 mi, Alpine Slide & Gondola ride ½ mi, rock climbing 2 mi.
★ no
⚐ yes
→ Hostel is former CCC work camp built in 1930s; only state-operated ski lodge in East.
DIRECTIONS: 8 mi N of Stowe Village on Rt 108; 10 mi S of Jeffersonville on Rt 108.
🏠 Waterbury Center 15 mi S,

WARREN Homestead, Box 118 Warren, VT 05674
🏠 Thelma Ricketts
☏ 802-496-3744
▬ 45
● $2.50 S
SN Check for ski lodge rates in winter
🚰 Hot & cold
🏪 E. Warren Grocery 2.5 mi
🚚 yes
🚌 Montpelier
🚂 Montpelier 26 mi
🚲 Waitsfield 6 mi
✈ ½ mi
∗ Sugarbush ski area, polo field, airport, hiking Longtrail & Roxbury Mt, Sardi Mt, Prickley Mt, Bundy Art Gallery & concerts (free).
★ I $1.50-$2.00, III $5
DIRECTIONS: 2½ mi on E War-

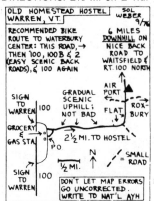

OLD HOMESTEAD HOSTEL   SOL WEBER 9/76
WARREN, VT.

ren Rd from Rt 100. Ask anyone in town for directions.

🏠 Waterbury Center 22 mi N, Rochester 25 mi S

WATERBURY CENTER 🏨 Ski Hostel Lodge, Waterbury Center, VT 05677

🏠 Martha Guthridge
☎ 802-244-8859
🛏 80 ⚓ 40 ⚓ 40
🏠 Hostel Summer, Ski Lodge, Winter, open hostel rates May 1-Nov 15
🍽 $4 S, $18-$22 W, inc. B & dinner
✉ yes
🚌 Waterbury 4 mi

🚂 Waterbury 4 mi
🚲 Stowe 6 mi
🚗 At hostel
✈ Montpelier 15 mi
∗ Hiking, swimming (lake), Alpine slide.
🛏 $1.50

DIRECTIONS: 4 mi N of Waterbury, look for sign on Rt 100. 4th house beyond traffic light.

WOODFORD 🏨 Greenwood Lodge, Rt 9, Woodford, P.O. Box 246, Bennington, VT 05201

🏠 Ed & Ann Shea

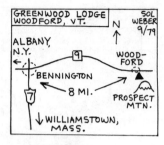

☎ 802-442-2547
🛏 40
🏠 July, Aug
⚓ Advance reservation recommended
◑ 197 Lyons Rd, Scarsdale, NY 10583
🍽 $5.80 in Lodge, tax included
SN Open 4:30 PM, close 9 AM
🚿 Hot & cold
🍴 Williams Market 7 mi on Rt 9, Twin Brooks Motel Groceries 3.8 mi E on Rt 9
✉ yes
🚌 Bennington 10 mi
🚂 Amtrak 50 mi
🚲 Giards & Up & Down Hill 10 mi
🚗 At Greenwood Lodge
✈ Bennington 15 mi
⚒ yes, $3.15 tax included
∗ Appalachian & long trail hiking 3 mi, winter alpine & cross country skiing Prospect Mt. & National Forest, Somerset & Wilmington reservoirs, summer theater 10 mi & 17 mi.
★ Advance reservations required.
🛏 $1.50 including 5 percent tax

DIRECTIONS: Approx. 8 mi E of Bennington off Rt 9, adjacent to Prospect Ski Mt. Enter thru ski area parking lot. Go past 2 posts, turn left, continue 1000 ft to hostel.

🏠 Lake George, NY 40 mi W; Pittsfield, MA 40 mi S; Ludlow 50 mi N; Keene, NH 50 mi E

VIRGINIA
Potomac Area Council, 1520 16th St., Suite A, NW, Washington, DC 20036 (202) 462-5780

LEESBURG ⌂ Caldwell, 88 Shenandoah St, Leesburg, VA 22075
🏠 Frank B. Caldwell
☎ (703) 777-1234
🛏 2
🔼 yes, all year
⊝ $4.50
SN Always call before coming
♨ Hot & cold
🍴 Safeway ½ mi
⚐ yes
🚌 Jock's Exxon 1 mi
🚍 Washington, D.C. 35 mi
🚶 ½ mi
🚲 ½ blk
✈ Dulles 19 mi, Washington 35 mi
⚓ no
* In historic Leesburg, 35 mi Washington, D.C., 40 mi Winchester, 35 mi Front Royal (entrace to Skyline Dr), 100 mi to Charlottesville, University of Virginia, Monticello, etc.
★ no
🖼 no
🎯 Washington, D.C. 35 mi SE

🏠 William Wade Douglas
☎ 804-776-6500. Transportation furnished weekdays from Williamsburg bus station 4 PM. Call 887-2500 (leave message).
🛏 5
🍽 30
⊝ $4.50 S, $5.75 W
▲ William Wade Douglas, Executive Director
♨ Hot & cold
🍴 Tall Chief Market 2.5 mi
⚐ Washer & dryer, dishwasher
🚍 Saluda 8 mi or Gloucester 10 mi
🚌 Williamsburg 40 mi
🚶 Williamsburg 40 mi
🚲 At hostel
✈ Newport News 40 mi, Richmond 60 mi
* Colonial Williamsburg, Busch Gardens, Mariners Museum, Kings Dominion (amusement park), 1781 Yorktown Hist. Revol. War Battlefield, (1607, 1st perm. English settlement) Jamestown Isl., Colonial Parkway 30 mi, protected bike path.
** Offers complete ocean sailing program advanced/beginners sailboats, nature trails, beach, arranges for historic tours, canoe or bicycle rental.
★ Private rooms
🖼 yes

CALDWELL HOME HOSTEL LEESBURG, VA.
SOL WEBER 9/80
RT. 7
RT. 15
↑ N
ARLINGTON 25 MI. →
¾ MI.
¾ MI.
SCATOCTIN CIRCLE
HARRISON ST.
ST.
SHENANDOAH ST.
ROANAKE ST.

URBANNA Sangraal-By-The-Sea, P.O. Box 187, Urbanna, VA 23175

SANG-RAAL-BY-THE-SEA HOSTEL URBANNA, VA.
SOL WEBER 9/80
↑ N
RAPPAHANNOCK RIVER
FREDERICKS-BURG
WAKE ☐ P.O.
626
SALUDA
33
17
↓ NEWPORT NEWS

VIRGINIA

🔦 I-$2 II-$2.50 III-$3
🛏 $1.50
➡ "Start where it all began — Historic Virginia dating back to 1607."

DIRECTIONS: Greyhound bus from Washington or Williamsburg to Saluda. Off Main Rt. Wash. D.C., Richmond, Norfolk I-64, heading S, take Hwy 301 or 17 to Saluda, N take I-64 & 17, from Saluda S on 33 to Farm Rd 626. Left from Wake Post Office. 2 mi to Waterfront Landing Mill Creek (10 mi from Urbanna).
🏠 Washington, D.C. 140 mi N

WASHINGTON
Washington State Council, 1431 Minor Avenue, Seattle, WA 98101 (206) 382-4180

ASHFORD The Lodge Youth Hostel, Box 86, Ashford, WA 98304
🏠 M/M Everett Woodward
☎ 206-569-2312
🛏 10
⊝ $3 S, $4.50 W
🚰 Hot & cold
🎵 Suver's Country Store, Ashford 5 mi
♂ yes
🚌 Tacoma 55 mi
🚂 Tacoma 55 mi
🚲 Puyallup 50 mi
✈ Seattle-Tacoma 75 mi
⛺ yes
* Mt. Ranier National Park. Excellent location for cross country skiing & snowshoeing.
➡ Oldest hostel in Washington state, 13 years.

DIRECTIONS: On Hwy 706, ¼ mi outside the Nisqually entrance to Mt. Ranier National Park; 54 mi SE of Tacoma; 90 mi SE of Seattle.
🏠 Seattle, SeaHaven 90 mi NW; Enumclaw

CARNATION 🏠 Carnation Hostel 32611 NE 50th, P.o. Box 238, Carnation, WA 98014
🏠 Don & Darcy Newman
☎ 206-333-4978, 333-4465, 333-4903
🛏 12 ♂ 6 ♀ 6
🛏 6 ♂ 3 ♀ 3
🕐 If we're gone, go around the blk & ask our neighbors
⊝ $3 S, $3.50 W
🚰 Hot & cold
🎵 IGA 5 blks 9-7 PM
♂ yes
🚌 Greyhound, Bellevue 20 mi, Metro Bus, 3 blks from Seattle
🚂 Seattle 30 mi
🚲 Redmond 14 mi
🚤 At hostel
✈ Seattle 30 mi
* Swim, float, hike, bike, read, talk, garden & spin wool in the country.
✦ yes

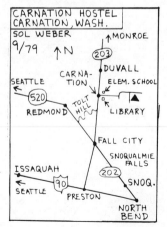

THE LODGE YOUTH HOSTEL ASHFORD, WASH.

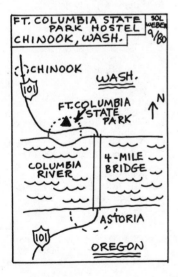

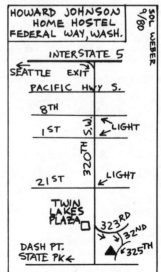

 yes

DIRECTIONS: In Carnation, turn E between grade school & library. Go 2 blks to a "T" turn left & immediately right. Go 2 blks to light brown house on right.

Seattle 30 mi W

CHINOOK Ft. Columbia, Box 224, Chinook, WA 98614

Frank Ross, Kaaren Black
(206) 777-8755
3 3
11 19
June 1-Sept 31
Oct 1-June 1; groups only
Washington AYH Council, 1431 Minor Ave, Seattle, 98101
$3 S
SN Check in at 5 PM & out 9 AM, unless other arrangements previously made.
Hot & cold
1 mi at Chinook
Utensils, elec. stove, refrig.
Astoria, OR 6 mi
Portland, OR 110 mi SE
Astoria, OR 6 mi away across toll bridge
Across the street
Portland, OR 110 mi SE
On Pacific Coast Bike Route, on grounds with Art Gallery, historic museums & hiking trails. Historic fort overlooking Columbia River estuary.

1 room
yes
I-75¢ III-$1
50¢ linens, pillow case, top sheet or blanket
DIRECTIONS: Hostel located in Ft. Columbia St. Park 2 mi E of Chinook. Hostel is 6 mi from Astoria, OR across bridge to N, take left turn off bridge, W 2 mi.

Lilliwaup 145 mi NE, Port Townsend 298 mi NE, Seattle 250 mi N

FEDERAL WAY (A) Howard Johnson Home Hostel, 3600 SW 325, Federal Way 98003

Mr. & Mrs. Howard Johnson
(206) 838-0587
3
2
Oct-May
yes
Olympic, WA; (206) 866-9007
$2 S
Hot & cold
Johnnys ¾ mi
yes
Tacoma, Seattle
Schwinn Federal Way 3 mi
driveway (2 cars)
Seattle

** Family members & college students occasionally may do own looking on private golf course.

★ no

🔊 no

🍴 I-50¢ II-$1 III-$2 I-III-$3.50

DIRECTIONS: Bus to Federal Way 320th & Prepe Hwy W on 320th to 323rd (past Trinlaces Plaza). Turn left, next 2 rights puts you on 325th, down a few blks on right. 3600, name on garage.

FEDERAL WAY (B) ⌂ 28th SW, Federal Way, WA 32021

🏠 Don & Edna Franklin

☎ (206) 927-1121

🛏 2

🏠 May-Sept

📞 Call on days to come

🍴 $3 S

🚿 Hot & cold

🚩 no

🚌 2 mi

🚉 Furview 10 mi

🚲 2 mi

✈ Seattle International 15 mi

⚓ no

* Rural setting. Private home on private gold course ½ mi from Puget Sound saltwater beach.

★ no

🔊 no

🍴 I-$1 II-$1 III-$2 I-III-$3

DIRECTIONS: 25 mi S of Seattle, 10 mi N of Tacoma, take 320th exit from I-5 & telephone. We pick up.

FEDERAL WAY (C) ⌂ A.W. Johnson (SA), Federal Way, WA

🏠 Adolph & Viola Johnson

☎ (206) 927-1558

🛏 ‍1 2

📞 yes, always

🍴 $3 S

▲ Adolph & Viola Johnson

🚿 Hot & cold

🚌 10 mi

🚉 10 mi

🚲 3 mi

🚏 our yard

✈ 10 mi

⚓ no

** Suburban home

★ no

🔊 no

🍴 I-$1.50 III-$2.50

DIRECTIONS: Directions will be given when reservation is made.

FRIDAY HARBOR Elite Hotel (yes, also a hotel), P.O. Box 555, Friday Harbor, WA 98250

☎ (206) 378-5555

🛏 45

● $8 S, $8 W

▲ Elite Hotels, Inc.

🚿 Hot & cold

🚩 Kings/Whiteys 1 blk

🚲 Island Bicycles 1 mi

🚏 At hostel

✈ Friday Harbor 1 mi

⚓ no

* Sailing, horseback riding, hiking trail (6 mi), hill climbing, biking. Tidepools, Island City Jazz Band Sat 1-5 at the Electric Co. Tavern.

** Modeled after the European hostel. Hot tubs & saunas available for rent.

★ By reservation

DIRECTIONS: 2 blks from Ferry Terminal, up Spring St & right on 1st (35 1st St).

🏠 Victoria, BC, Canada 4 hrs W, Vancouver, BC, Canada 4 hrs N

LILLIWAUP Mike's Beach (SA, no kitchen), Rt 1, Box 95, Lilliwaup, WA 98555

🏠 Robert & Trudy Schultz

☎ (206) 877-5324

🛏 ‍1 36 ‍1 10

🏠 April 15-Oct 15

● $3.25 S

🚿 Hot & cold

🚩 Mike's Beach Grocery, Eldon Store, 1.5 mi

🚩 yes

🚌 Shelton 30 mi

🚉 Shelton 30 mi

🚲 Clinton's, Shelton 30 mi

✈ Shelton 30 mi

* Olympic National Park, Gateway Hamma (2000′ on fjord-like arm of beach to mountain setting).

DIRECTIONS: 15 mi N of Hoodsport on Hwy 101.

🏠 Port Townsend 50 mi N, Nordland 40 mi N

NORDLAND ⌂ Fort Flagler State Park, Nordland, WA 98358

🏠 Joseph Iuro & Katy Iuro-Guthridge

☎ (206) 385-1288

🛏 8 ♦ 8 ♦ 4

🛏 8 ♦ 8 ♦ 4

🏠 May 1-Sept 30, rest of year by reservation

🔒 Oct 1-April 30

● $3

♨ Hot & cold

🍴 Nordland Trading Co. 4 mi

ℹ yes

🚌 Hadlock 9 mi

🚃 Seattle 60 mi

🚲 Port Townsend 20 mi

🛠 At hostel

🚐 Port Townsend 14 mi

* Historic bunkers & gun emplacements ½ mi. Miles of saltwater beaches.

🔺 yes

→ "The Hostel is located in Fort Flagler State Park, which is listed in the National Historic Register."

DIRECTIONS: From Port Townsend, take Hwy 20 or Discovery Rd (bike route) out of town, turn left where road forks to go to Chimicum & Fort Flagler. Stay for another 4 mi or so & make another left where a sign post points to Marrowstone Island, Indian & Fort Flagler State Park. Follow through the intersection in Hadlock onto 2nd left (first left goes to lower Hadlock). Continue on over Indian Island & onto Marrowstone Island. Follow road all the way through (about 6 mi) till you enter Fort Flagler State Park.

Keep on going straight past ranger office. Hostel is first bldg on left past open field. AYH sign on side of building.

🏠 Port Townsend 20 mi, Seattle 60 mi

OLYMPIA 🏠 Olympia on the Water, Olympia, WA

🏠 Dotty & Howard Johnson

☎ (206) 866-9017

🛏 4

🛏 2

🏠 Summer only, June 1-Sept 1

🔒 Call first

● $1 S, $4 with meals

♨ Hot & cold

🍴 Safeway 1½ mi

ℹ yes

🚌 107 E. 7th 2 mi

🚃 Amtrak Service to E. Olympia 3 mi

🚲 Falcones, 222 Division 2 mi

🛠 On property

🚐 7647 Old 99 Hwy SE, Tumwater 4 mi

🔺 yes

* Evergreen College 1 mi, State capitol 2 mi, swim, boat on property.

** Kayaking, clams, 5 other water sports

★ no

🔺 no

🗝 I-$1   II-50¢   III-$1.50 I-III-$4.00

DIRECTIONS: Phone & we will meet you.

PORT TOWNSEND 🏠 Fort Worden Youth Hostel, Fort Worden State Park, Port Townsend, WA 98368

🏠 Woody & Hiroko Dennis

☎ (206) 385-0655

🛏 30 ♦ 13 ♦ 12, (2 family rooms 5 beds)

🏠 Jan 4-Dec 16, except Thanksgiving

● $3.50

▲ Washington State AYH Council, 1431 Minor, Seattle 98101

♨ Hot & cold

🍴 Buy food from stores on Water St before coming to hostel.

ℹ yes

🚌 Greyhound 1 mi

🚲 Repairs: John Marckworth 385-4425 (weekend), Jan Dahline 385-4544; Parts:

Olympic Bike Shop, Western Auto
- Park laundromat
- Sea-Tac 70 mi
- Olympic National Park 63 mi, historical port town. Wooden boats, historical fort, beach, bus route between Victoria & Seattle ferry.
- ✶ 1 room, 3 beds, 1 room, 2 beds
- yes
- 75¢

DIRECTIONS: Rt 20 into Port Townsend, from edge of town follow signs to Fort Worden State Park. AYH Bldg 272 is 600 ft behind Park Office. Hostel is 2 mi from downtown.

Fort Flagler 21 mi, Lilliwaup 50 mi S

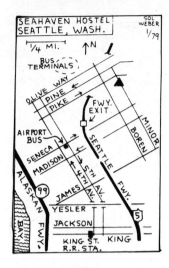

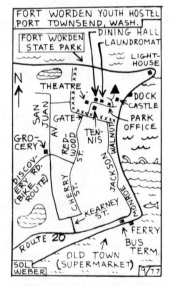

SEATTLE Sea Haven Youth Hostel 1431 Minor Ave, Seattle, WA 98101

- Gail Falkenhagen
- (206) 382-4170
- 200 (88 rooms)
- June-Sept (suggested)
- $5.50
- SN By referral through Sea Haven Hostel, visitors may go to any of 4 Home Hostels in the Seattle area.
- ▲ Sea Haven Hostels, Inc.
- Hot & cold
- 1 blk
- yes, no utensils provided
- Municipal bus 1 blk
- Amtrak 1 mi
- Pine St. Cycle 3 blks
- 1 blk
- Sea-Tac, 15 mi
- ✶ Lake Washington 3 mi, Cascade Mts. 40 mi, Olympic Mts. & Rain Forest 60 mi. Space Needle 2 mi, Pike Place Market 8 blks.

DIRECTIONS: Located on corner of Pike & Minor, 2 blks E of freeway.

Pt. Townsend 65 mi NW, Carnation 30 mi E

WEST VIRGINIA
Pittsburgh Council, 6300 Fifth Ave., Pittsburgh, PA 15232
(412) 362-8181

MORGANTOWN Chestnut Ridge Camp, P.O. Box 590, Morgantown, WV 26505

🏠 Les Studgel

📞 (304) 292-4773

🛏 Dormitory accommodations with/without blankets, can accommodate groups.

● $1.25 S

SN Camp is approx. 15 mi E of Morgantown. No public transportation from town to Hostel.

⌂ Sand Springs Campgrounds adjacent to Hostel.

⚑ Complete

🚌 Morgantown 15 mi

� Grafton 30 mi

🚲 Pathfinder 15 mi in Morgantown

🚢 Morgantown 15 mi

✳ Swimming, fishing, skiing. Surrounded by 13,000 acres of State Forest with numerous hiking trails.

DIRECTIONS: US Rt 48 from Morgantown to State Rt 73 to Chestnut Ridge Camp.

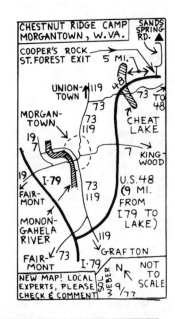

WISCONSIN
Wisconsin Council, 7218 W. North Avenue, Wauwatosa, WI
53213 (414) 257-2323
Minnesota Council, 475 Cedar Street, St. Paul, MN 55101
(612) 292-4126

CABLE Ches Perry Youth Hostel, Box 164, Cable, WI 54821

🏠 Mark Leonard

📞 715-798-3367

🛏 60 ♂ 30 ♀ 30

🏠 Ski season, from Thanksgiving until end of April, after April by reservation only.

⬆ April-Nov

● $2.50 S, $3.50 W

SN Reservations requested, 3712 N. Clark St, Chicago, IL 60613

⌂ Hot & cold

⌂ Rondeau's 3 mi W

⚑ yes

🚌 Cable 4 mi

🚆 Duluth 100 mi

🚲 Ashland 42 mi

🚗 At Hostel

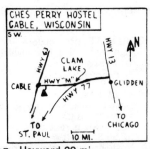

🚢 Hayward 20 mi

✳ Telemark Lodge Resort, skiing, canoeing, horseback riding, tennis, bicycling, 18 hole golf course, indoor & outdoor swimming pool, saunas.

** Ski lockers
→ I-$1.75 III-$3.25

DIRECTIONS: 2 mi E from Cable on County Rd M, then 2 mi S on Mt. Telemark Rd, next to Telemark Lodge.
⌂ Turtle Lake 82 mi SW, Hurley 72 mi NE

DODGEVILLE (A) ⌂ Spring Valley Trails, (SA, no bunks, pads only) RR 2, Box 156, Dodgeville, WI 53533
⌂ Rev. Philip & Lucille Yaeger
☏ 608-935-5725
⊨ 25 either sex
⬆ All year
● $4 S, $4 W
▲ Rev. Philip & Lucille Yaeger
⌂ Hot & cold, summer only
⌒ Lone Rock 8 mi
🚆 13 mi
🚌 Dubuque & Madison 45 mi
🚲 Barneveld 33 mi
🚑 On premises
🚐 Madison 50 mi
⚖ yes
* House on Rock 7 mi, Cave of Mounds 35 mi, Pendarvis House & Shake Rag Alley 22 mi, Swiss Village 33 mi, Wisconsin River 8 mi, Governor Dodge State Park 20 mi.
** Ecology rides, Sat summer only. Small general store & gift shop in summer.
✗ yes
→ "Heart of tourist area — end of driftless area & home of Wolfgap Rock & Exeriences."

⌂ Madison 45 mi E

DODGEVILLE (B) Folklore Village Farm, Rt 3, Dodgeville, WI 53533
⌂ Jane Farwell
☏ (608) 924-3725
⊨ ⚥ 12 ⚥ 13
⬆ Open all year, Sat overnights only. Closed Christmas.
🛏 Reservations required
● $2.50 S, $3.00 W
SN Hostelers welcome to our pot luck supper & community folk dance (with instruction) every Sat 7:30 PM.
▲ Wisconsin Council
⌒ Davis Grocery 3 mi E
⚖ yes

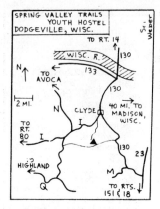

🚌 Greyhound 3 mi
🚌 Columbus 60 mi E
🚲 Barneveld 7½ mi E of Hostel
🚑 outside hostel
🚐 Madison 50 mi E
⚖ yes
* Recreation room with piano, record player, shuffleboard, folk music & folk dancing sessions. Fireplace & outdoor folk dancing platform. Swimming 3 mi, canoeing 8 mi, horseback riding at Gov. Dodge State Park, hiking, biking, skiing, all within 10 mi. Cave of the Mounds 10 mi, Little Norway Outdoor Museum 12 mi, Bl. Mound State Park 11 mi, Folk Music Festivals at Folklore Village.
** Rural Folk Arts Center
⌂ $1
DIRECTIONS: Go 2 mi W of Ridgeway on Hwy 18 & 1 mi S on Country Rd BB. The Hostel is 3 mi SW of Ridgeway, VT.
⌂ Dodgeville 20 mi NE, Madison 39 mi E

HURLEY Crystal Springs Dairy YH, 223 Silver St, Hurley, WI 54534
⌂ Irene & Don Mildren
☏ (906) 932-2222
⊨ ⚥ 20 ⚥ 20
⬆ Dec 15-Dec 31
● $3.25 S, $4.25 W
⌂ Hot & cold
⌒ Erspancer Super Market 1½ blks E
⚖ yes
🚆 1 mi

⚖ Giovaoni Hardware across street

🍴 7 mi

* Recreation room with radio, record player, quiet games. Swimming pool, sailing, canoeing, water skiing; horseback riding, hiking trails, biking trails, skiing. Four major ski areas are within 12 mi. Mt. Zion, Rainbow Falls, Lake of the Clouds, Greenwood Falls, Presqueisle, Copper Peak.

DIRECTIONS: 1 blk W of the intersection of US 51 & 77, on 77 which is also called Silver St, within city. The hostel is 24 mi N of Mercer.

🏠 Bessemer, MI 6 mi E; Cable 50 mi W

MADISON University YMCA, 306 North Brooks, Madison, WI 53715

🏠 Jeanette Fiefarek for women; Larry Gleasman for men

📞 (608) 257-2534

🛏 ⚡ 5 ⚡ 5

🌙 May 15-Aug 15

● $3 S

🚰 Hot & cold

🍴 International House of Foods, 1½ blks E

🚌 Madison 8 blks

⚖ Yellow Jersey, 419 State St, 5 blks

* Fireplace, piano, ping pong, pool table, TV. Outside recreation includes softball & tennis court. Sailing 2 blks; hikng, biking trails, skiing at Devil's Head in Baraboo, WI 30 mi

DIRECTIONS: The hostel is located in the center of the University of Wisconsin, Madison Campus

MILWAUKEE (Greendale) The Red Barn Youth Hostel, 6750 W. Loomis Rd, Greendale, WI 53129

🏠 Al & Joan Vitense

📞 (414) 529-3299

🛏 ⚡ 18 ⚡ 18

🌙 May 1-Oct 31

🔥 Requested

● $3 S, Day fee 50¢

▲ Milwaukee County

🚰 Hot & cold

🍴 1 mi NE in Greendale

⚑ yes

🚌 Greendale 2 mi

🚆 Milwaukee 12 mi

⚖ 1 mi NE on Loomis Rd

🚲 On hostel grounds

✈ Mitchell Field 5 mi

⚞ yes

DIRECTIONS: On Hwy 36, 10 mi SW of downtown Milwaukee. Corner of Root River Pkwy & Loomis Rd.

🏠 Dodgeville 100 mi W; Madison 80 mi W; Whitewater 40 mi SW; Chicago, IL 90 mi S

TURTLE LAKE 🏠 Timberlake Lodge, RR2, Turtle Lake, WI 54889

🏠 Jake Hoyer

📞 715-986-2484

🛏 20 ⚡ 10 ⚡ 10

🍴 10

🌙 Dec 1-Mar 15

● $3.25 S, $4.50 W

🚰 Hot & cold

🍴 Riley's 6 mi

⚑ yes

🚌 Turtle Lake 10 mi

🚆 Mpls.-St. Paul 75 mi

⚖ Amery 16 mi

✈ Mpls.-St. Paul 75 mi

⚞ yes

* Recreation room w/fireplace; Badminton, softball, swimming, sailing, canoeing, hiking & biking trails. (Local back roads only), skiing, ice skating. Hostel is on 900 acres of recreational educational center; nature trails, ski touring.

DIRECTIONS: 75 mi E of St. Paul, MN on Hwy 8, to Range, N on county road D to V, E 2½ mi.

WHITEWATER The Dock (SA, is part of resort), Rt. 2, Whitewater, WI 53190

🏠 Neil & Beverly Ferguson

📞 608-883-2856

🛏 ⚡ 8 ⚡ 16

🍴 ⚡ & ⚡ flexible

🔥 not required, but is desired

● $4.50 S

SN Reservations are recommended in summer, required rest of year. Send self-addressed stamped envelope for confirmation. $4.50

WYOMING

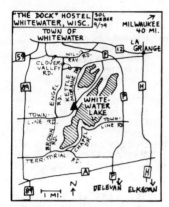

per person deposit required. Phone reservations accepted when followed by

- deposit.
- ⌂ Hot & cold
- ♫ on premises
- ☞ yes
- 🚌 Whitewater 6 mi
- 🚲 Whitewater 6 mi
- 🚗 on premises
- ✈ Milwaukee 50 mi
- ∗ Hostel is on Whitewater Lake in Kettle Moraine area. Fish, swim, boat, hike, bike, ski.
- ✷ yes

DIRECTIONS: From where 12 curves on S side of Whitewater, go 5 mi to P. Turn right. Go 3.4 mi to Kettle Moraine. Turn right & go 2.6 mi to resort.
- 🏠 Greendale 50 mi E

WYOMING
Rocky Mountain Council, 1107 12th Street, P.O. Box 2370
Boulder, CO 80306 (303) 442-9304

JACKSON HOLE (Teton Village), The Hostel (SA, no kitchen), Box 546, Teton Village, WY 83025

- 🏠 Colby & Joey Wilson
- ☎ 307-733-3415
- 🛏 240 ♂ & ♀
- 🔥 for winter
- ● 10% discount from rates
- ⌂ Hot & cold
- ♫ Village Store 100 yds
- 🚌 Jackson 12 mi
- 🚲 Jackson 12 mi
- 🚗 adjacent
- ✈ Jackson 22 mi
- ∗ 90 mi S of Yellowstone National Park. Teton Mtns. Skiing, fishing, trout fishing; movies nightly.
- ✷ yes

DIRECTIONS: Just N of Jackson. Midway between Moose & Wilson.

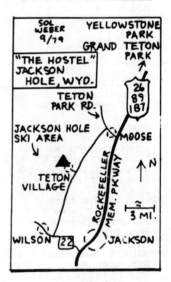

Hostel Locator
Maps

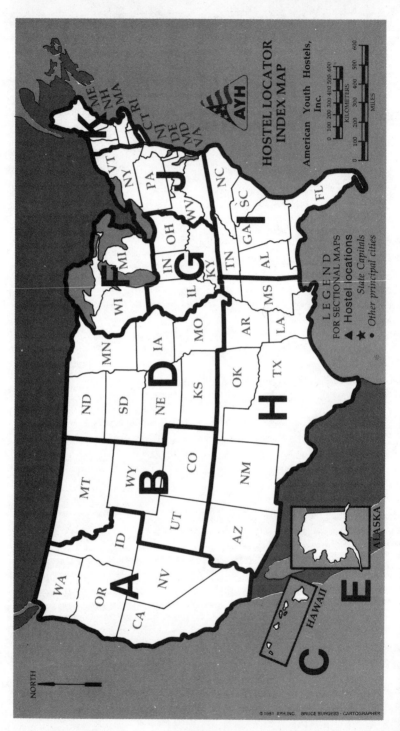

HOSTEL LOCATOR INDEX MAP

American Youth Hostels, Inc.

L E G E N D
FOR SECTIONAL MAPS
▲ Hostel locations
★ State Capitals
• Other principal cities

KILOMETERS
0 100 200 300 400 500 600

MILES
0 100 200 300 400 500 600

NORTH

© 1981 AYH, INC. BRUCE BURGESS - CARTOGRAPHER

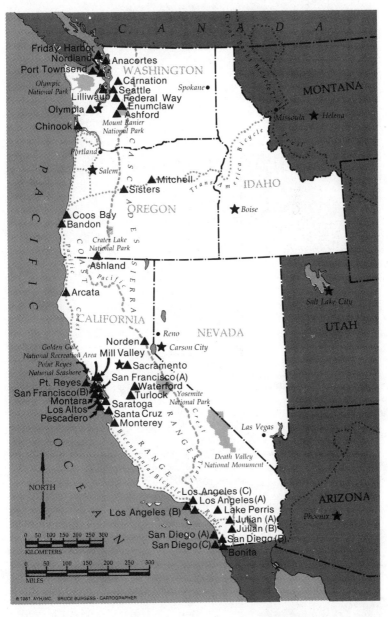

Map A

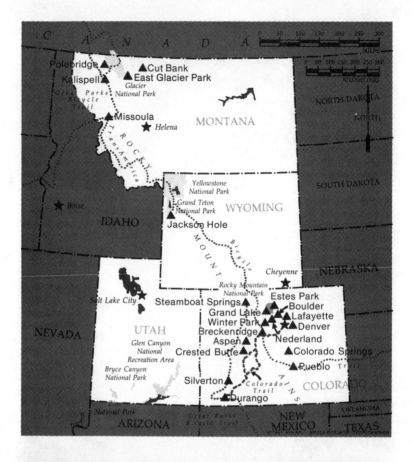

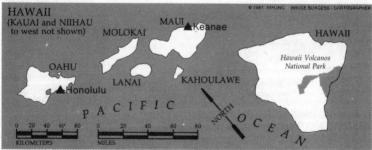

Maps B ☐☐ **D** ☐☐

C ☐☐ **E** ☐☐

Voyageurs National Park
Boundary Waters Canoe Area
LAKE SUPERIOR

NORTH DAKOTA
★ Bismarck
North Country Trail
Great River Trail
▲ Grand Marais
▲ Nimrod
▲ Duluth
▲ Barnum
Bicycle
St. Croix National Scenic Waterway

SOUTH DAKOTA
★ Pierre
▲ Rapid City
▲ Hamel ▲★ St. Paul
Wabasha
MINNESOTA
WISCONSIN
Madison ★

NEBRASKA
▲ Sioux City
IOWA
Des Moines ★
▲ Iowa City
ILLINOIS
Springfield ★

Lincoln (B) ▲★
Lincoln (A) ▲★

TransAmerica
KANSAS
Topeka ★
Southwest America Bicycle Trail
▲ Marion
Bicycle
▲ Kansas City
Jefferson City ★
MISSOURI
St. Louis (A)
St. Louis (B) ▲
Ozark National Scenic Riverways
Trail

NORTH

0 50 100 150 200 250
KILOMETERS

0 50 100 150 200 250
MILES

▲ Fremont

© 1981 AYH, INC. BRUCE BURGESS · CARTOGRAPHER

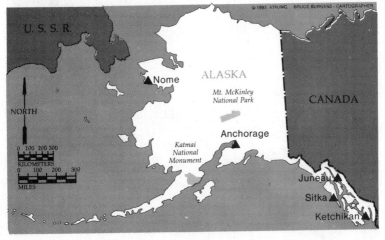

© 1981 AYH, INC. BRUCE BURGESS · CARTOGRAPHER

U.S.S.R.

ALASKA

▲ Nome

Mt. McKinley National Park

CANADA

NORTH

Katmai National Monument

▲ Anchorage

0 100 200 300
KILOMETERS

0 100 200 300
MILES

Juneau ▲
Sitka ▲
Ketchikan ▲

207

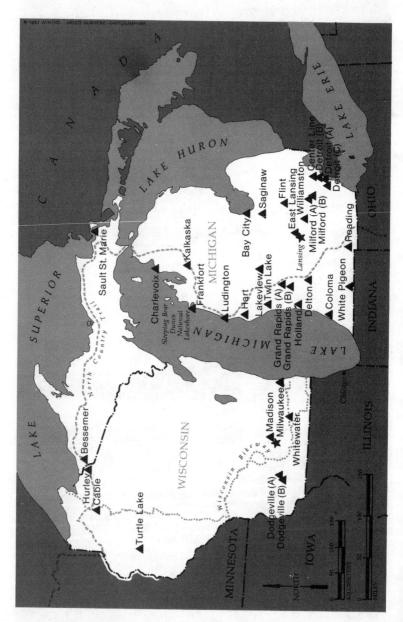

© 1981 AYLING BRUCE BURGESS CARTOGRAPHER

CANADA

LAKE HURON

LAKE ERIE

OHIO

MICHIGAN

LAKE SUPERIOR

Sault St. Marie

North Country Trail

SUPERIOR

LAKE

Bessemer

Hurley
Cable

Turtle Lake

Sleeping Bear Dunes National Lakeshore

Kalkaska

Frankfort

Charlevoix

Ludington

Hart

Twin Lake

Lakeview

Grand Rapids (A)

Grand Rapids (B)

Holland

Delton

Bay City

Saginaw

Flint

East Lansing

Williamston

Lansing

Milford (A)

Milford (B)

Center Line

Detroit (B)

Detroit (A)

Detroit (C)

Reading

Coloma

White Pigeon

INDIANA

LAKE MICHIGAN

Chicago

Madison

Milwaukee

Wisconsin Bikeway

Whitewater

WISCONSIN

Dodgeville (A)

Dodgeville (B)

IOWA

MINNESOTA

ILLINOIS

KILOMETERS
MILES

NORTH

Map F

208

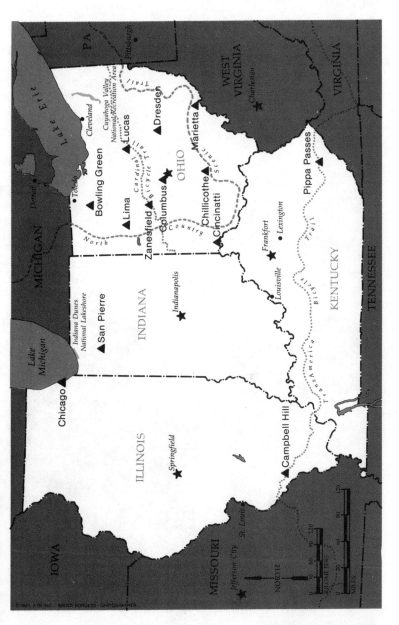

Map G

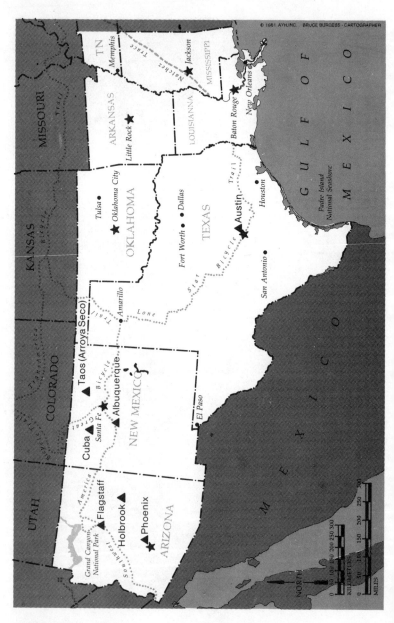

Map H

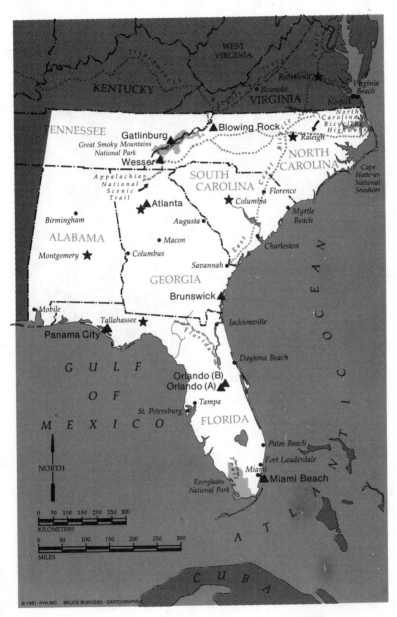

Map I

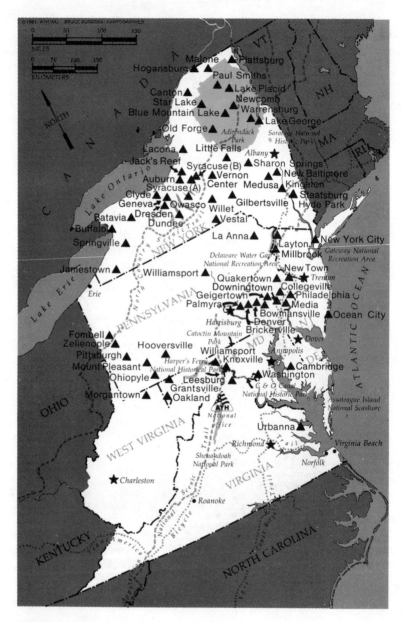

© 1991 ATHUS   BRUCE BURGESS CARTOGRAPHER

MILES
0   50   100   150

KILOMETERS
0   50   100   150

NORTH

CANADA

VT

NH

MA

RI

Malone
Plattsburg
Hogansburg
Paul Smiths
Canton
Lake Placid
Star Lake
Newcomb
Blue Mountain Lake
Warrensburg
Old Forge
Lake George
Adirondack Park
Saratoga National Historic Park

Lacona
Little Falls
Albany
Jack's Reef
Syracuse (B)
Sharon Springs
Vernon
New Baltimore
Auburn
Center Medusa
Kingston
Syracuse (A)
Clyde
Staatsburg
Geneva
Owasco
Willet
Gilbertsville
Hyde Park
Batavia
Dresden
Vestal
Buffalo
Dundee
Springville
La Anna
Layton
New York City
Lake Ontario

NEW YORK

North Country Scenic Trail

Jamestown
Millbrook
Gateway National Recreation Area
Delaware Water Gap National Recreation Area
New Town
Williamsport
Quakertown
Trenton
Downingtown
Collegeville
Geigertown
Philadelphia
Palmyra
Media
Bowmansville
Ocean City
Denver
Brickerville
Harrisburg

Lake Erie
Erie

PENNSYLVANIA

North Country Trail

ATLANTIC OCEAN

Fombell
Hooversville
Zelienople
Williamsport
Pittsburgh
Knoxville
Cambridge
Mount Pleasant
Catoctin Mountain Park
Annapolis
Ohiopyle
Harper's Ferry National Historical Park
Washington
Morgantown
Leesburg
Dover
Grantsville
C & O Canal National Historic Park
Oakland
Assateague Island National Seashore

OHIO

MD
DE

AYH
National Office

WEST VIRGINIA

Urbanna

Richmond
Virginia Beach
Shenandoah National Park
Norfolk

VIRGINIA

Charleston

Roanoke

National Scenic Trail

American Trail

Bicycle Trail

East Coast Bicycle Trail

KENTUCKY

NORTH CAROLINA

Map J

212

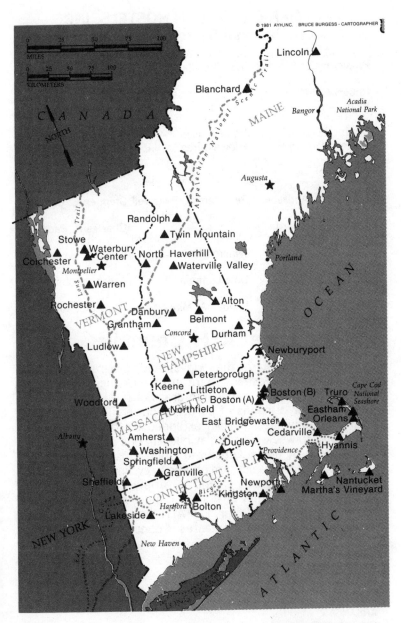

© 1981 AYH,INC. BRUCE BURGESS - CARTOGRAPHER

CANADA

MAINE

Lincoln

Blanchard

Bangor

Acadia National Park

Appalachian National Scenic Trail

NORTH

Augusta

Randolph

Twin Mountain

Stowe

Waterbury Center

North Haverhill

Colchester

Montpelier

Warren

Portland

VERMONT

Long Trail

Rochester

Danbury

Waterville Valley

Alton

Belmont

Grantham

Concord

Durham

OCEAN

NEW HAMPSHIRE

Ludlow

Newburyport

Peterborough

Keene

Littleton

Boston (A)

Boston (B)

Truro

Cape Cod National Seashore

Woodford

Northfield

Eastham

Orleans

East Bridgewater

MASSACHUSETTS

Cedarville

Albany

Amherst

Washington

Springfield

Dudley

Providence

Hyannis

Granville

CONNECTICUT

Appalachian Trail

R.I.

Sheffield

Newport

Nantucket

Kingston

Martha's Vineyard

NEW YORK

Lakeside

Bolton

Hartford

Bicycle

New Haven

ATLANTIC

LONG ISLAND

Map K

213

Local AYH Councils

Local Councils are the widespread program arms of American Youth Hostels. There are 27 Councils located in most of the major metropolitan areas of the United States. Councils offer a means of participation in the full range of hosteling activities . . . from extended bicycle tours across the U.S.A. to weekend and day hikes in one of the metropolitan parks near home. Organized group trips, often with free instruction in the basics, are offered in cycling, hiking, skiing, caving, sailing, canoeing, and a variety of other outdoor adventures. There may be an AYH Council near you. In order to receive their newsletter, join AYH, and participate in the activities, call or write the nearest Council listed below:

ALASKA:
Alaska Council Box 1543 Juneau, 99802

ARIZONA:
Arizona State Council 14049 N. 38th Place Phoenix, 85032

ARKANSAS:
Ozark Area Council 5400 A Southwest St. Louis, MO 63139

CALIFORNIA:
Central California Council P.O. Box 28148 San Jose, 95159

Golden Gate Council Bldg. 240, Ft. Mason San Francisco, 94123

Los Angeles Council 1502 Palos Verdes Dr., N. Harbor City, 90710

San Diego Council 1031 India St. San Diego, 92101

COLORADO:
Rocky Mt. Council 1107 12th St. P.O. Box 2370 Boulder, 80306

CONNECTICUT:
Yankee Council P.O. Box 10392 W. Hartford, 06110

DISTRICT OF COLUMBIA:
Potomac Area Council 1520 16th St., N.W. Washington, 20036

ILLINOIS:
Metropolitan Chicago Council 3712 N. Clark Chicago, 60613

Ozark Area 5400 A Southwest St. Louis, MO 63139

INDIANA:
Northwest Indiana Council 8231 Lake Shore Dr. Gary, 46403

Tri State Council 5400 Lanius Lane Cincinnati, 45224

or: **Friars,** 65 W. McMillan, Cincinnati, 45219

IOWA:
Northeast Iowa Council 139 West Green St. Portsville, 52162

KANSAS:
Ozark Area Council 5400 A Southwest, St. Louis, 63139

KENTUCKY:
Tri State Council 5400 Lanius Lane, Cincinnati, 45224

or: **Friars** 65 W. McMillan Cincinnati, 45219

MARYLAND:
Potomac Area Council 1520 16th Street, NW Washington, DC, 20036

MASSACHUSETTS:
Greater Boston Council 251 Harvard St. Brookline, 02146

MICHIGAN:
Metropolitan Detroit Council 3024 Coolidge Berkley, 48072

Western Michigan Council 1013 W. Burton Grand Rapids, 49509

MINNESOTA:
Minnesota Council 475 Cedar St. St. Paul, 55101

MISSOURI:
Ozark Area Council 5400 A Southwest St. Louis, 63139

NEBRASKA:
Nebraskaland Council Wesley House 640 North 16th St. Lincoln, 68508

NEW HAMPSHIRE:
Greater Boston Council 251 Harvard Street Brookline, 02146

NEW JERSEY:
Delaware Valley Council 35 South 3rd St. Philadelphia, PA 19106

Metropolitan
New York Council 132 Spring Street New York, 10012

NEW MEXICO:
Rocky Mountain Council 1107 12th Street P.O. Box 2370 Boulder, 80306

NEW YORK:

Metropolitan New York Council 132 Spring St. New York, 10012

Northern New York Council 65 Park St. Malone, 12953

Syracuse Council 459 Westcott St. Syracuse, 13210

OHIO:

Columbus Council 160 S. Dawson Ave. Columbus, 43209

Erie-Ana Council 304 N. Church St. Bowling Green, 43402

Lima Council Box 173 Lima, 45802

Toledo Council 3440 Lawrin Dr. Toledo, 43623

Tri-State Council 5400 Lanius Lane Cincinnati, 45224

or: Friars 65 W. McMillan Cincinnati, 45219

OREGON:

Oregon State Council 4212 SW Primrose St. Portland, 97219

PENNSYLVANIA:

Delaware Valley Council 35 South 3rd St. Philadelphia, 19106

Pittsburgh Council 6300 Fifth Avenue Pittsburgh, 15232

RHODE ISLAND:

Greater Boston Council 251 Harvard Street Brookline, 02146

SOUTH DAKOTA:

Minnesota Council 475 Cedar Street St. Paul, 55101

VIRGINIA:

Potomac Area Council 1520 16th St., NW Washington, DC, 20036

WASHINGTON:

Washington State Council 1431 Minor Ave. Seattle, 98101

WEST VIRGINIA:

Pittsburgh Council 6300 Fifth Ave. Pittsburgh, 15232

WISCONSIN:

Wisconsin Council 7218 West North Ave. Wauwatosa, 53213

Minnesota Council 475 Cedar Street St. Paul, 55101

WYOMING:

Rocky Mountain Council 1107 12th Street P.O. Box 2370 Boulder, 80306

MEMBER ASSOCIATIONS OF THE
INTERNATIONAL YOUTH HOSTEL FEDERATION

Name and Address

Argentina
Asociacion Argentina de Albergues de la Jucentud, Corrientes 1373 10A, Buenos Aires

Australia
Australian Youth Hostels Association, 383 George St., 7th Floor, Room 2 Sydney, N.S.W. 2000

Austria
Osterreichischer, Jugendherbergs-Ring, 1010 Vienna, Schottenring 28

The above "Umbrella organization" consists of:

Osterreichischer Jugendherbergsverband, Hauptverband, A 1010 Vienna, Schottenring 28

Belgium
Centrale Wallonne des Auberges de la Jeunesse, Rue van Oost 52, 1030 Bruxelles

Vlaamse Jeugdherbergcentrale, Van Stralenstraat 40, 2000 Antwerpen

Bulgaria
Youth Travel Bureau 'ORBI-

216

TA', 45 Blvd., Alexander Stamboliiski, Sofia

Canada
Canadian Hosteling Association, 333 River Rd, Vanier City, Ottawa, Ontario K1L 8B9

Cyprus
Cyprus Youth Hostels Association, P.O. Box 1328, Nicosia

Czechoslovakia
Club of Young Travellers (KMO), Zitna 12, 121 05 Prague 2

Denmark
Herbergs-Ringen, Vesterbrogade 35 DK-1620 Copenhagen V

Egypt
Egyptian Youth Hostels Association, 7 Dr. Abdel Hamid Said Street, Maarouf, Cairo

England and Wales
Youth Hostels Association (England and Wales), Trevelyan House, St. Stephens Hill, St. Albans, Herts AL1 2DY

Finland
Suomen Retkeilymajajarjesto Yrjonkatu 38 B 16, 00100 Helsinki 10

France
Federation Unie des Auberges de Jeunesse, 6 rue Mesnil, 75116 Paris

Germany
Deutsches Jugendherbergswerk, Hauptverband, Bulowstrasse 26, Postfach 220, 4930 Detmold

Greece
Greek Youth Hostels Association, 4 Dragatsaniou Street, Athens 122

Hong Kong
Hong Kong Youth Hostels Association, 12B Watson's Estate, North Point

Hungary
Magyar Ifjusagi Hazak, Express, Budapest V. Szabadsag ter 16

Iceland
Bandalag Islenzkra Farfugla, Laufasvegur 41, 101 Reykjavik

India
Youth Hostels Association of India, 5 Nyaya Marg, Chanakya Puri, New Delhi 110 021

Ireland (Eire)
An Oige, Irish Youth Hostel Association, 39 Mountjoy Square, South, Dublin 1

Ireland (Northern)
Youth Hostel Association of Northern Ireland, 56 Bradbury Place, Belfast BT7 1RU

Israel
Israel Youth Hostels Association, P.O. Box 1075, Jerusalem,3 Dorot Rishonim Street

Italy
Associazione Italiana Alberghi per la Gioventu, Palazzo della Civilta del Lavoro, Quadrato della Concordia, 00144 ROMA/E.U.R.

Japan
Japan Youth Hostels, Inc., Hoken Kaikan, 1-2 Sadohara-cho, Ichigaya, Shinjuku-ku, Tokyo 162

Kenya
Kenya Youth Hostels Association, P.O. Box 48661, Nairobi

Korea
Korea Youth Hostels Association, 407 RM, Central Youth Center, 27-1 Soopyo-Dong, Joong-Ku, Seoul

Luxembourg
Centrale des Auberges de Jeunesse Luxembourgoises, 18 Place d'Armes, Boite postale 374

Malaysia
Malaysian Youth Hostels Association, P.O. Box 2310, 9 Jalan Vethavanam, Kuala Lumpur 13-12

Morocco
Federation Royal Marocaine des Auberges de Jeunes, 6 Place Amiral Philibert, Casablanca

Netherlands
Stichting Nederlandse Jeugdherberg Centrale, Professor Tulpplein 4, 1018 GX Amsterdam

New Zealand
Youth Hostels Association of New Zealand, Inc., 28 Worcester (Arts Centre of Christchurch), Box 436, Christchurch

Norway
Norwegian Youth Hostel Association, Dronningensgate 26, Oslo 1

Pakistan
Pakistan Youth Hostels Association, 110-B-3 Gulberg-III, Lahore

Phillipines
Youth and Student Hostel Foundation of the Phillipines (YSHFP), 2456 Taft Avenue, Malate, Manila

Poland
Polskie Youth Hostel Society, 00 971 Warszawa, Chocimska 28

Portugal
Associacao Portuguesa de Pousadas de Juventude, Rua Andrade Corvo 46, Lisboa

Scotland
Scottish Youth Hostels Association, 7 Glebe Crescent, Stirling, FK8 2JA

Spain
Red Espanola de Albergues Juveniles (REAJ), c/o Jose Ortega y Gasset 71, Madrid 6

Sri Lanka
National Youth Hostels Association of Sri Lanka, 50 Haig Road, Colombo 4

Sudan
Sudanese Youth Hostel Association, P.O. Box 1075, Khartoum

Sweden
Svenska turistforeningen (STF), Box 7615, Stureplan 2, 103 94 Stockholm

Switzerland
Schweizerischer bund fur Jugendherbergen, CH 8958 - Spreitenbach AG

Syria
Syrian Youth Hostels, Saleh el Ali Street 66, Damascus

Thailand
Thai Youth Hostels Association, The Bangkok Planetarium, Sukumvit Road, Bangkok 11

Tunisia
Association Tunisienne des Auberges de la Jeunesse, 63 Avenue Habib Bourguiba, Tunis

U.S.A.
American Youth Hostels, Inc., National Headquarters, Delaplane, VA. 22025

Uruguay
Asociacion de Alberguistas del Uruguay, Pablo de Maria 1583/008, Montevideo

Yugoslavia
Ferijalni savez Jugoslavjo, Mose Pijade 12/1, 111000 Belgrade

AFFILIATED ASSOCIATIONS

The youth hostel associations listed below are not yet members of the International Youth Hostels Federation.

Brazil
Federacao Brasileira dos Albergues de Juventude, Praca Anna Amelia 9, ZC 39 Castelo, Rio de Janeiro GB

Chile
Asociacion Chilena de Albergues de la Juventude, Estados Unidos 359 B, Santiago

Colombia
Albergues Juveniles de Colombia, Bogota Youth Hostel, Carrera 16A, No. 22A 16

German Democratic Republic
Jugendreiseburo der DDR "Jugendtourist," 102 Berlin, Alexanderplatz 5

Ghana
Youth Hostels Association of Ghana, P.O. Box 3339 Accra

Iraq
The Ministry of Youth, Baghdad

Jordan
Jordan Youth Hostels, P.O. Box 1794, Amman

Lesotho
Lesotho Youth Hostels Association, P.O. Box 970, Maseru 100, Lesotho

Libya
Libyan Youth Hostel Association, 69 Amru Ben Al Aas Street, P.O. Box 8886 Tripoli, Al-Jamahiriya

Malta
Valetta Youth Hostel Association, 17 Tal Borg Street, Pawla

Mexico
(AMAJ) Asociacion Mexicana de Albergues de la Juven-

tud,A.C., Madero No. 6, Despachos 314 y 315, Mexico 1, DF

(CREA) Red Nacional de Albergues Touristicos, Serapio 10, Rendon 10, Mexico 4 DF

Nepal
Mahendra Youth Hostel, Jawalakhel, Lalitpur

New Caledonia
Association des Auberges de Jeunesse de Nouvelle Caledonie, Rue Orly, B.P. 767, Noumea

Nigeria
Nigerian Youth Hostels Association, c/o African Centre, 76 Finbarrs Rd., Akoka, P.M.B. 1150, Yaba, Lagos

Saudi Arabia
Saudi Arabian Youth Hostels Association, Riyadh, P.O. Box 2359

South Africa
South African Youth Hostel Association, P.O. Box 4402, Cape Town 8000

Leseding Youth Hostel Association, P.O. Box 48, Orlando, Johannesburg

United Arab Emirates
United Arab Emirates Youth Hostel Society, Deira, Dubai 54/51

Zimbabwe
Youth Hostels Association of Zimbabwe, P.O. Box 8521,m Causeway, Salisbury

Index to Hostel Listings

East Woods Press Books

Backcountry Cooking by J. Wayne Fears
The Complete Guide to Backpacking in Canada by Elliott Katz
Florida By Paddle and Pack by Mike Toner and Pat Toner
The Fructose Cookbook by Minuha Cannon
The Grand Strand by Nancy Rhyne
The Healthy Trail Food Book by Dorcas S. Miller
Honky Tonkin' by Richard Wootton
Hosteling U.S.A. by Michael Frome
Inside Outward Bound by Renate Wilson
Just Folks by Jerry Bledsoe
The Living Land by Marguerite Schumann
The Maine Coast by Dorcas S. Miller
The New England Guest House Book
   by Corinne Madden Ross
New England: Off the Beaten Path
   by Corinne Madden Ross and Ralph Woodward
Roxy's Ski Guide to New England by Roxy Rothafel
Sea Islands of the South by Diana and Bill Gleasner
The Southern Guest House Book by Corinne Madden Ross
Steppin' Out by Susanne Weil and Barry Singer
Sweets Without Guilt by Minuha Cannon
Train Trips by William G. Scheller
Trout Fishing the Southern Appalachians by J. Wayne Fears
A Vacationer's Guide to Orlando and Central Florida
   by Judi Foster Grove
Walks With Nature in Rocky Mountain National Park
   by Kent and Donna Dannen
Wild Places of the South by Steve Price
You Can't Live On Radishes by Jerry Bledsoe

East Woods Pak-Books™

Adirondack Rock and Ice Climbs by Thomas Rosecrans
Berkshire Trails for Walking and Ski Touring by Whit Griswold
Campfire Chillers by E.M. Freeman
Canoeing the Jersey Pine Barrens by Robert Parnes
Exploring Nova Scotia by Lance Feild
Hiking Cape Cod by J.H. Mitchell and Whit Griswold
Hiking Virginia's National Forests by Karin Wuertz-Schaefer
Rocky Mountain National Park Hiking Trails
   by Kent and Donna Dannen
Southern Rock: A Climber's Guide by Chris Hall
Tennessee Trails by Evan Means
Walks in the Catskills by John Bennet and Seth Masia
Walks in the Great Smokies by Rod and Priscilla Albright

AYH MEMBERSHIP APPLICATION
AND MEMBERSHIP RENEWAL FORM

Mail to AYH, 1332 I Street NW, 8th Floor, Washington, D.C. 20005.

Enclosed is my check or money order for $_____ in payment of the items checked below.

Charge my membership amount of $_____ to my VISA_____or my MASTERCHARGE _____ with expiration date of _____, in payment of items checked.

Please note – most Councils do not accept charges.
Please remit in the form of a check or money order.

Date of Departure_____ Date of Birth_____
                                                  mo/day/year

Name_____
                        Please print clearly

Street_____ County_____
           (Permanent home address)   (Please)

City_____ State_____Zip_____

Mail Address _____
                              (If different)

NOTE: Individual AYH membership cards are valid in 50 countries. All such memberships expire on December 31st of the year issued except that cards purchased in October, November and December of the year of issue will expire on December 31st of the following year. Cards are not transferable and no refunds are given.

- ☐ Junior Membership (17 years and under) $7
- ☐ Senior Citizen Membership (60 years and over)...........$7
- ☐ Senior Membership (18 years and over) $14
- ☐ Family Membership (it includes children of the family up to 18 years, and must be accompanied by one parent) $21
- ☐ Organization Membership (this membership may be used only in the U.S.A. and Canada by recognized non-profit organizations and is valid for not more than 25, with a leader for each group of 10 persons)....................................$35
- ☐ Life Membership (individual) $140

☐ New Member   ☐ Renewal
☐ My tax-deductible contribution of $_____

Explanation of Symbols

⌂	Shelter grade hostel
⌂	Simple grade hostel
♠	Standard grade hostel
♠♠	Superior grade hostel
⌂	Home hostel
SA	Supplemental Accommodation
⌂	Name of houseparents or managers
☎	Hostel telephone number
▬	No. of beds with blankets; ♂ males, ♀ females
▬	No. of other beds: ♂ males, ♀ females
⌂	Hostel not open all year, open . . .
⌂	Advance reservations required during . . .
◑	Address during hostel closed period
●	Overnight charge
SN	Special rule or condition at this hostel
▲	Hostel owned and/or operated by (If different from hostel or houseparent name)
⌂	Type of showers
⌂	Nearest grocery/Name and/or distance
♥	Type of kitchen, or fully equipped
⛟	Location and/or distance of nearest bus station
🚂	Location and/or distance of nearest train station
🚲	Nearest bicycle shop
🚗	$ Nearby parking and fees, if any
✈	Location of nearest airport served commercially, distance
⛺	Camping on hostel grounds
✳	Special attraction and distance from hostel
✳✳	Any special features of the hostel facility
✶	Special accommodations available for families
⌂	Hostel is AYH pass selling agency
✎	Meals provided I Breakfast and $ II Lunch and $ III Supper and $ I-III inclusive price
⌂	Price for rental linens or sleeping sacks
➡	Any interesting historical fact about hostel
⌂	Nearest hostels—by name of town and distance

NOTE: Symbols for which information is not available or which do not pertain to a particular hostel will not appear in the listing.

Most of these symbols are used internationally and have the same meaning when used in the International Youth Hostel Handbook, Vol. 1 & 2.